The *Frances Smith*

The *Frances Smith*

Palace Steamer of the
Upper Great Lakes, 1867–96

SCOTT L. CAMERON

Foreword by C. Patrick Labadie

NATURAL HERITAGE BOOKS
TORONTO

Published by Natural Heritage / Natural History Inc.
P.O. Box 95, Station O, Toronto, Ontario M4A 2M8
www.naturalheritagebooks.com

Cover illustration: The *Frances Smith*, artist Doug Wood, courtesy of Jane Wood
and Phillip Smith; Capt. W.H. Smith, courtesy of Phillip Smith; newspaper
advertisement from *The Owen Sound Comet*, May 16, 1867, courtesy of the
Owen Sound Union Library. *Back cover:* Killarney or Shebahononing, 1853,
LAC Acc. No. R9266-72, Peter Winkworth Collection of Canadiana; Menagerie
Island Lighthouse, photo by Jason Funkey; Timetable of Collingwood
Lake Superior Line of steamers, TRL, Baldwin Room, BR 385.20971 N59.
All maps and sketches, unless otherwise identified, are by the author.

Cover design by Neil Thorne Design
Text design by Blanche Hamill, Norton Hamill Design
Edited by Jane Gibson

The text in this book was set in a typeface named Granjon.

Printed and bound in Canada by Hignell Book Printing

Library and Archives Canada Cataloguing in Publication

Cameron, Scott L., 1937–
The Frances Smith : palace steamer of the upper Great Lakes, 1867–1896 /
Scott L. Cameron ; foreword by C. Patrick Labadie.

Includes bibliographical references and index.
ISBN 1-897045-04-2

1. Frances Smith (Steamboat). 2. Steamboats – Ontario – Georgian Bay Region –
History. 3. Steam-navigation – Ontario – Georgian Bay Region – History.
4. Georgian Bay Region (Ont.) – History – 19th century. I. Title.

VM395.F74C34 2005   386'.22436'0971315   C2005-903955-8

Natural Heritage / Natural History Inc. acknowledges the financial support of the
Canada Council for the Arts and the Ontario Arts Council for our publishing program.
We acknowledge the support of the Government of Ontario through the Ontario
Media Development Corporation's Ontario Book Initiative. We also acknowledge the
financial support of the Government of Canada through the Book Publishing Industry
Development Program (BPIDP) and the Association for the Export of Canadian Books.

To all those who labour to preserve the past

Contents

List of Maps

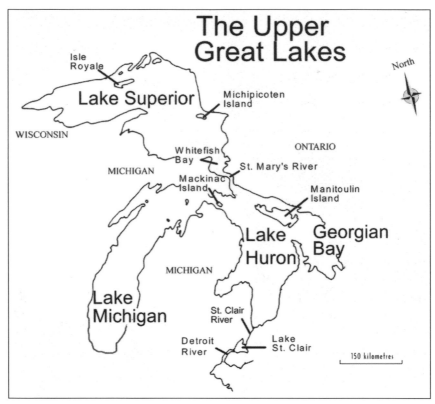

Map of the Upper Great Lakes. In 1855, a set of two locks was constructed at Sault Ste. Marie, Michigan, on the St. Mary's River. This construction opened up Lake Superior and the western lands of Canada and the United States to commerce and travel from the heartland of the continent.

Map of Georgian Bay and North Channel Communities. Before 1870 the *Frances Smith* served only the communities of Owen Sound and Collingwood, with occasional sailings to Penetanguishene and Killarney. When the railway came to Owen Sound, her scheduled trips were extended to the North Channel, Sault Ste. Marie and Lake Superior ports.

Foreword

At the time of Confederation in 1867, the Georgian Bay district was Canada's western frontier. Georgian Bay was expansive and dangerous, its shores sparsely populated and virtually without navigation aids. The only available charts were incomplete and badly outdated. Northern Ontario and the western provinces all lay largely unsettled and untamed by agriculture and industry. Their minerals and timber and their vast prairies had until a few years before, been beyond the reach of settlers and entrepreneurs, who were largely kept at bay by the rapids of the St. Mary's River and the raging waters of Lake Superior. However, by the heady days of the 1860s, the rich resources of the Canadian west were widely acknowledged and the forces had already gathered in eastern cities and across the Atlantic to exploit them. A new era of immigration and westward expansion was dawning.

If Georgian Bay, with its ten thousand islands, was a challenge to mariners, Lake Superior was still even more so. Lake Superior stretched westward from Sault Ste. Marie 450 kilometres (280 miles) to Fort William and the ancient fur trade portages. Its rugged shores were treacherous under the best of conditions, with boulders, shoals, islands and points of land thrown in the path of whatever watercraft dared trespass its waters. Its depths ranged from hundreds of metres to mere centimetres, sometimes within very short distances of each other. Its waters were swept by impenetrable fogs in spring and summer, by powerful gales in the fall and by thick floes of ice in the winter and early spring. Ferrous metals under the lake and around its shores made compasses useless in some regions. Mosquitoes and blackflies often made waterborne travel unpleasant, but it was infinitely more difficult by land.

Until 1855 access to the Big Lake was barred except for canoes and small boats by the six-metre (twenty-one feet) fall of water at St. Mary's Rapids. In that year the State of Michigan constructed the St. Mary's Falls' ship canal around the mile-long rapids and opened Lake Superior to waterborne commerce. This changed forever the character of America's Midwest and Canada's prairie provinces. The old North West Company had portaged around the falls at Sault Ste. Marie for more than a hundred years before they constructed the first primitive navigation locks there in 1784, but those were suitable for only the smallest boats at best, and were in ruins by the last days of the fur trade in the 1830s. The American locks brought large ships to Lake Superior's shores, but, in its first years, those were almost exclusively American ships. It was only after 1870, with the completion of railroads from Duluth towards the Red River and Winnipeg that Canadian shippers in appreciable numbers began to take advantage of the canal. Not surprisingly, most of the Canadian steamers connected with eastern rail lines at Collingwood or Sarnia. The organization of those steamboat companies in association with railways from Toronto and Montreal set the stage for one of the most exciting periods in Canada's history.

Transportation in that pivotal era was not at all as we know it today. Passenger accommodations were tiny, most of the berths measuring two-and-a-half square metres (about three square yards). There were bunk beds one above the other and, on the facing wall, a bench and a small closet. A wash basin was squeezed between, with "running water" piped to the cabin from a tank on the hurricane deck above; hot water was provided only in the "gentlemen's saloon" normally located at the forward end of the ship or in the "ladies' cabin" at the after end. Capacious "thundermugs" were placed discreetly beneath the bunks to obviate the embarrassing need to leave the berth during nighttime hours. Most of the berths had windows for light and ventilation. Passenger comfort was compromised by stops at all hours to offload freight or to take on cordwood for fuel. It didn't help any that most of the steamers of the day carried livestock on board as well – including horses and cattle, pigs and sheep, chickens and geese, sometimes by the dozens, and they were as much subjected to sleeplessness and seasickness as were the passengers on the decks just above. Many immigrant passengers travelled in "steerage" on the freight deck, where the livestock were penned and the cargo was stowed. They had only bedrolls and hammocks and whatever provisions they brought with them.

In the pages that follow, Scott Cameron has breathed life into that colourful era when people of means and people of vision came together to make Canada what it is today. This book on the *Frances Smith* is the result of inspiration, dedication and years of prodigious research. The author has uncovered a treasure-trove of records, official documents, journalism and personal reminiscences to paint this wonderful portrait in words of the ship, the men who ran her and the Ontario communities that were touched by her travels.

– C. PATRICK LABADIE, HISTORIAN
Thunder Bay National Maritime Sanctuary,
Alpena, Michigan

Preface

My fascination with the steamer *Frances Smith* came circuitously. I have had an interest in Upper Lake's shipping since I was a young boy, sailing on my grandfather's steam tug, the *T.J. Scott*. He had a steam shovel fitted with a giant clam bucket mounted on a scow, which he towed into Lake Superior. I watched from the safety of the pilot-house as "Indian Joe" Biron and my uncles dug underwater gravel off Gros Cap just north of Sault Ste. Marie. At our summer cottage at Pointe Aux Pins near the entrance to Whitefish Bay I spent lazy summer hours watching freighters plough past, downbound, low in the water with heavy cargo. On Sundays tall gleaming passenger boats steaming upbound signalled every nearby youngster to run for the beach shouting, "Passenger, Passenger." We would launch our row-boats into deep water to catch raking waves cast from the sterns of the *South American*, the *Noronic* and the CPR passenger ships, *Assini-boia* and *Keewatin*.

When my father took me to the government dock on Sundays I dreamed of working on one of those magnificent boats. The insides seemed like great palaces. I recall plush carpets in the forward saloons, gleaming brass on every cabin door, pungent cigar smoke in the draw-ing room, and the deep-throated blast from the ship's whistle. Luxuriously appointed, these ships were an elegant and romantic way to travel on the Great Lakes.

My first real summer job was as a bellhop on the *Assiniboia*, sailing from Georgian Bay to Port Arthur each week. Later I became a waiter on the *Keewatin*. It was a wonderful experience – a dream come true.

Today those passenger ships are gone: burned, scrapped or occasionally made into museums, which decay while grounded in shallow water – a sad reflection of their former lives.

I am still transfixed, watching modern freighters, those "one thousand footers," glide silently to destinations in Michigan, Ohio, Illinois, Wisconsin and Ontario. There is magic in their passage through narrow channels and open water. But they do not have the romance of the old passenger steamers. But by 1965 these ships could not compete with high-speed air travel and the convenience of the automobile. One hundred and fifty years of passenger travel on steamers of the Upper Great Lakes ended.

A few years ago while trying to discover how the Scottish-born John Muir, the founder of the Sierra Club, came to Canada in 1864, I read the passenger manifests of the sidewheel steamer *Clifton*. Captain William Henry Smith owned the *Clifton*. I found nothing of Muir, but I found much about mid-19th century steamboats and Captain Smith. This piqued an interest in passenger ships of the 1880s.

This is a story about a boat, and it is also a story of Upper Great Lakes shipping when steamboats, railways and telegraphs were still new. It is an exploration of a special part of our past.

Acknowledgements

Writing a book is a much more complex task than it first appears. Not only is there a huge commitment to the preliminary writing and the assembling of mountains of material into some sense of order, there is, for most ordinary people, the task of keeping everything tidy. I recall university days when we kept everything on filing cards to be shuffled and reorganized as a scholarly paper evolved. That was always difficult because tidy I am not. Nowadays we have databases and word processors, but I do not think it makes life any easier. My files remain rather messy. As I approached the end of this project, my hard drive made growling noises just minutes before it "went west." In panic I took my machine to our local computer store, Harbour Microtrends, where a young man performed some technological wizardry and recovered about eighty percent of the files I had not regularly backed up. To Evan I owe a deep debt of gratitude.

Having cursed the technology, one must give recognition to and offer thanks for its wonders. The resources posted on the Web by Library and Archives Canada, the Archives of Ontario, The Michigan State Archives, the U.S. National Archives and Records Administration and countless universities, museums and small town libraries around the world have enriched my understanding and appreciation of modern research. Their databases with direct links to primary resources or the location of relevant information were invaluable in the writing of this book. One of the most useful (for me) new resources on the World Wide Web is Walter Lewis's "Maritime History of the Great Lakes." This ambitious project is evolving into an essential tool for maritime historians.

For getting me started, Captain Gerry Ouderkirk, of the Toronto Islands ferry, deserves credit. He shared his initial research on the *Frances Smith*. His generosity and encouragement is sincerely appreciated.

Once I started reading marine history on the Great Lakes seriously, David Swayze, Walter Lewis and Bill McNeil were touchstones who helped me in my research. Patrick Labadie at the Thunder Bay National Marine Sanctuary and Underwater Preserve, National Oceanic and Atmospheric Administration, U.S., in Alpena, Michigan, was exceedingly charitable with his comments, advice and counsel. He spent hours constructively reviewing the manuscript. Marine historian Patrick Folkes also reviewed the original manuscript, making valuable observations and suggestions. I cannot thank these two mentors enough. Robert Touhy at the U.S. National Archives and Records Administration in Chicago and Robert Graham at Bowling Green University kindly went the extra mile digging about in their faraway collections. They were as close as the next e-mail message.

Stamp collectors Bob Parsons, Gus Knierm and Bill Longley helped add a dimension to the story of the *Frances Smith* that initially I did not think about. They pointed me to the Royal Mail Files in our national archives. In Ottawa, staff at the Library and Archives Canada was most helpful during my personal visits. In particular, Sandy Ramos spent extra time assisting with my research. At the Archives of Ontario, Gabrielle Prefontiane helped me find some of the more obscure materials that I found difficult to source. Staff at the Baldwin Room of the Toronto Reference Library equally provided much assistance.

Microfilm resources and interlibrary loan materials were made available through the Meaford Public Library and the Owen Sound Union Library. Without the assistance of their many staff members, I could not have documented much of the material in the narrative. Librarians Rita Orr, Marion Mower and Lynn Fascinato at Meaford allowed me extra privileges with the use of their resources. At the Owen Sound Union Library, Judy-Beth Armstrong, Karen Teeter, Patricia Redhead, Janet Isles and Pat Frook managed to obtain most of my interlibrary loan requests as well as offering research advice.

In my travels around the Great Lakes I found the staff at each museum and archive helpful and willing to assist. Anita Miles and Susan Warner at the Collingwood Museum were the source of valuable images. At the Gore Bay Museum, Nicole Weppler gave me an interesting photo that led me to insights about the operation of the *Frances Smith*. A special thank you to the Town of Bruce Mines for use of the photo of the 1871 sketch by William Armstrong.

Special mention must be made to recognize the help I received at Grey Roots, through both the Museum and Archival Collections. Joan Hyslop, Karen Foster and Stacy McLennan were most accommodating in responding to my requests for resources. The Sault Ste. Marie Ontario Library and Kim Forbes at the Sault Archives gave me access to their image files. The Bruce Mines Museum, the Great Lakes Shipwreck Museum Centre at Whitefish Bay and the Archives of Nova Scotia were obliging as well. Archivist Tory Tronrud at the Thunder Bay Archives was helpful in responding to my requests.

My research in England at the British Museum, the British National Archives, the British Newspaper Archives and the Victoria and Albert Museum added a number of important items of information to the *Frances Smith* story. Their well-informed staffs were most accommodating.

In addition, Laura Jacobs at the Jim Dan Hill Library, University of Wisconsin; Neil Garneau and Mary Smith at the Owen Sound Marine and Rail Museum; the staff at the Bruce County Museum and the Midland Museum, all helped me find information I could never have found on my own. Sandy McGillvery, former librarian in Little Current, Manitoulin Island, allowed me access to his personal collection of photographs. Thanks also to Susan Corbett-Cyr, curator at the Marine Museum in Kingston; Margaret Evans, the historian for the Royal Canadian Mounted Police; Dr. Robert Wightman, University of Western Ontario, and Dr. John Willis at the Canadian Museum of Civilization.

And to Susan Godwin, who knew the story of her ancestor Chase Godwin; lawyer Brian Renken, who researched some of the legal documents; fisherman Walter White of Collingwood and his confirmation of the location of the elusive One Tree Island; Bruce Shepperd, retired captain of Algoma Central, and John B. Aird for nautical explanations; a sincere thank you.

To those dozens of other people at institutions and associations around the Great Lakes who devote their efforts to preserving our heritage and keeping watch on our collective story, a heartfelt thank you. Your contributions make the bones and sinew of our history come alive.

Phillip Smith of Oshawa supplied several hitherto unpublished photographs of the Smith family. Stuart Robertson kindly loaned me the private correspondence of his great-great-grand uncle, Captain William Tate Robertson. Their generosity added flesh to the bones of the story.

My wife Margaret, whose forbearance allowed me to follow my bliss, is deeply appreciated. She humoured me, corrected many errors and gave me sound advice. Margaret accompanied me on many of my visits to faraway places. She waited for me as I rummaged in archives and libraries from Canada to the United Kingdom. My companion was my most honest critic and I thank her for that.

If errors remain, I take full responsibility. I'll not blame my computer, those who assisted with research, my editor Jane Gibson, my friends, my counsel, my publisher Barry Penhale, his assistant Shannon MacMillan. I offer them only my thanks for their dedication and support of my efforts.

To those who may find errors, both my publisher and I would be grateful if you would tell us. Corrections will be made in subsequent editions.

The *Frances Smith*

1

Steamboats on the Upper Lakes

FROM FIFTEEN KILOMETRES (about nine miles) offshore the town of Collingwood, Ontario, squats on the horizon, barely distinguishable from the flat lands of Wasaga Beach bearing southeast and the rising hills of the Blue Mountains to the southwest. On a clear day the white grain elevator is the landmark to bear on while keeping an eye out for the Nottawasaga Light just off the starboard bow. It is only from a distance of about one kilometre out that the town's old name, "Hens-and-Chickens," makes any sense, the harbour area having been named for the one large island with its nearby clutch of four small islands.

Collingwood's old name hints at the harbour's dangerous underwater topography. When the level of Georgian Bay is low, as it is every so often, there are scores of small sharp limestone shoals that become tiny grey islands. One of the islands that used to be a shoal was One Tree Island.[1] Today this island has been joined to the mainland and is called "Brown's subdivision."[2] The bass fishing used to be good there, good not just because it was a shoal, but because the scattered remains of the sidewheel steamer *Frances Smith* provided underwater refuge for fish. Now the steamer's remains are buried under a housing development. Any remaining parts of the vessel have been crushed under the blade of a bulldozer, paved over with asphalt or turned into somebody's lawn.

Most local fishermen don't know anything about the *Frances Smith*. A few of the old-timers from around Nottawasaga Bay, an extension

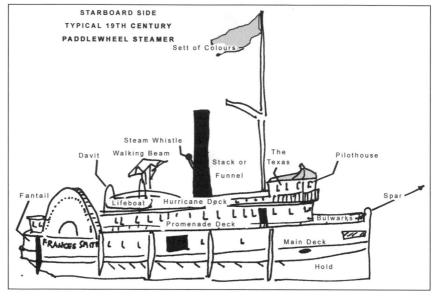

STARBOARD SIDE
TYPICAL 19TH CENTURY
PADDLEWHEEL STEAMER

Sett of Colours

Steam Whistle
Walking Beam
Davit
The Texas
Pilothouse
Stack or Funnel
Fantail
Spar
Lifeboat
Hurricane Deck
Bulwarks
Promenade Deck
FRANCES SMITH
Main Deck
Hold

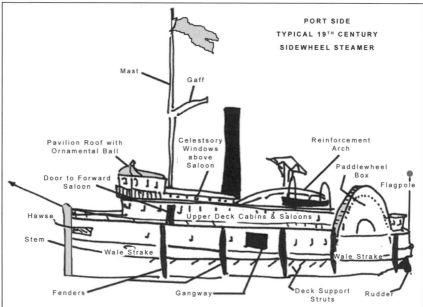

PORT SIDE
TYPICAL 19TH CENTURY
SIDEWHEEL STEAMER

Mast
Gaff

Pavilion Roof with
Ornamental Ball
Celestsory
Windows
above
Saloon
Reinforcement
Arch
Paddlewheel
Box
Door to Forward
Saloon
Flagpole
Hawse
Upper Deck Cabins & Saloons
Stem
Wale Strake
Wale Strake
Fenders
Gangway
Deck Support
Struts
Rudder

Top: Sketch of the port side of a typical nineteenth-century sidewheel passenger steamer. *Bottom:* Sketch of the starboard side of a typical sidewheel steamer showing several parts of the vessel.

of the much larger Georgian Bay, recall that the *Baltic* rested on the bottom near the island. Fewer still know that the *Baltic* and the *Frances Smith* are one and the same.

The *Frances Smith* was the first steam passenger ship to be built in Owen Sound on Georgian Bay. Back then, in 1867, she was called "a palace steamer," "the pride of her ports" and "a first-class upper-cabin steamer." In her glory days she was advertised as " a splendid and commodious steamer."

In her time the *Frances Smith* was the queen of Upper Great Lakes shipping. She was a gleaming, white, oak-framed, wooden sidewheel steamer, whose characteristic whistle was a familiar sound for thirty years from Collingwood to Thunder Bay. She was fast, sleek and extremely stable in heavy seas. Her stability came from the huge paddles on each side acting like sponsons, insuring that the 27.7-foot-wide vessel did not roll as severely as a screw-propeller ship would in rough weather. Inside each of the 30-foot paddle boxes mounted on the sides of the ship was a great wheel fitted with paddles over six feet wide, churning in tandem. Her small pilothouse, perched 24 feet above the waterline, was set immediately forward of a 50-foot mast that could be fitted with a gaff-rigged sail. Abaft the mast, a raised curved platform on the hurricane deck was fitted underneath the curve with transom windows, which allowed light into the saloons below.[3] The most prominent features on the upper hurricane deck were the tall twin smokestacks (reduced to one in 1869) and the iron walking beam connected to the engine deep in the ship's hold. When under full steam, black wood smoke and sparks spewed from the stacks while the walking beam rocked back and forth like a giant metronome, driving the paddlewheels by means of a massive crank.

At the bow of the ship was a hinged spar that could be raised or lowered to an almost horizontal position for steering guidance. At the broad round curved stern on the main deck was an open fantail from which a perpendicular flagpole was mounted. Above the fantail on the promenade deck were the upper cabin sleeping quarters, each marked with twin arched windows.[4] Each window was fitted with a sliding shutter built into the outside wall of the cabin. The shutter could be raised for privacy, for security against violent weather and for darkening the cabin.

The 181-foot *Frances Smith* was launched in 1867, just two months before the date of Canadian Confederation. From bow to stern, she was state-of-the-art in ship design. By the time her remains were towed to their final resting place at One Tree Island, she had become a legend on the Great Lakes. She had a record of service unmatched by any other steamer around

Georgian Bay. She had endured her share of troubles along the rocky coasts of the upper lakes, both from the natural elements and from events aboard ship, and, like many 19th century vessels without 21st century communication technologies, she had experienced several accidents and near disasters. Like the Victorian society she served, the *Frances Smith* displayed both pomp and circumstance when the occasion demanded. This then is a the story of a grand lady of the steamship era and the tough reality of shipping on the Upper Great Lakes in the 19th century.

*   *   *

The story of the *Frances Smith* begins with events far from Georgian Bay where she was built and where she sailed throughout her entire life. Her creation was the dream of one man, Captain William H. Smith, who was responding to emerging economic and social forces in Europe and North America in the mid-1800s.

By the time Lord Cardigan and his six hundred men rode into the "Valley of Death" during the Crimean War in October 1854,[5] life in Canada West (Ontario) had changed from just two decades earlier. In the 1830s, pioneers were still hacking primitive roads into the wilderness north of Lake Ontario. By the 1840s the first paddle steamboats[6] had chugged and splashed their way around the upper Great Lakes, and there were now several steamers making routine trips from Penetanguishene to Lake Huron, Manitoulin Island, the North Channel and Lake Michigan ports. Schooners on similar routes would continue to outnumber steamers for another four decades, yet steamers were making serious inroads into the way transportation systems on the upper lakes operated. Their increased speed, capacity and reliability more than offset their high capital cost and relatively high operating expenses.

One consequence of the Crimean War was that prices for grain soared in Britain. In Canada the price of grain reflected the demand/supply economics across the ocean. The rising price in turn redoubled the efforts of the new settlers on the south shore of Georgian Bay to clear-cut the forests and plant crops for export. At the same time, Collingwood was just about to complete its railway link to Toronto. When the Ontario, Simcoe and Huron Union Railway (OS&HUR) (popularly known as the Northern Railway) was completed in 1854, the hinterland of southern Georgian Bay became hitched to both the world economy and the developing transportation network with connections to Lake Superior and beyond.

Each lock at Sault (Soo) Michigan had a lift of just over three metres (about ten feet). Steamers and schooners carried grain, ore, package freight and passengers from both American and Canadian ports around the whole Great Lakes basin. After 1870 there was pressure to construct a Canadian lock to insure clear passage for Canadian vessels. *Courtesy of the State Archives of Michigan, Negative No. 05595.*

A growing urban population in the eastern United States sent grain prices even higher. In addition, an insatiable demand for lumber in Chicago and an irresistible pressure for new farmland from immigrants turned the southern shore of Georgian Bay into a tumultuous real estate market. Speculators and land agents promoted the region with claims that enticed prospective farmers from eastern Ontario as well as immigrants from Britain.

On June 18, 1855, a set of two locks on the St. Mary's River at Sault Ste. Marie, Michigan, allowed the first steamer, the *Illinois*, to pass upbound into Lake Superior.[7] The event opened the lake to serious commercial activity. The two locks with a lift of twenty-one feet allowed ships to bypass the rapids that blocked easy passage between Lake Superior and the lower water levels of lakes Huron and Michigan. The cities of Detroit and Chicago, as well as Collingwood, were now directly connected to Lake Superior destinations. Emigrants, freight and mail had an efficient course to the ports of Duluth and Thunder Bay, and to the new mines on the shores of Superior and to western North America.

Top: This sketch of Bruce Mines by William Armstrong (1822–1914) originally appeared in the *Canadian Illustrated News* on December 23, 1871. The original is at the Library and Archives Canada. The *Frances Smith* was a regular visitor to Bruce Mines after 1871. By that time the economy of the area had shifted from mining to agriculture. However, whenever there was a delay at the dock passengers made a point of walking to the old mine, still an attraction for today's visitors. *Courtesy of Bruce Mines Museum. Bottom:* The Bruce Mines dock as it looks today, a reminder of the time when the town was a supply centre for shipping copper to Great Britain. *Photo by Scott Cameron.*

In the 1840s, the Montreal Mining Company began production of copper at its new mine at Bruce Mines on the North Channel, the body of water that stretches from Killarney to the Sault. The rich copper ore was shipped across the Atlantic Ocean to Wales for smelting. Initially, some ore was sent across lakes Huron and Erie by schooner, but increasingly Collingwood, as the terminus of the new railway, became the important hub for copper export activity. The growing town also became the supply depot for Bruce Mines and for prospectors attracted north in search of new mineral deposits.

The timber business in Michigan was fully matured by 1855, and entrepreneurs began to look to the vast reserves around the east coast of Georgian Bay, from Penetanguishene to Parry Sound and as far north as the La Cloche Mountains. Two decades later, estimates of twenty-four billion board feet of lumber in the area near the Spanish River alone attracted dozens of Canadian and American investors.[8]

By 1854 the Royal Mail for all points north and west in Canada converged at the port of Collingwood. Competition for mail contracts was fierce. As well, the communities along the southern shore of Georgian Bay from Wiarton to Meaford were moving beyond the "roughing it in the bush" pioneer stage and onto the cusp of a period of anticipated commercial and industrial prosperity. The growing villages put pressure on the transportation system for agricultural necessities, dependable business communications and regular mail delivery. Small town businesses became the bread and butter of the evolving lake traffic.

One of the first steamboats on Georgian Bay, the *Penetanguishene* (1833),[9] was described as "a wretched little boat, dirty, and ill contrived."[10] By the 1850s larger and faster ships replaced both it and the 125-foot *Gore* (1838). Sidewheel steamers like the *Ploughboy* (1851), the *Kaloolah* (1852) and the propeller *Rescue* (1858) were either built for, or migrated to, Georgian Bay in order to participate in the opportunities created by the economic boom. Scores of schooners worked the bay with cargoes of lumber and grain destined for Toronto by way of Sarnia, the Welland Canal and Lake Ontario. Others sailed only from Georgian Bay to Chicago. Tools, cookstoves, ploughs, whisky, dry goods, salt and manufactured goods poured into the ports of Collingwood, Meaford, Cape Rich and Sydenham[11] to support the early settlers moving into the surrounding townships. Lumber, peas, apples, fish and potash intended for markets as far away as New York and Britain returned in the emptied holds.

The primitive roads of 1855 were almost impassable in spring and fall. Deep ruts, raging streams and bogs near the shore meant that heavy freight could not be moved easily on the muddy and poorly constructed roads. Even roads that were passable in dry summer and frozen mid-winter were narrow, rutted and ungravelled. Between spring breakup in April and freeze-up in early December, the water highway was the best way of transporting people and goods. The construction of railways linking Collingwood to the communities along the Georgian Bay shore would have to wait another decade or more to give steamers competition.

During the mid-19th century, sailing on the Great Lakes was a perilous business. Marine records show a shocking number of accidents and shipwrecks in their annual reports. In 1872, Captain J.W. Hall documented just how dangerous sailing the lakes was:

> The number of marine disasters on the Northern Lakes during the season of 1871, so far as known, was 1,167. Of this number, 225 were caused by collisions, 280 vessels went ashore, 81 were burned, 26 capsized, 19 foundered, 182 sprung a leak, 65 waterlogged, 60 were dismasted, 110 lost deck-loads and 10 exploded their boilers. There were also other disasters of a minor character, which are not included in the above enumeration unless serious damage to hull or outfit was sustained.[12]

The number of disasters from earlier years are every bit as shocking:

1871	Total number of disasters	1,167
1870	No report.	
1869	Total number of disasters	1,914
1868	Total number of disasters	1,164
1867	Total number of disasters	931
1866	Total number of disasters	621
1865	Total number of disasters	421
1864	Total number of disasters	880
1863	Total number of disasters	850[13]

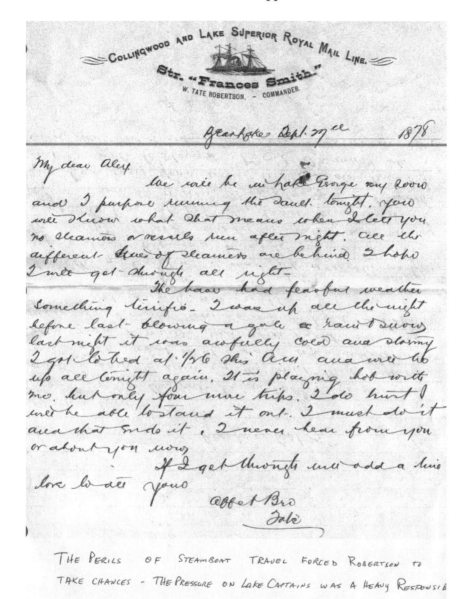

Letter from William Tate Robertson, captain of the *Frances Smith*, to his brother Alexander Rocke Robertson, 1878. The demands of steamboat travel forced Captain Robertson to take chances by sailing the dangerous waters of the St. Mary's River in treacherous weather and at night. He is expressing his discomfort with his decision to attempt to reach the Sault first, taken because he felt compelled to arrive ahead of his competition. The pressure on all lake captains to make "good" time often resulted in bad decisions and tragedy. *Courtesy of Stuart Robertson.*

Only a few scattered lighthouses existed on Georgian Bay before 1860. By today's standards they were poorly illuminated.[14] Erected in 1858, the ones at Cove Island, Griffith Island, Christian Island and Nottawasaga Island were the first to be built. On Lake Superior the Americans had already established a lighthouse at Whitefish Point in 1848 and another the same year at Copper Harbour on the Keweenaw Peninsula.[15] The first on the Canadian side of Lake Superior at Michipicoten was not completed until 1872.[16] There were only occasional harbour lights and docking flag signals at scattered villages along the shore. Nor were there any bobbing red and green spars and buoys to mark the channels. Range lights were not yet in existence as guides through narrow passages and straits in the North Channel. There was neither ship-to-shore radio nor any government weather information system; full and accurate sets of charts were non-existent. There were no lightships, channel guides or spotlights on the ships to penetrate the darkness. The development of radar and Global Positioning System (GPS) was still more than a century away.

In foggy weather a seaman stood at the bow and peered into the mist, shouting observations to the captain standing outside the pilothouse. A wheelsman responded to the captain's orders, turning the large wheel as directed. A sounding lead was heaved over the bow to measure the depth of water. On the bottom of the lead was a wax core to pick up debris from the bottom in order to identify sand, mud or rock below the surface.

By far the greatest threat to navigation was the lack of good charts. Before the sinking of the *Asia* in 1882, and the subsequent demand for improved charts, the basic tool of the mariner's trade, an accurate chart, was not available in Georgian Bay. Lieutenant Henry Wolsey Bayfield's charts of Lake Huron and Georgian Bay, drawn between 1819 and 1822, were the foundation of all charts until recent times.[17] These were excellent for the period, but lacked detail on the inner passages, shoals, and harbour extensions. The revision of 1863 was an improvement, but it too was not adequate for the dangerous waters of the east coast of Georgian Bay.[18] As a result, running onto a shoal or bar was a normal hazard for vessels on the upper lakes. Often this was not a real problem if the grounding occurred in a sheltered and well-travelled route. For example, when the steam propeller *Quebec*, owned by the Beatty family[19] of Sarnia, was almost new she hit a shoal in October 1878 on an upbound trip at False Detour Channel between Cockburn Island and Drummond Island. The passengers and freight were taken off by a steam tug and then transferred to the *Ontario*, another of the Beatty ships. The *Ontario* carried the cattle, freight and passengers to Bruce Mines where she intercepted the *Frances Smith*.[20] Here the load was transferred once more and carried on to Prince Arthur's Landing on Lake Superior by the *Smith*.

Forest fires were also a constant danger to marine navigation. As land was clear-cut and burned, the conflagration spilled curtains of smoke into the narrow passages along the North Channel and smothered the inlets of Georgian Bay with acrid fumes, reducing visibility to zero. *The Detroit Post and Tribune*, of September 5, 1878, reported that the steamers *St. Louis, Northern Queen, R. Holland* and the *Frances Smith* all ran aground in the St. Mary's River just below Sault Ste. Marie because of "smoky weather." This may have been a reference to fog, but it is likely there was smoke in the air from fires where land was being cleared. Certainly when the *Quebec* again ran into trouble in Bear Lake near St. Joseph Island in July 1885, the cause was a forest fire. The *Quebec* ran onto a shoal during a day obscured by dense smoke and slid quickly into forty fathoms of water.[21] Conveniently, the *Ontario* was again nearby and able to rescue all on board. A week later, Captain William Tate Robertson on the *Frances Smith* reported that he passed within 15 feet of the wreck and there was no trace of the *Quebec*.[22] Fortunately, the salvagers, the Detroit Tug & Transit Company, were able to raise her in 1886 to sail another day. Less fortunate was the two-masted schooner *Cascaden* that sank in shallow water near Tobermory in October 1871. Losing sight of land in the smoke, the captain anchored in shallow water, and subsequently the schooner was driven ashore and totally wrecked during a gale.[23]

In 1877, in a letter to his brother Alexander, Captain Robertson on board the *Frances Smith,* wrote, " We have experienced an unusually rough trip not only a stormy one but a very smoky one. The whole country is one mass of fire and the smoke so dense and thick… navigation is difficult. I had to be up nearly all the time and was regularly used up last night."[24] Five years later, Robertson would also observed, "The whole of the country on Lake Huron must be on fire judging by the amount of smoke."[25] In 1882, a huge forest fire burned for weeks at Grand Marais pouring billows of smoke out over Lake Superior while arching flames spewed ash and sparks for miles around.[26]

In very heavy fog, particularly in the St. Mary's River and the North Channel, all engines stopped, sails were furled and ships sat dead in the water for hours, the captains hoping that other ships in the channel were likewise stopped. The river immediately above and below the rapids at the "Soo" was particularly dangerous because of fog in spring and fall. A crewman rang the forward bell at regular intervals as a warning. The standard three long blasts on the steam whistle as a fog warning was not agreed upon until 1890.[27] In rain and snow, when spray froze solidly on every rope and block, a watchman or officer stood on deck day and night, bundled in sweaters and sheepskin covered by oilskin outerwear, completely exposed to the weather. Tons of water poured over the bulwarks in heavy storms. The glass in the pilothouse was usually covered in ice, eliminating any possibility of the wheelsman being able to see without the eyes of those on the open deck. In order to keep gear running, the crew smashed the ice from the superstructure with axes to prevent the ship from becoming top heavy and capsizing. October and November storms were notorious for encasing the forward superstructures and the bow in layer upon layer of ice. The decks would become glazed, making footing treacherous. To avoid being washed overboard, the crew strung safety lines to grasp, but even then moving about on deck was a treacherous undertaking.

In very cold weather the alcohol-filled compass with its directional floating card was sluggish and unresponsive.[28] Even in the best of times, the compass of 1869 was an idiosyncratic thing, thrown off its reading by metal objects in the ship, another nearby compass or the distance from the floor. *Thompson's Coast Pilot*, a handbook for Great Lakes navigators stated emphatically: "I have found great differences in the compasses on these lakes – hardly two will agree....There is no remedy for this difference, except by constant running on a route, when you will find out how your compasses will lead you; and by strict observation, the use of a LEAD and a good lookout...."[29] The ultimate solution to this navigation problem, the gyroscopic compass, was not invented until 1911.[30]

In the 1860s, life vests were not standard. The most effective vests were awkward blocks of cork tied with ribbons front and back, with straps over the shoulder.[31] They had a tendency to push the wearer's face into the water when the back cork rode up on the sailor's shoulders. There were few government regulations about safety on board ship, fewer still boat drills, no printed instructions for emergencies and no standard procedures in case of an accident. As late as 1899, the *Marine Review*, an annual report and directory published in Cleveland and listing all Great Lakes ships along with any accidents for the year, as well as historical information, advertised a "floating mattress" as a solution to survival in the frigid lakes when a ship went down. There is no record of its effectiveness. The woodcut in the ad showing the floating mattress could not possibly inspire confidence. In reality, when dumped into the frigid lake, non-swimmers without life preservers simply died faster than swimmers with life preservers.

The number of lifeboats was calculated on the basis of a ship's length, not the potential number of passengers. Boats were always overloaded. Inspectors were more interested in boilers, hulls and mechanical things than in passengers. In the late 1860s, no Canadian life-saving stations were in place ashore to meet emergencies. On-board communication systems were often unreliable in stormy conditions. Standardized signals between passing ships were still not fully developed. As a result, the lives of both the crew and passengers aboard Great Lake's vessels were in jeopardy with each sailing.

Devices used to measure distance were at best rough instruments. A propeller-like mechanism called a log was pulled behind the boat, spinning as the vessel moved. Each revolution was calibrated and translated into distance covered. The device was useless in the twisting North Channel and the St. Mary's River.

Instinct, experience and a sixth sense were more valuable. "The sturdy navigator learned the lessons of caution and alertness, and acquired skill in piloting, through the rough and dangerous school of experience, which as in many other occupations often ended in 'the survival of the fittest.' It was from these ranks of survivals that the skilled pilots were chosen to guide the early steamboats and the larger brigs and schooners through the uncharted highways of the fresh waters."[32]

A clear night sky above the open waters of Lake Superior was as good as it got for navigational purposes. In tight spots along the shore, captains sniffed the breeze for the smell of pine trees or the industrial smoke of a sawmill to give themselves location clues.

Although running aground was almost routine, it could be disastrous. In Lake Superior the 257-foot steamer *Planet* ran aground three times between 1862 and 1863. The last accident was fatal for the thirty-five persons on board.[33] The names of ships grounded on unmarked shoals in the Great Lakes in the 19th century run into the thousands. Naturally myths and legends creep into the stories of shipping in these perilous times and frequently are perpetuated by museums, folklore and outright fabrication. There are several stories about the *Frances Smith* for which no corroborating evidence has been found. The Marine Museum of Kingston, Ontario, claims that in 1877, the *Frances Smith* ran aground at Silver Islet in Lake Superior and, after extracting herself from the shoal, proceeded to Owen Sound with a rock in her timbers to stop the flow of water.[34] The legend, while interesting, remains unsubstantiated.

Legends also grew around the captains who, along with their title, carried prestige and stature in the community. An aura of authority, a smart uniform and a mantle of power were accoutrements of being a captain. In addition, Captain William H. Smith, the first captain and owner of the *Frances Smith*, was handsome, congenial and generous. He became a local hero in Owen Sound. While he was master of the *Canadian* in the 1850s, his popularity resulted in his election to the Owen Sound Municipal Council in 1859 and 1860. Tales of his efforts to put Owen Sound on the map are the stuff of local folklore.[35]

In the spring and fall ice was a constant problem. It interfered with shipping schedules and was a potential cause of serious damage, particularly to a sidewheeler steamer. Propeller-driven vessels without exposed propulsion faced less risk. For sidewheelers like the *Frances Smith* floating ice would be swept into the paddlewheels where it broke the wooden buckets. The result could be a major breakdown leaving the ship helpless in the water. In mid-May of 1876, the *Frances Smith* was one of the first vessels to reach the lakehead communities of Port Arthur and Fort William. The propeller steamers, *Quebec* and *Asia*, managed to punch their way to the dock, but the heavy ice forced the *Frances Smith* to wait for two days before the captain was able to manoeuvre his way to the wharf.[36] Two days of precious running time was an expensive delay.

At the end of the season there was always pressure to make just one last trip. Shipowners often made their year-end profit with one final voyage. In those days captains had less discretionary power to resist the pressures of owners than they do today. They took chances with the deadly gales of November in making that last voyage, always keeping in mind that the Sault locks closed in mid-November, trapping tardy vessels for the winter in Lake Superior. In 1873, the propeller *Annie L Craig* (later named the *City of Winnipeg*) did not make it through these locks in time.[37] She was forced to off-load her cargo and tie up at the Sault for the winter. This was an expensive miscalculation.

In 1880, the *Frances Smith* was almost trapped at the head of Lake Superior in the same way. She arrived at Prince Arthur's Landing at noon on November 12 with two hundred tons of freight, some of which was consigned to the Canadian Pacific Railway (CPR) at Fort William.[38] She had to leave quickly in order to make it to their docks, up the Kaministiquia River before the river froze. The wharf at Port Arthur was alive with dockmen unloading other vessels. Already there were the *Sovereign*, the *Ontario* and the *City of Winnipeg*, having arrived within hours of each other, each demanding to be unloaded so they could strike out for their homeport on the lower lakes.

When the *Frances Smith* arrived, Henry Smith, the purser, threw a tantrum when told he could not simply dump the CPR freight on the dock in Port Arthur. Amid "a great deal of cussing," he was forced to advise Captain Robertson that the ship had to move on to Fort William to deliver its load.[39] He later claimed that it was his honour that forced him to make the delivery to the CPR dock. Honour or not, the trip was not a good one. As the *Frances Smith* headed up the river, she was able to move less than one mile per hour through the fast-forming ice. It took ten hours of precious time and considerably more "cussing" to reach her destination. Once there, the crew unloaded the vessel and Captain Robertson hightailed it directly back to the Sault just beating the year-end seasonal closing of the locks.

Perils were not just natural and physical. Indeed, the clients were a tough lot who lived and worked in a rough and ready pioneer community. Fighting was a common occurrence. A case in point was a dispute over a seventy-five-cent passenger fare. In July 1856, William White of Sullivan Township (just south of Owen Sound) boarded W.H. Smith's *Canadian*, along with a gang of co-workers at Owen Sound, for the ship's regular trip to Collingwood. The purser claimed that White attempted to avoid paying his full share of the fare. An argument followed and Captain W.H. Smith commanded his first mate, William Myers, to extract payment. As the argument became heated, Smith turned the vessel

toward a small dock at Squaw Point a short distance from Owen Sound
and ordered Myers to put White ashore. When they landed, White refused
to step across the gangway. First Mate Myers attempted to push him onto
the dock. At this point White's friends got into the act. As they began to
shove back, Captain Smith moved in to support the agitated Myers. He
ordered his crew to get White off his boat. A melee developed. Fists flew
and shoving escalated to full-scale fighting. Amid the shouting, pushing
and fisticuffs, White pulled out a pistol and shot Myers point-blank in
the stomach.[40] As Myers reeled backwards into the arms of the crew, White
ran off the dock leaving the first mate for dead. Fortunately Myers survived the attack. He later became master of the *Silver Spray* (also owned
by the Smith family). There are no court records to indicate what, if anything, happened to White.

Death and injury on the Great Lakes in the mid-19th century came
in full measure from the natural elements, the lack of navigation aids
and even the passengers themselves. Sailing was an occupation for only
the courageous. As masters of the *Frances Smith*, both Captain W.H.
Smith and Captain William Tate Robertson were outstanding exam-
ples of the heroic commanders who opened the upper lakes to inland
commerce. By so doing, they helped to build a nation.

2

Captain W.H. Smith Arrives on Georgian Bay

CAPTAIN WILLIAM HENRY SMITH saw his chance in 1855.[1] He moved the 90-foot steamer *Oxford*, built in Montreal in 1840, from Chatham, Ontario, to Georgian Bay. Prior to this, he and his future two brothers-in-law, William and Walter Eberts, had run the *Oxford* on the Thames River between Chatham and Detroit. The Eberts were a well-connected and established family in Upper Canada with military roots on the British side that dated back to the American Revolution. Most of all, they had entrepreneurial know-how. They owned several businesses in Chatham as well as valuable property along the Thames River. Captain Smith, originally from Cornwall, Ontario, married Frances Jane Eberts in Detroit in 1853, and thereby secured access to solid financing on for his 1855 venture into Georgian Bay

He had acquired his initial maritime experience as commander aboard the steamer *Ploughboy* when it too was on the Chatham to Detroit route, under the ownership of the Park brothers of Amherstburg.[2] When he moved north with the *Oxford,* he ran a service between Collingwood and Owen Sound on alternate days. The wood-fired sidewheeler *Mazeppa,* under Captain E. Butterworth of Collingwood, complemented this service and competed with W.H. Smith by operating the same route on the days the *Oxford* did not run.

In November 1855, a syndicate organized by a Mr. Moberly of Barrie, Ontario, called a meeting of businessmen to purchase the 188-foot *Kaloolah*

Captain William Henry Smith, circa 1866. Captain William H. Smith was an Owen Sound booster, a visionary and astute businessman. His initiatives set the foundation for Owen Sound's prosperity as a lake port for half a century. A staunch Anglican, town councillor, justice of the peace and congenial host, he was highly respected in the community. *Courtesy of Phillip Smith.*

in order to compete with the *Mazeppa* and the *Oxford*. It was his belief that a larger vessel could take over the route. Since 1853 the *Kaloolah* had worked the Penetanguishene/Manitoulin Island/Sault Ste. Marie route with occasional stops at Collingwood, Meaford and Owen Sound.

At the same time as Moberly and his colleagues were organizing their syndicate, Captain Smith and the *Oxford* left Owen Sound bound for Chatham for winter layover. The weather was rough and he had to shelter at Colpoy's Bay for four days to escape a storm. With temperatures dropping to below freezing, one of the pumps froze and the ship returned to Owen Sound for repairs. Again he set out for Chatham. This time the *Oxford* was battered by a southwest gale. As the ship pounded her way farther north along the east coast of the Bruce Peninsula,[3] the wind shifted to the northwest. Smith pointed his ship into the wind while huge waves slowed his progress. Near Cabot Head his fuel supply was running desperately low. Since Wingfield Basin, a perfect modern small craft shelter tucked in behind Cabot Head, was too small and too dangerous to enter, Smith continued to battle his way to the small harbour at Tobermory, then an isolated little fishing hamlet at the northern-most tip of the peninsula. Located in a deep cleft at the northern terminal of the Niagara Escarpment, Tobermory offered first-class protection from the heavy seas surging between there and Manitoulin Island. There, the *Oxford* waited an additional five days, loading wood for the trip down the west coast to Southampton and eventually to Sarnia and Chatham.

Smith set out again to round the tip of the peninsula at Cape Hurd, a low-lying limestone dagger pointing into Lake Huron. The gale force

northwest winds hurled huge breakers onto the shore, and "to the surprise and horror of all on board, she struck what is called Big Reef,
which she completely jumped at a second bound, landing inside in 18
feet of water...."[4] The *Oxford* was imprisoned for four days, straining
at her anchors and gradually being dragged toward the sharp knife-
like edges of the layered limestone ridges just below the surface.

Captain Smith contemplated putting up steam and attempting to
catch a wave in order "to jump" the shelf back into the lake. In consideration for the safety of his crew (and the boat), he decided on an
alternate action. To resolve his conundrum he scuttled the *Oxford* and
left her there until next spring when he would refloat her for the new
season. Once the *Oxford* was safely on the bottom, the anchors set and
lines tied to the shore, the crew began their walk of over one hundred
kilometres (about sixty miles) along the desolate coast to Southampton
where they arrived several days later.

After a short rest, Smith made his way to Chatham. Here he worked
out a deal with his in-laws, the Eberts family, who had recently purchased the 162-foot steamer *Canadian Lily* and renamed her the *Canadian*.
Their initial intent was to augment their growing business in the Detroit
River and lower Lake Huron area,[5] but with the *Oxford* possibly doomed,
Smith and the Eberts decided that if necessary they would alter plans
and send their new ship to Georgian Bay. When they returned to Big
Reef in April 1856, their worst fears were confirmed. Over the winter
the *Oxford* had been smashed to bits. They decided to initiate the move
of the *Canadian* up to Owen Sound.

*   *   *

Meanwhile, Moberly was busy in Barrie getting his *Kaloolah* syndicate
organized. To check out what was going on, Captain Smith made his way
to Barrie in January 1856. During a meeting there at May's Hotel,[6] he
revealed to the *Kaloolah* group that he would likely be putting the newly
purchased sidewheeler *Canadian* on the Collingwood/Meaford/Owen
Sound route with daily service starting in May of 1856. The meeting broke
up without the syndicate raising sufficient money for Moberly's project.[7]

Not to be outmanoeuvred by Smith, William Gibbard[8] representing
the stockholders of the *Kaloolah,* held a meeting in Collingwood in early
February 1856 to solicit additional backers. Along with F. Charles Thompson,[9] they went to Owen Sound and offered shares to investors there as

well. By mid-February they had enough money from thirty-seven businessmen to compete with Smith and his *Canadian* in the forthcoming
shipping season. They then hired Captain Edmund Butterworth, formerly
of the *Mazeppa,* as the new master of the *Kaloolah,*[10] which by now was
known as the *Collingwood.*

The *Collingwood* did not stand a chance despite the glowing expectations of potential profits as printed in the Collingwood newspapers. The
Kaloolah's boilers, originally from the *Lexington* built in 1838, were notoriously inefficient and noisy. The ship itself was later described as being
constructed of pasteboard. To complicate matters, her thirty-seven investors
were scattered across several communities making management a problem.[11] But the most serious factor was the competition from Smith and his
Canadian, which had not been anticipated when the project was initiated.
There would not be enough money to make the venture profitable.[12]

Smith got the jump on the spring business when the *Collingwood* did
not get out of the starting gate until several weeks after the opening of
navigation. With his more modern and faster *Canadian*, he was able to
corner most of the business. All in all, the investment in the old *Kaloolah*
was not a wise one despite the £3000 laid out over the winter to improve
her. The syndicate was in trouble from the beginning.

The people of Owen Sound, however, rejoiced at having this new
transport. Travel time measured in days a decade earlier was now measured in hours. With the *Canadian* operating out of their port, passengers
now could get to Toronto in a single day by shipping out on the 8 a.m.
boat for Collingwood and catching the afternoon train to Toronto. The
through travel time to Toronto was only nine hours. For this service,
Captain Smith became an instant Owen Sound hero.

Faced with such stiff competition, the owners of the plodding *Collingwood (Kaloolah)* shifted plans to sail to Duluth, Minnesota, leaving Smith
almost in sole control of the Collingwood/Meaford/Owen Sound route.
Further clearing the way for Smith was the fact that Captain Butterworth's former steamer, the *Mazeppa,* was wrecked at Chantry Island
off the coast of Southampton in November 1856.[13] There would be no
competition from that quarter the next year. By the spring of 1857 the
owners of the *Collingwood* were losing so much money that they were
forced to put her up for sale by auction under a court order.[14] The backers of the former *Kaloolah* lost their investment.

In 1857, Captain Smith mounted an aggressive marketing campaign in the local newspapers, advertising his new steamer *Canadian* as a "Fast sailing low pressure steamer." In his advertisements he listed every township within seventy kilometres (forty-three miles) of Owen Sound as his target for customers. He claimed that his was the cheapest and most direct route from Toronto to the townships of St. Vincent, Euphrasia, Artemesia, Holland, Glenelg, Sullivan, Brant, Bentinck, Grenoch, Kincardine, Bruce, Saugeen, Elderslie, Arran, Derby and the new townships of Kepple and Amable. Despite the ambitious campaign, Smith was caught in the down-draft of the 1857 depression that began in the United States. Many American ship operators in the Great Lakes faced bankruptcy and ships were laid up early that year. Wages for seamen were pushed to under $20 per month and ship construction on the Great Lakes all but halted.[15]

In Georgian Bay the depression was not as serious, but lake traffic was hurt. Despite hard times, the Collingwood Line[16] along with the Northern Railway from Collingwood, was able to raise capital for new vessels to meet the future needs of anticipated traffic between Collingwood and Chicago.[17] Although Smith's business was down, he was somewhat protected because he was providing a ferry service rather than just competing with other lake steamers. With the *Collingwood* gone, he had a stranglehold on local traffic along the south shore. However, as his reduced income was not sufficient to make ends meet, Captain Smith took the unprecedented step of asking the Grey County Council for financial assistance. He petitioned the Finance Committee of the county for help, claiming the volume of trade on his route did not pay expenses.[18] He argued that his service was "a material advantage" to the people of Grey County and neighbouring Bruce County. Although the Finance Committee sympathized with Smith and recognized his "prayers" for "pecuniary aid," they claimed they had no jurisdiction to authorize assistance to a business.[19] Captain Smith left the council chambers empty-handed.

The bankrupt old *Kaloolah*, now in the hands of Captain McGregor of Goderich,[20] having been purchased at a "fire-sale price," was no longer in the picture. She moved north to participate in the growing trade to the Sault. With the *Mazeppa* wrecked and the other vessels sailing out of Collingwood (*Ploughboy, Algoma* and *Rescue*) not offering daily service along the southern reaches of Georgian Bay (their focus was the north shore route from Collingwood to Sault Ste. Marie), Smith would remain in control of southern Georgian Bay transportation during the 1860s.

He struggled through 1858 and the next year renewed his aggressive advertising campaign. Smith remained convinced that there was significant potential for profit in Georgian Bay. By this time his wife and small family had joined him in Owen Sound. Whether or not William H. was able to count on the continued financial support from the Eberts family in Chatham is not known, but the family connection was still solid. "Effie" (Eberts) Robertson, Smith's widowed sister-in-law, moved to Owen Sound in 1864 with her children in order to be with her sister Frances. The Robertson family and the Smith family eventually became partners in steamboat operations out of Owen Sound.

In 1859, Captain Smith was elected to the Owen Sound Council and was re-elected for a second term in 1860. There he worked closely with John Creasor, a lawyer who had connections to the government, and with whom later owners of the *Frances Smith* (the Robertson family) would have even closer connections, both legal and familial.

William Henry Smith, circa 1865, with his wife and five of his seven children. *Back row, left to right:* Frances Jane (Eberts) Smith, Henry Eberts Smith, William Henry Smith, Cornelia Smith; *front row, left to right:* Elizabeth Smith?, unnamed child. Frances Smith was the namesake for her husband's new vessel. Cornelia christened the ship when it was launched on April 30, 1867. Henry became a purser and part owner later in life. He went on to become involved in the Collingwood shipyards. *Courtesy of Phillip Smith.*

Council records for the period of Smith's short political career reveal a sudden and intense interest in council's attention to Owen Sound's harbour. There were long discussions about dredging, shipping contracts, appeals to government for funding, bylaws relating to wharfage, employment of a harbour master, the erection of a harbour light, the setting of navigation buoys and, most important for passenger steamer traffic, the construction of a municipal dock. Clearly Smith's hand was in these discussions, and the council made significant harbour improvements while he was a member.[21]

William Henry Smith understood where his niche business existed. He was also aware of the larger prospects on the upper lakes. He was competitive and shrewd enough to adapt to conditions when times were difficult. If money was in short supply, business acumen and vision would tide him over the rough times. He firmly believed that money was to be made by having the fastest local service on the water. By pushing this theme and racing any steamer on the bay, Captain Smith made his point. Fast boats got recognition and business. For the winners, there was Her Majesty's Royal Mail to be contracted, prestige to be won, bragging rights to assume and advertising puffery at stake.

Steamboat races asserted status and power for the winner. Smith was up to a race anytime, anywhere. His former ship, the *Ploughboy*, which, by 1856, had moved to the Georgian Bay/Sault Ste. Marie route, was obvious competition. In a collision off Cape Rich in September of 1859, after a race between the *Canadian* and the *Ploughboy*, Captain Smith was arrested for unsafe seamanship.[22] In his diary, Peter Fuller claimed that the *Ploughboy* was in the wrong and was responsible for the damage. He claimed the conduct of the ship's captain was "disgraceful."[23] He even claimed that the bartender, standing on the hurricane deck of the *Ploughboy,* threw some undefined objects at Captain Smith and his passengers. No matter, the court saw otherwise. Smith was judged to be the wrongdoer.

Races were common on the lakes, and captains went to extreme lengths to gain every pound of pressure from the ship's boilers. Fires were stoked so hot that paint burned off the stacks. There were even reports that wood soaked in coal oil was used to gain additional combustion in the boilers. In mad races across the lakes, collisions were not uncommon. Despite the genuine fear expressed by some passengers, the competitive blood of crew and officers fuelled the aggressive spirit of many on board. Crowds gathered at the rails, cheering as racing steamers churned in tandem from port to port. Men checked their pocket watches as they passed familiar landmarks, while down in the throbbing engine room, cord after cord of wood was heaved into the hungry furnaces.

Heroism, bravery and altruism were also part of nineteenth century steamboat life. Captain Smith and a few of the crew of the *Canadian* were recognized as brave sailors when, in July 1859, they rescued the prime minister of Canada, John A. Macdonald, from what the *Leader* of Toronto referred to as a rescue from the "Very jaws of death."[24] The prime minister, along with several dozen dignitaries and their families, had taken an excursion from Collingwood to Sault Ste. Marie aboard the *Ploughboy* with Captain Duncan Rowan at the helm. Near Lonely Island, the crossheads of the walking beam snapped[25] causing the captain to shut down steam, leaving the ship adrift as storm clouds mounted in the west. Stiff winds turned into a gale and the vessel appeared to be about to crash on the nearby rocks. As the drifting *Ploughboy* was swept toward certain disaster and the passengers toward their deaths, families said their final farewells. They held hands, offered prayers and huddled together. Just fifteen metres from the shore where breakers surged over the rocks, the anchors of the *Ploughboy* miraculously caught on an underwater ledge. The swells heaved the ship about, but their appointment with disaster was averted.

Some of the ship's crew volunteered to take the open yawl, a small two-masted sailboat that was used as a lifeboat, and sail the 100 kilometres (sixty miles) to Owen Sound for help. Some ten or so hours later, the yawl landed north of Owen Sound and the crew walked the balance of the way to town. There they found the *Canadian* and Captain Smith in port, having just returned from Collingwood. Smith immediately set out for Lonely Island with a skeleton crew and found the distraught passengers encamped in a makeshift shelter. After they were returned to the *Ploughboy*, he secured a towline to the vessel and towed the disabled steamer back to Collingwood.[26] Passengers and local citizens around the bay praised Smith's bravery.

William Henry Smith was not above a bit of puffery of his own. He told *The Owen Sound Comet* that Edward, the Prince of Wales, would take a trip around Nottawasaga Bay on the *Canadian* when he visited

Photograph of the *Clifton*, circa 1865. With her dual smokestacks and great churning paddlewheels, the *Clifton* under Captain W.H. Smith was a familiar sight along the coast of Georgian Bay in the early 1860s. The 187-foot steamer became a barge in 1867 when she had her engine removed and placed in the newly constructed *Frances Smith*. *Courtesy of the Meaford Museum.*

Collingwood in September 1860. The Collingwood papers of the week do not confirm his confidence. Instead they claim the Prince took a tour on board the *Rescue*, one of the *Canadian's* competitors. However, Smith did offer to take residents of Owen Sound to greet Edward at Collingwood for the special return price of $2.00.[27] His offer attracted about one thousand passengers. He also managed to serve them lunch on board, which was not included as part of the bargain price.

By late 1860 the economy was once again booming so Smith decided to put the *Canadian* up for sale and purchase a larger vessel. Increased steamer activity in the upper lakes meant growing competition. It had to be met with a better boat. Thus, in October 1860, he moved the *Canadian* to Chatham for the winter, and immediately entered into negotiations to replace her.

In March 1861, Smith purchased the 187-foot *Clifton*,[28] a fourteen-year-old sidewheel steamer originally designed by Thomas Collier, a highly respected marine architect who worked for the Macklems, ship builders of Chippewa, Ontario, near Hamilton. With two tall smoke stacks and sleek lines, the *Clifton* took over the Owen Sound to Collingwood route, carrying general cargo, passengers and livestock.[29] The *Clifton* dominated this run for five years. She left the port of Owen Sound

Poster for the steamer *Clifton*. The *Clifton* provided
essential service between 1860 and 1866 for citizens of
Grey County, sailing from Owen Sound, Leith, Cape
Rich and Meaford to Collingwood. From there passengers were connected to Toronto and the world. *Taken
from W. Wye Smith,* Gazetteer & Directory of the County
of Grey for 1865–6 *(Toronto: Globe Stream Press, 1865).*

daily and met the train at noon in Collingwood and was back in Owen
Sound by early evening. She also held a Royal Mail contract and carried large quantities of mail back and forth from May until late
November, at which point it was contracted out to a land carrier who
carried mail by sleigh or on horseback. Given the fact that the *Clifton*
ran on a sheltered part of Georgian Bay, Smith kept regular timetables,
much to the satisfaction of the local communities.

In his first decade on the bay, Captain Smith and his steamers were
the most recognized participants in the emerging economy of Grey and
Simcoe counties. As he considered his second decade, Smith began to
dream about a new vessel that would be the "pride of her ports" and
become a favourite on Georgian Bay.

3

Economic Prospects Around Georgian Bay, 1865

B Y THE END OF 1858 the economy of the United States had recovered from the 1857 depression and an era of prosperity for the Great Lakes region began. As the political positions of the American North and South drifted toward their "irrepressible conflict,"[1] pre-Civil War economic activity ushered in demand for agricultural products, raw lumber and manufactured goods. When war broke out in 1861, it began a decade of prosperity for Canada.

Although political relations between the United States and British North America were often strained during the war, the spin-off economy had a positive effect on the finances of communities around the Great Lakes. The demand for a range of goods from railway ties to foodstuffs was creating a buoyant economy in Canada. This was particularly true of the Georgian Bay communities where the mainstay of their economy was grain and wood products. In the light of growing prosperity, Captain William H. Smith began to dream about a replacement for the *Clifton*.

OWEN SOUND

Smith's vision of investing heavily in a brand new vessel was based on his belief in future economic growth along the south shore of Georgian Bay. By 1865 Owen Sound had a population of 2400 people[2] with as many again within its compass of 20 kilometres (about 13 miles). Only four years earlier, *The Owen Sound Comet* remarked that, "Owen Sound

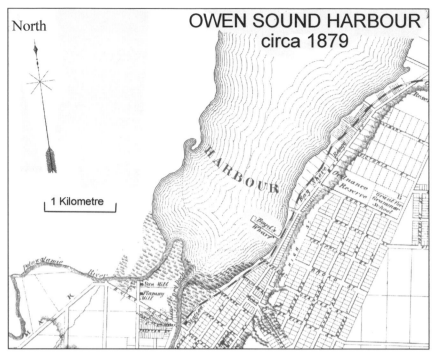

Map of Harbour at Owen Sound. This excerpt from an 1877 map of Owen Sound shows the low-lying marshy area around the mouth of the Sydenham River. A bar often formed near the station of the Toronto, Grey & Bruce Railway, forcing rail passengers to disembark at Boyd's Wharf and then walk to town. Major dredging efforts between 1860 and 1884 eventually made the harbour accessible for larger vessels. Map taken from the *Illustrated Atlas of Grey & Bruce Counties*, H. Beldon & Co., 1880.

is just emerging from that chrysalis state, peculiar to all rapidly rising villages when the filthy vendor of bad whiskey holds an illegitimate influence by virtue of ruffians..."[3] It is true the town was rough, but the community boasted a vibrant manufacturing sector supported by an expanding agricultural hinterland. Solid citizens were striving to make the town work as a good place to live and do business.

The Harrison brothers (John, William and Robert) had a substantial flourmill with three run of stones, and were shipping hundreds of barrels of flour to Collingwood by boat during the summer and by horse-drawn sleighs in the winter. Their sawmill was state of the art, complete with a large circular saw. The result was that they were able to produce tens of thousands of board feet of lumber for sale to the United States and Canada. In addition they operated a successful and modern carding and fulling mill, which produced finished cloth.

John Quinn's tannery was also state of the art and produced extensive leather goods for export. The demand for leather was high in the
days of the horse and buggy and, with growing populations, the demand
was expected to accelerate. Robert Crawford Jr. ran a second large tannery. Cabinet factories, blacksmith shops and pearl ash[6] factories
employed dozens of workers. There was even a melodeon factory owned
by John Sloan who had a large client list of well-to-do citizens.

The most significant indicator of future economic growth was found
in iron and metal works. David Christie's Owen Sound Iron Works manufactured threshing machines, steam engines, stoves and ploughs. A
second foundry owned by George Corbet manufactured potash kettles,
mill gearing and sawing machines. Although not assembly line operations, they were highly sophisticated for the times. Given that these
factories were essentially small industries, there was a great deal of lat-
itude for invention and adaptation in production. The manufacture of
iron products on site in Smith's hometown was a bonus when a custom-
made vessel was to be built. W.H. Smith had ready access to experienced
carpenters, millwrights and ironworkers – a perfect combination for the
eventual realization of his dream.

Eight hotels and eleven taverns in the town were a clear testimony
to the vibrant commercial activity even though the coming of the railway to Owen Sound was still several years away. Successful breweries,
carriage factories and several wagon shops demonstrated to an observer
of the Owen Sound economy that growth and potential reward was at
hand in 1865. A fast steamer along the south shore of Georgian Bay
would serve the business community well. Indeed, the passenger lists
for the *Clifton* in 1864 show that sales agents and businessmen from all
over southern Ontario significantly augmented local traffic. It was clear
to W.H. Smith that passenger service as well as freight movement and
storage would have excellent prospects.

Transportation, storage and distribution industries offered significant
opportunities for expansion. Already Smith had built a substantial ware-
house near his home on the east side of Owen Sound harbour near Peel
Street, and at least another half dozen wharves and storage sheds were
spread along both sides of the harbour and the Sydenham River.

The river had recently been dredged in 1860 while Smith was a member of council, allowing large boats access to the centre of the town.

Map of Meaford Harbour, 1864. Taken from the "Plan of Town Lots Adjoining Meaford…" *Reproduced by Knight Press, Courtesy of the Meaford Museum.*

However, Boyd's Wharf,[7] a half kilometre away from the heart of the village remained the major docking facility for deep draft vessels. The new municipal dock, completed in 1863, was used by shallow draft boats. All in all, these conditions seemed propitious to Smith, and he began planning his new steamer service.

MEAFORD

At the same time in Meaford,[8] just thirty-three kilometres (about twenty-one miles) to the east as the crow flies, the citizens were equally optimistic. The community had a new wharf, albeit a poorly located one, a new 80,000 bushel grain storage elevator, a new town hall and a growing population that had expanded in thirty years from a score of settlers to more than 1,100 people.

Land agents like Cyrus R. Sing[9] actively promoted the town as a "beautifully situated" community "surrounded by an excellent wheat growing country." Jesse Purdy, an aggressive entrepreneur owned a sawmill, a gristmill and a woollen mill on the Big Head River. A second gristmill owned by Moses Chantler was also in operation upstream from Purdy's wool factory. Further up river, William Trout operated a sawmill and broom handle factory near the log house where John Muir, the founder of the Sierra Club, lived in 1865.

Like Owen Sound, Meaford had a carriage works and tanneries, augmented by potash factories, blacksmiths and cabinet makers. There were four hotels and assorted shops as well as a small professional class of lawyers and doctors. W.H. Smith could see commercial gain in a steamer service to Meaford and its becoming vital to the growing prosperity of the community. C.R. Sing's map of 1864 displays Smith's *Clifton* prominently, approaching the new Stevenson's Wharf. By offering fast freight and passenger service, and with the contract for the Royal Mail, Smith had a major opportunity at hand in Meaford.

COLLINGWOOD

Located forty kilometres (about twenty-five miles) east of Meaford, Collingwood was a booming centre for the lumber trade. Logs in huge booms clogged the waterfront. The smell of fresh sawdust and the sharp aroma of pine resin hung over the harbour. Schooners lined the wharves waiting to be loaded with sawn lumber and squared timbers. Mills along

View of Collingwood Harbour, 1875. Taken from a map of Collingwood published by J.J. Stoner. Note the grain elevator to the right. *Courtesy of Scott Cameron.*

the shore ran long hours to fill the holds of schooners destined for Saginaw, Chicago and Detroit. Huge piles of cordwood, telegraph poles and railway ties were piled high, awaiting shipment to the American mid-west where railway expansion seemed to have an insatiable appetite for Canadian wood products. Grain from the region filled the elevator for transshipment to Toronto and Montreal. Freight trains rumbled into town several times a day from Toronto. There were two regular passenger trains daily and a growing demand for additional railway lines to Hamilton. Collingwood, a boom town with apparent unlimited potential, was legitimately called the "Chicago of the North."

In town, Robert Kirk's planing mill supplied the growing community with building materials while Anderson & Jones met the community's need for beer with their Collingwood Brewery. The North American Hotel had livery stables for sixty horses. Its clients were travellers seeking superior class accommodation. Down the street, the Alma Hotel appealed to emigrants and those less well off. The International Hotel, under the management of Charles Cameron, appealed to customers who enjoyed good cigars, fine sherry and imported whisky.

Collingwood was a vibrant fifteen-year-old town with florists, booksellers, auctioneers, land agents and insurance salesmen. James Henry had a huge selection of tweeds, sweaters, broadcloth and sealskin wear for the sailors who landed in town. There were lawyers, dentists and surgeons. There were customs officers as well as government inspectors of ships, taverns, weights and measures. There were freight forwarders, dressmakers, harness makers and blacksmiths. Messers Butler and Jackson sold ploughs and stoves. Thomas Bowles imported chewing tobacco, brandy, whisky and English sauces.[10]

In short, Collingwood was a town exploding with economic prospects for those with vision. William Henry Smith believed in that vision.

ON THE NORTH SHORE

In 1865, the communities along the north shore of Georgian Bay were not developed. Their agricultural hinterland was limited and the lumbering industry was just on the brink of exploiting its forest reserves.

At Killarney[11] plans were on the drawing board for lighthouses at both the east and west entries to the hamlet. A Jesuit missionary, Father A. Kohler, was assigned to minister to the local Ojibwe community. Their economy was essentially based on the fur trade and the fishing industry, as it had been for the previous century, with cordwood cutting to supply steamers being the only significant addition to their livelihood.

By 1865, at the narrows between Manitoulin Island and the mainland to the north (Algoma), the village of Little Current was about to have some limited growth. That year the Hudson's Bay Company had moved its trading post from Fort La Cloche, a few kilometres away, to Little Current.[12] Although the fur trade held little interest for steamers involved in mid-1800s commercial trade, a dock for a steamer stop was built there. It was used essentially as a fuelling station and was on every steamer's path through the North Channel. Within a few years a major influx of European settlers began moving to Manitoulin Island.

Killarney or Shebahononing, North Shore of Lake Huron, 1853, a watercolour over pencil by J.H. Caddy. As southern Georgian Bay developed as a successful agricultural community in the 1850s and '60s, Killarney and the outposts in the north became important as fishing and lumbering centres. Killarney was a routine stop for passenger vessels sailing from Collingwood to Sault Ste. Marie from 1855 until 1950. *Courtesy of Library and Archives Canada, Acc. No. R9266-72, Peter Winkworth Collection of Canadiana.*

Captain Smith may have anticipated this migration, but the fact that initially he was uninterested in Manitoulin suggests his anticipation of better prospects in southern Georgian Bay.

Further along the North Channel, Bruce Mines was still operating as a copper mine, although the West Canada Mining Company had bought out the Montreal Mining Company in 1865 and scaled down operations. Several Cornish families[13] were living there and involved in the mining operations. A major dock whose pilings are still visible, was a convenient supply station for the small community.

At Hilton Beach on St. Joseph Island a small community flourished but was insignificant for the steamer trade. At that time even Sault Ste. Marie was essentially only a transit location for vessels heading for Lake Superior as there was no worthwhile trade beyond the town limits at this time. Even the Hudson's Bay post at the Canadian Sault had lost its importance to the post at Michipicoten. Furs were shipped from there through the river systems north to Hudson Bay and thence on to Europe, entirely bypassing the new locks at the Sault.

Given the poor economic prospects in the thinly populated north shore communities, Captain Smith made the prudent decision to stay in southern Georgian Bay where his financial prospects were obviously better.

4

The Construction of the *Frances Smith*

B Y 1866 W.H. SMITH decided that business opportunities were suf-
ficiently positive on Georgian Bay to allow him to build a new ship
to replace the *Clifton*. He had spent considerable money on repairs over
the winter of 1864–65,[1] but by the end of 1866 realized that the ten-
year-old vessel was not up to further extended use. After removing the
boiler and some of the machinery, Smith sold the *Clifton* as a barge.

Over the winter he engaged a highly experienced and skilled ship-
builder, Melancthon Simpson, to build his new steamboat. Simpson had
a shipyard in Thorold, Ontario, where he had built the barkantine *Jessie
Drummond* in 1864.[2] The *Drummond* was involved in the creation of a
through commercial sailing link from Canada to Europe, hauling cargo
directly to Germany and for this venture she had to be well-built to
withstand the rigours of ocean voyages. Hence the Simpson yard
appeared to be the obvious choice for good design and construction.
Unfortunately, the *Jessie Drummond*'s experiment in transatlantic trade
was not successful. However, it failed for economic reasons rather than
inadequacies in the design of the vessel. As a result, the owners realized that more money was to be made serving the exploding Great Lakes
trade than in transoceanic trade.

When Simpson and W.H. Smith teamed up to build the *Frances Smith*,
Owen Sound was chosen as the site for their venture. Although there
was no major shipbuilding facility there, the west side of the sound near

the mouth of the Sydenham River seemed to offer an ideal location. Using available craftsmen and labour already established in the booming town, Simpson created a launch site almost directly across the harbour from Smith's home on the opposite bank of the sound. It was at this new Simpson yard that Georgian Bay's first major shipbuilding tradition began. With the construction of the *Frances Smith* in Owen Sound the stage was set for an active industry that lasted for more than one hundred years on the bay. Collingwood's shipbuilding industry eventually eclipsed that in Owen Sound, but for fifty years Owen Sound set the pace. The rivalry that developed between the two communities spilled over into everything from politics to hockey and continued for more than a century.

Although there was a significant pool of skilled workers in Owen Sound, Simpson needed experienced help to build a 181-foot passenger boat. Fred Landon, in his classic book *Lake Huron*, stated that every plank on the *Frances Smith* was hand-sawed.[3] He claimed that French Canadians, possessing both stamina and experience with wood, were brought in as labourers, spiking the heavy timbers and planking the hull.

The hull construction was classified as carvel-built, meaning that each plank was laid edge to edge and hand-fitted to the plank above, as opposed to clinker planking in which boards were overlapped. This detail required careful planing and fitting along the edges of every plank. Shipwrights often had to take the planks down to refit them exactly to the plank below, a painstakingly slow business. Each set of planking or strake extended from bow to stern, and there would be more than forty strakes on each side. Each strake was comprised of three or four individual wooden planks. Oakum, made from loose jute fibre or sometimes from old rope and rope scraps, was unwound and the fibres then rolled and soaked in pitch before being driven into the planking seams. When properly done this ensured a well-built, water-tight and strong vessel. The *Frances Smith* was constructed to last, and it did for thirty years, a long time for wooden boats of this period.

In the centre hold where the engine and boiler rested, extra-heavy timbers were lagged crossways to support the concentrated weight of the massive machinery. A great metal "A" frame structure was bolted to the timbers in the hold to steady the walking beam, which drove the paddles. A large curved reinforcement arch called a hogging frame, spanned the ship from front to back, creating a bridge-like support for the heavy engine and boiler. Without the arch, a wooden ship would begin to sag (or hog) amidships over time. The twin smoke stacks were real chimneys, towering above the vessel to create a powerful draft to carry smoke and sparks well away from the wooden decks.

Sidewheel steamers gave up a great deal of space to machinery in the centre of the vessel. This bulky machinery was expensive but long lasting. Often engines were relocated from one vessel to another and the *Frances Smith* was no exception Her engine, originally made by the Macklem Iron Works of Chippewa, Ontario, was moved from the *Clifton* into the *Frances Smith*. This low pressure engine had a forty-two-inch cylinder and a piston stroke of one hundred and thirty-two inches. Her boilers were wood-fired and fed by hand.

Officially, the vessel was 181 feet 8 inches long and 27 feet 9 inches wide. She was painted white above and below the wale strakes and normally carried six timber fenders on each side to protect the vessel from rubbing against the wharf. These were lowered by ropes when the ship approached a dock.

The superstructure was made entirely of wood. The octagonal-shaped paddlewheel house [4] was located well forward on the upper deck. Perched over the promenade deck where the passenger cabins were located, it seemed isolated. The multiple windows were placed so that visibility was good in all directions. In good weather the windows could be lowered into pockets for ventilation. On the roof was a decorative ball, a standard fixture for ships of the period. It was usually painted gold.

The inside was equipped with a large hand-crafted wheel connected to a system of chains on a drum. These chains in turn ran the entire length of the ship where they connected with the rudder at the stern. The rudder movement was assisted by a set of tackles (pulleys) to increase the mechanical advantage of the wheel in the pilothouse. A barometer was fixed to the wall above a small chart table and a compass housed in a binnacle was mounted to the floor. A rope with a wooden pull was attached to the ship's whistle on one of the stacks. Another rope with a pull ran to the signal bell in the engine room. As there was no electricity, the only illumination by day and night down in the hold would come from a kerosene lantern or the open doors of the roaring furnace.

All winter long, Smith watched the giant ribs rise above the heavy keel and then each patiently fitted plank spiked into place. In order to

Author Scott Cameron holds the framed parchment given to Captain W.H. Smith by the citizens of Owen Sound and area on April 30, 1867, on the occasion of the launch of the *Frances Smith*. The original parchment is now part of the Grey Roots Archival Collection. *Photo by Joan Hyslop, curator of Grey Roots Museum.*

launch the ship sideways into the river, huge wooden forms were constructed to hold her securely until launching day. The ship itself was wedged in place by heavy hardwood chocks spaced about every four metres along the length of the hull. On the upper side, cables anchored into solid footings held the ship upright and in place. By spring the deck was laid and the superstructure was almost completed. The launch date was set for April 30. In the town of Owen Sound skeptics and "wiseacres" shook their heads and said, "She would not be off so soon."[5]

At last the launching day approached. A collection was taken in Owen Sound to furnish a "Sett of Colours"[6] to be flown by the new ship. Advertisements were run in *The Owen Sound Comet* for citizens to meet at the Davis Hotel to finalize the details for the flag presentation. The formal presentation was to be an Owen Sound event like no other.

April 30, 1867, was a cool and cloudy day. A light drizzle began in early morning and continued until noon. But the raw weather did nothing to dampen the spirits of the local citizens who gathered all morning to see the launching of Smith's new ship. Along the harbour banks the townsfolk and farmers from the countryside turned out to watch the event. Both sides of shore were lined with spectators. A special excursion sidewheeler from Collingwood, the 28-year-old steamer *Algoma,* lay downstream at Boyd's Wharf with hundreds aboard. Passengers disembarked and walked closer to the launch site to get a better view. This was to be the biggest event ever to happen in Owen Sound. *The Daily Leader* of Toronto estimated the crowd at between four thousand and five thousand spectators.[7] At the time the population of the town was under two thousand eight hundred.

The *Frances Smith* stood above the water's edge, her great frame's base line squatting on the shore. The huge greased timbers sloping to the harbour were like fingers waiting to slide the weight of her 1,324 tons into the harbour. On board, a brass band waited nervously for the moment when the colossus on which they perched would slip into the basin in a giant shock of waves. Only when her floating body stabilized would they strike up the music to mark the grand event.[8]

About 1:30 p.m. labourers below set to work pounding the chocks holding the ship in her timbered cradle. At each of a dozen positions men hammered with heavy mauls at the wedges, pressing the 181-foot hull against the skids. By half-past two, the last block was knocked out of place and the ship was left with her cradle held only by ropes.

While the boat balanced in this precarious position, the speeches began, led by Mayor Thomas Scott. All the local businessmen gathered at the bow to present a large hand-lettered parchment to Captain Smith and a "Sett of Colours" for this "splendid steamer."

A grateful Captain Smith replied that he believed that his was only the first of many vessels to be built in Owen Sound. The town, he stated, was the best location on Georgian Bay for the expected growth of merchant marine service for the Canadian northwest. (The full text of the mayor's speech and Captain Smith's reply are in Appendix C).

At this point, Cornelia (later Mrs. William Brown), the eleven-year-old daughter of Captain W.H. Smith, and his wife, Frances Jane, prepared to smash the traditional bottle of wine on the bow. Cornelia recalled in an interview with the social editor of *The Owen Sound*

Cornelia Smith, daughter of W.H. Smith, at age 15, circa 1871. It was Cornelia who broke the bottle of wine over the bow of the *Frances Smith* to launch her father's dream on April 30, 1867. *Courtesy of Phillip Smith.*

This is the earliest known photograph of the *Frances Smith*, taken in 1867 or 1868. Boyd's Wharf was the only deep-water dock for large vessels at Owen Sound. Its location, just north of the village on the east shore, was a major inconvenience for steamer passengers. Owen Sound consistently pressured the government for financial support to dredge the harbour. Note that this rare photograph shows the two tall smokestacks still in place, but the "texas cabin" behind the pilothouse has not yet been built, and the transom above the cabin deck is nonexistent. Food stuffs (apples, eggs and vegetables) were often shipped in barrels in the hold of the ship. These are lined up on the dock, ready for loading. *Courtesy of Phillip Smith.*

Times when she was in her eighties, that she wore a "white muslin frock with ribbons." Before the ceremony she asked her father what his new ship would be called and he replied without letting the secret out, " I have chosen a nice name."

As the great wooden ship sat poised to slip down the ways, Cornelia smashed the bottle against the ship. The flag covering the nameplate was pulled aside revealing Captain Smith's "nice name." It was the name of his wife, Frances Smith.

A gang of men with axes above the frame cut the cables and "The great mass with a tremor and groan moved off and gliding down took her plunge, surging water back in a huge swell."[9] Small skiffs floating nearby bobbed in the harbour, and one took on several buckets of water.

The bandsmen on deck staggered, regained their balance and struck up the music. The crew raised the flag high on the mast and it fluttered in the raw spring wind. Crowds cheered and applauded Owen Sound's first passenger ship. They were sure the launch of the *Frances Smith* would bring a new prosperity to southern Georgian Bay.

Lines from the bow and the stern of the hull secured the new ship to the dock and crowds milled about for several hours. Excursionists from the *Algoma* took advantage of the afternoon to explore the town. Later in the evening the steamer sounded her warning whistle, and the visitors hiked back to the wharf and boarded for the return trip to Meaford and Collingwood.

Test runs were made into the sound and as far as Wiarton in early May. The maiden voyage was a short excursion to McLaren's Wharf at Cape Rich,[10] east of Owen Sound. The trip was uneventful, except for rough seas, causing some passengers to not enjoy the voyage as much as they had hoped. Cape Rich, by 1867, had only a population of about 100 people. Still an active fishing village, it was shipping over 1200 barrels of fish a year to Collingwood and Toronto. The substantial dock at the cape had plenty of depth but was exposed to the east and northeast, making it unsuitable for large-scale shipping. However, the spectacular views from the town site across Nottawasaga Bay to the sloping shoulders of the Blue Mountains gave the little community a "pleasant seat."

Unfortunately, the village was destined within two decades or so to become a ghost town. Nothing remains today at Cape Rich except the decayed remains of a few half-sunken foundations softened by rows of common lilacs along the rocky shore. Like the graceful schooners and sidewheel steamers on Georgian Bay, the village of Cape Rich and the memory of the maiden voyage of the *Frances Smith* are all nostalgic footnotes to the past.

The village remains are inaccessible today, as it is located inside the confines of an 8000-hectare military training area run by the Department of National Defence Canada.[11]

By May 23 the ship's cabins were fully completed and the vessel was ready to begin regular trips to Collingwood. On May 24, 1867, Captain Smith pulled the bell cord in the pilothouse to signal slow ahead to Engineer A.J. Cameron in the boiler room below. The engineer in turn pulled a large lever to engage the engine, and a huge crank plunged up and

The New, Fast, Commodious and Splendid Steamer

1867.   1867.

"FRANCES SMITH,"

Will commence making daily trips between Owen Sound and Collingwood, on Thursday, the 23rd, leaving Owen Sound (Sundays excepted) at 7 a.m., calling (weather permitting) at Cape Rich and Meaford, arriving in Collingwood in time to make connection with the afternoon train for Toronto ; leaving Collingwood at 1:30 p.m., or immediately after the arrival of the morning train, calling at Meaford and Cape Rich, and arriving at Owen Sound the same afternoon.

FARES :

Through tickets from Saugeen.Starks Corners, Invermay and Arkwright,only........... $4.50
Return tickets........................ 8.50
From Owen Sound to Toronto.............. 4.50
Return tickets........................ 8.00

RATES OF FREIGHT THROUGH TO TORONTO AND VICE VERSA.

| 1st Class, | 2nd Class, | 3rd Class. |
| 46c., | 40c., | 32c. |

☞ For further information see Tariff, or apply to Miller & Moe, Agents, Owen Sound ; Robinson & Layton, Meaford, or the Purser on board.

W. H. SMITH, Master.

Owen Sound, May 16, 1867.   436 tf.

The first advertisement for the *Frances Smith*, published in *The Owen Sound Comet* in May 1867. With the launch of the *Frances Smith* in April 1867, a new steamer age began in Georgian Bay. The first passenger steamer built in Owen Sound, the *Frances Smith* initiated a major ship building industry in the region. Positioned to be a major carrier of immigrants to settle the west, Captain Smith and his steamer became the leading force in the integration of steamer and rail service for the nation. *Courtesy of the Owen Sound Union Library.*

down inside the ship. The walking beam, with one end of its crossheads connected to the engine, and the other to a crank, rocked back and forth driving the paddles in the enclosed paddle boxes on each side of the ship. A new era in Canadian upper lakes shipping had begun.

As the paddles increased rotational speed, water and mist fanned out from the air slots in the paddle box. The *Frances Smith* steamed out of Owen Sound harbour, the finest passenger ship built on Georgian Bay. On her first run, the *Frances Smith* left Owen Sound at 1:30 p.m. and arrived at Collingwood at 6:50 p.m.,[12] complete with a brass band on board, but once again the heavy seas detracted from an otherwise pleasant voyage. With this maiden trip successfully completed, daily service began on May 26, 1867.

5

Aground in Georgian Bay

A<small>T THE END OF</small> the 1868 navigation season, lumber camps along the eastern coast of Georgian Bay prepared for winter tree cutting. Huge tracts of virgin white pine stood waiting to be felled on government assigned timber limits. American and Canadian timber companies, using "harvesting" techniques that to-day are unacceptable, cut, slashed and burned vast swaths of Ontario's forests. They clear-cut their assigned land limits to meet the demands of insatiable British and American markets. Fortunes were to be made. It was an uncontrolled, wild-west economy with huge rewards for those in on "the ground floor." There was work for able-bodied men willing to spend the winter in the bush. Frequently, the loggers were recent immigrants from Britain and Ireland adding to the large numbers from Quebec. Some were Ontario farm boys, otherwise unemployed in winter.

During the last week of November, the *Frances Smith* took on over one hundred lumberjacks and several teams of horses for the trip north from Collingwood. In addition, Captain Smith loaded fodder, tools, cookstoves, tobacco, tents and barrels of salt pork, sugar, flour and beans.[1] The men on board the *Frances Smith* represented the crews of three bush camps located just north of present-day Parry Sound. These men would work all winter, felling giant trees, trimming them into logs and skidding them to the riverbanks to wait for spring thaws when the logs would be swept into the bay. Once there, the floating logs would be

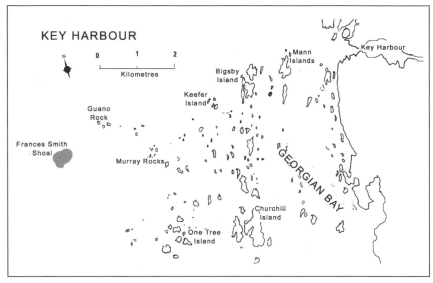

Map of Key Harbour. The tens of thousands of shoals and tiny islands along the eastern coast of Georgian Bay were poorly marked on charts of 1868. The treacherous coast was extremely hazardous for large vessels like the *Frances Smith*. The steamer ran onto the Frances Smith Shoal in November 1868 and remained hard aground until April 1869.

loaded onto schooners, lumber hookers and barges for transport to Saginaw, Michigan, or Collingwood, Ontario.

The heavily loaded *Frances Smith* steamed north past Christian Island where John Hoar manned one of Georgian Bay's first official lighthouses, established just eleven years earlier.[2] From Christian Island, Captain Smith set his course NNW toward Byng Inlet. Using dead reckoning, a decade of experience on Georgian Bay and navigational skill, Smith was confident that he would arrive at his destination, Key Harbour, in a few hours. He steamed past the Western Islands, a low-lying set of granite rocks well off the coast, and then past Red Rock where no light was yet erected at the outer entrance of Parry Sound. The *Frances Smith* churned her way northward at full speed, with thick black wood smoke pouring from the dual funnels. Beyond the Mink Islands and the Limestone Islands just a few kilometres offshore from Pointe au Baril, Captain Smith plowed forward. At a point just beyond Gereaux Island, he set his course on the entrance to Key Harbour, still churning at full speed despite a light fog. Beyond the Murray Islands were Bigsby Island and Mann Island and finally Key Harbour itself.

The entrance to Key Harbour is difficult to navigate from offshore. Thousands of low windswept islands and glacially scarred granite fingers reach into Georgian Bay, presenting a confusion of obstacles like guards in a labyrinth. Blasted pines cling to rock surfaces, barely able to anchor their roots on the solid pink surface of a scattering of stone scarcely visible above the water's surface. In 1868, many of these hazards remained uncharted although the original 1822 map by Lieutenant H.W. Bayfield had been updated between 1861 and 1863.[3] On deck keeping watch were the captain, one of the officers and two coastal pilots hired especially for the trip.

Beneath the surface of the channel a few kilometres from the harbour, an unmarked shoal was hidden a metre below the choppy November water. With a sickening crash and a severe jolt, the *Frances Smith* slammed into the submerged rocks. Men were thrown about and cargo spilled. The *Frances Smith* was firmly stranded.

This was a painful reminder of Captain Smith's experience fourteen years earlier when he lost the *Oxford* on the west coast of the Bruce Peninsula. There is no doubt that the memory of this calamitous event shaped Smith's decision as he contemplated his options in November of 1868. After assessing the damage, he instructed the engineer to put the engine full astern. He did not want to lose his ship to the winter storms on this treacherous coast. The paddles on each side of the ship whipped the water into a foam but the boat would not budge. The *Frances Smith* was hard aground.

Smith pondered his options and decided he had to escape this dangerous position at all costs. He ordered his purser, William Tate Robertson, along with a few of the crew and the two coastal pilots, to sail the ship's yawl to Killarney, seventy-five kilometres (about forty-seven miles) northwest along the coast, to attempt to intercept the *Algoma* and ask for assistance. It was a risky and desperate mission along the uninhabited and shoal scattered coast. An open sailboat setting out in mid-November on Georgian Bay would be considered by many to be foolhardy, but they had no choice. After thirty-five hours they returned to the *Frances Smith,* their efforts having been in vain.[4] Meanwhile, fierce November weather closed in with heavy winds and rough seas, forcing Captain Smith's hand. Realizing that November storms from the west might soon drive his new ship further onto the shoals and the rocky Georgian Bay coast, where she would become a total loss, Smith made a desperate decision. He scuttled his ship. Then he set out anchors and lines to secure his life's dream and began making salvage plans. With any luck he would get help before winter closed off any possible escape from an icy tomb. He knew that he had to have assistance to pull his ship off the shoal and tow her to safety. Time for a salvage attempt was rapidly fading.

With the *Frances Smith* firmly anchored, Captain Smith ordered lifeboats to be swung from the hurricane deck. The lumberjacks and crew ferried much of the cargo to shore and halter-led the horses over the stern, into the water, forcing them to swim. Then, leaving a couple of watchmen aboard and several crew and lumberjacks on shore, they sailed their small boats south to Parry Sound. As luck would have it, the 135-foot paddle-wheel steamer *Waubuno* was about to sail on her last trip of the season back to Collingwood. Smith's crew got on board and sailed south.

Upon arriving there, Smith immediately made arrangements with his insurance company to conduct salvage operations before the weather closed in. While he was engaged in this process, the steamer *Algoma* arrived from the north. Smith explained his desperate position to Captain Leach and convinced him to make one more dangerous trip north. Consequently, the *Algoma* was loaded with men, equipment and machinery needed to attempt a rescue by pulling the *Smith* off the shoal. Just before departure there was a snag. As *The Kingston Daily News* reported on December 18, 1868, "Everything was ready for a start to the site of the sunken vessel when a difficulty arose between the insurance companies respecting the risk upon the *Algoma*, the owners being desirous of insuring to the amount of $1,400, which two out of five of the companies refused to entertain, and her owners refused to allow her to depart on other terms."5

It was a crushing blow to William Smith. Without the *Algoma's* help, the *Frances Smith* was doomed to spend the winter stranded in shallow water, open to storm waves, mountains of ice and the possibility of being swept to a final grave in the cold waters of Georgian Bay. As the desperate Captain Smith negotiated with other captains in the harbour, the master of the 111-foot sidewheeler *Bonnie Maggie* agreed to take a run north to off-load some of the cargo and return it and the remaining crew to Owen Sound.6 It was fortunate that they were successful as winter weather suddenly closed in on Georgian Bay. Mr. Donnelly of the insurance company, Calvin & Breck, reported that there was more than four feet of snow on the ground when he inspected the *Frances Smith* on December 2. The *Frances Smith* was then abandoned for the winter. For the next four months, Captain Smith agonized over his ship.

On April 30, 1869, the second anniversary of the launch of the *Frances Smith*, W. H. Smith returned to Key Harbour with a salvage crew. The steamer *Magnet* and the tug *Okonra* battled the ice for three days as they pushed their way north from Collingwood to Key Harbour where the *Frances Smith* had remained scuttled in the water over the winter.[7] What greeted Captain Smith was his ship, badly battered but still unbroken. The wooden superstructure was smashed and ice had destroyed some of the gear on deck. The upper deck cabins and saloons were in shambles. Deck and pilothouse windows were smashed. Everything was soaking wet inside. Bedding, furniture and linens were ruined. Several bottom planks were damaged, but it appeared that the hull was sound. Machinery was rusted but still operational. The boat was still firmly aground on the shoal, but the boiler was intact, the water level in Georgian Bay was high and the paddles were operational – all good news for Captain Smith.

The salvage crew and Smith's officers immediately went to work. A mate started to pump water from the hold. The chief engineer fired up the boilers and soon heavy smoke billowed from the stacks. As water from the hold was discharged back into Georgian Bay, the ship gradually recovered from the list she held all winter. The ship floated a few centimetres above the rocks below. On orders from the captain, the *Frances Smith* backed off the shoal under her own power.[8] Lines were made to the steamer *Magnet* for the return voyage for repair. The beleaguered vessel was soon under tow and heading west.

In 1869 there were no drydocks on Georgian Bay. Even in Owen Sound where the *Frances Smith* was built and a modest shipbuilding industry was underway, there were no facilities for major repairs. The *Frances Smith* was therefore towed immediately to Campbell & Owen's shipyard in Detroit.[9] She remained there, out of service, for over a month and a half.

To fill in the gap in passenger service, the small 53-foot steamer *Quail* was brought up to southern Georgian Bay from Chatham where she had been built the year before. Under her new owner, Captain Charles Hunt of Thornbury, she made her way to Owen Sound after the ice left and was soon ready to run a daily service from Meaford and Thornbury to Collingwood, charging $1.25 for a full return fare.[10] As with the *Clifton* and the *Canadian* before her, the schedules were coordinated

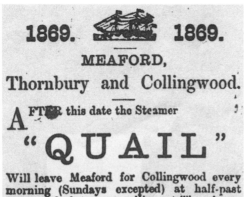

1869. **1869.**

MEAFORD,
Thornbury and Collingwood.

AFTER this date the Steamer

"QUAIL"

Will leave Meaford for Collingwood every morning (Sundays excepted) at half-past Seven o'clock, a. m., calling at Thornbury. Returning will leave Collingwood on the arrival of morning train from Toronto.

FARE—From Meaford to Collingwood, 75 cents ; return ticket $1.25.   From Thornbury to Collingwood 50 cents ; return ticket 75 cents.

CHAS. HUNT, *Master.*
Meaford, May 11th, 1869.   46

Advertisement for the steamer *Quail,* from *The Meaford Monitor,* May 14, 1869. While the *Frances Smith* was laid up in Detroit, the Chatham-built (1868) 53-foot *Quail* was given a contract to run from Meaford to Thornbury to Collingwood. The *Quail* eventually was sold and enlarged to 77 feet in 1871, and finally burned in 1873 on the Bay of Quinte. *Courtesy of the Meaford Public Library.*

to meet the morning train from Toronto, arriving at Collingwood at noon. Owen Sound was not included in the schedule in the early part of the spring, so the community was anxious for the *Frances Smith* to swing back into service.

The incident at Key Harbour was not to be the last time the *Frances Smith* ran seriously aground on the upper lakes. Counting her final resting place, she was grounded seriously at least six times in her career. There were many other times when a little manoeuvering was required to remove her from light groundings on a sandbar. This was normal for shallow draught ships moving in and out of unmapped and poor harbours in the 19th century. Shallow draught paddle steamers were adept at this and were well suited for uncharted water. But the Key River grounding was by far the most serious during the *Smith's* life on the lakes.

*   *   *

A general frustration with the early performance of the *Frances Smith* resulted in local rumour mills churning out stories about the poor reliability of the vessel, the questionable competence of Captain Smith and the inability of the company to live up to service expectations. In Meaford the talk around the harbour was that the insurance carriers were going to lower the boat's insurance rating and that Captain Smith himself was to be replaced:

We remember reading in an old almanac under the weather predictions something to this effect: "Storm about this time; if it doesn't come, keep on expecting it." People have learned to apply this philosophy to the announcements concerning the Frances Smith. From the day she was first announced to be launched it was fully six weeks until she was afloat; she was equally behind time in commencing her trips and now we have been daily expecting her arrival during the last three weeks and yet she is not here.[11]

*   *   *

The *Frances Smith* was delayed at Detroit because the damaged bottom planks needed repairs beyond what was originally anticipated. In addition, the dual twin smokestacks were replaced with a single, shorter funnel. A "texas cabin" was added to the pilothouse, providing additional space for the captain. The cabin deck was completely reconstructed and reconfigured with additional interior space and a raised clerestory running its entire length. Captain Smith wanted his prized ship refitted and repaired properly before returning to home base. Although the delay was an unwelcome challenge for the strong-minded captain, there was nothing to do except exercise patience. This was not Smith's long suit, but wait he did.

On the morning of June 17, 1869, the *Frances Smith* arrived back in Owen Sound.[12] When she eventually steamed into the long sound, the whole community celebrated as though a conquering hero had returned.

Extensive repairs to the *Frances Smith* in the spring of 1869 completely changed the appearance of her upper decks. The cabin deck accommodation was enlarged and the twin smokestacks replaced with a single larger but shorter stack. A raised transom was added above the forward saloons to provide more interior light. An expanded pilothouse called a "texas" was added. *Courtesy of Grey Roots Archival Collection.*

As the *Frances Smith* came into sight off Cape Commodore, town and country folks crowded onto Boyd's Wharf on the eastern outskirts of Owen Sound to watch her return. Those who had small sailboats set the rigging and sailed off to meet her as she steamed into the harbour. It was a grand sight to see the newly painted, radiant white sidewheeler approach home shores with smoke pouring from the brand new red and black funnel. The side paddles churned the early morning waters with a steady throb, sending mist and spray through the side vents of the paddle box. Above the hurricane deck the walking beam set its regular pace, rocking back and forth.

Tugs and small steamers carried the local brass band and dignitaries out to meet the *Smith* while she was still several kilometres from the wharf. As the tugs pulled alongside, the dignitaries climbed on board through the open gangway of the still moving steamer. One by one the bandsmen scrambled aboard and mounted the stairwell to the upper decks. There they set up chairs, and the brass band began to play. With flags flying, the *Frances Smith* steamed up to the wharf.[13] At the dock there was cheering and hand-shaking as the smiling Captain Smith stepped ashore. Amidst waving banners and bunting, there were hearty ovations in anticipation of a restored service along the bay.

The day after her return the *Frances Smith* sailed to Meaford with the brass band from Owen Sound and Mayor Thomas Scott on board. Crowds stood shoulder to shoulder along Meaford's shore, waving and cheering as Captain Smith glided his steamer beside Stevenson's Wharf on the west side of the Big Head River. The *Frances Smith* was back on her old route and ready for business. The rumour mills of Meaford were silenced. The captain was once again hailed as a local hero.

Steamboat arrivals and departures in the mid-1800s were at the heart of small town entertainment. The arrival of friends, freight and mail was an anticipated event at the town dock. At the foot of every main street, crowds of children and adults turned out to participate in the landing. Always there were onlookers and helpers ready to heave heavy ropes around the bollards on the dock. Always there were extra hands to set loading planks into the open gangway. Always there were expectant eyes looking up to the promenade deck to see some passenger's familiar face. The captain in uniform added a sense of authority and importance to what in fact was a routine event. The reappearance of the *Frances Smith* on June 18, 1869, was so special that the whole community of Meaford came to the dock to welcome her.

However, it was not all clear sailing in early 1869. During the first week of July, between Meaford and Collingwood, there was serious engine trouble and the *Frances Smith* had to be towed back to Owen Sound for three days of repairs. But by the end of the week Captain Smith was in full swing on his Owen Sound, Cape Rich, Meaford, Collingwood schedule. During the summer he chartered special excursions for Orangemen, Sabbath schools and anyone else who wanted to have a pleasurable trip out on the bay. Moonlight excursions were popular diversions for citizens too. They normally left the dock around sunset and returned well after midnight. It made for a long day for the captain and his crew, but for the gregarious William Smith it was all part of the job.

Dominion Day excursions became a tradition. In 1869, the Pythagoras Lodge 137 of Meaford chartered the *Frances Smith* for the day. Leaving the town harbour at 8 a.m. sharp,

Thomas Scott, mayor of Owen Sound in 1867 and in 1875, was one of several dozen dignitaries present on the maiden voyage of the *Frances Smith* to Cape Rich. After his election to the Ontario Legislature as the member for North Grey, he took the first trip on the rebuilt *Frances Smith* in 1869. *Courtesy of Library and Archives Canada, PA28700.*

she sailed to Cape Rich where passengers disembarked and wandered through the small fishing community. She then sailed directly across Nottawasaga Bay to Penetanguishene, where passengers were able to visit the reformatory for young offenders. A brass band entertained the excursionists on the way over. On the return trip a quadrille band played for dancing. All this Captain Smith offered for the low price of 75 cents for gentlemen, 50 cents for ladies and 35 cents for children.

By late 1869 Captain Smith began advertising his ship as a "Splendid, fast and commodious steamer."[14] He picked up the headline from the Owen Sound papers and used it to his advantage in his advertisements for many years thereafter. During the year, the account books for the port of Owen Sound show the *Frances Smith* hauling everything from live pigs to nail kegs, cases of boots to card tables, bags of barley to grindstones. All these things were essential supplies for the growing communities around the bay.

Yachting regattas were a particularly popular pastime in the latter half of the nineteenth century. Small sailboats from communities around the bay gathered every summer for competition. The long sound between Vail's Point and Cape Commodore was a particularly popular venue for these events. There was enough protection from the head-lands to keep the wave height reasonable and ample sweep to the north for a good wind and, best of all, the races were visible from the high points of land on both the east and west shores. Larger craft with bunting draped along the decks served as platforms for watching the events up close. Captain Smith was involved in organizing these regattas, and, in the September 1869 competitions, the *Frances Smith* was the flagship. A small payment of fifty cents was charged to help the "Grand Excursion" to at least break even. Unfortunately, this grand excursion was not well-attended because of foul weather and the townsfolk knew enough to stay off the bay. Very little money was made from the event.

In bad weather and good, the *Frances Smith* worked her regular route along the south shore of Georgian Bay, moving passengers and freight without much serious competition. Excursions only generated extra revenue for an already profitable business.

6

The Red River Affair

W HEN THE *Frances Smith* was laid up for the winter in Owen
Sound at the end of November 1869, events in the Canadian
northwest were devolving into a national political crisis. Louis Riel, the
Métis leader, was about to challenge the new Dominion of Canada over
the Red River territory near present-day Winnipeg. In the spring of
1870 the *Frances Smith* would be swept up briefly in a crisis known as
the "Chicora Affair."

The new government of Canada was to assume the transfer of land in
the northwest from the Hudson's Bay Company on December 1, 1869.
The Métis in Manitoba, with Louis Riel as their leader, posted a List of
Rights to protect Métis culture, not only from English-Canadian immigration pressure but from fear of expansionist sentiment in the United
States. Riel, frustrated by the lack of response by the Canadian government, proclaimed a provisional government. While his intentions may have
been worthy, his actions were seen as rebellion in Ontario. Prime Minister John A. Macdonald refused to pay the Hudson's Bay Company on
December 1 because of the disturbance. Since the company no longer
owned the land, Riel's provisional government became the *de facto* authority in the territory. Through a series of what was seen as provocative actions,
English-Canadian prisoners were taken by Riel, tried by his provisional
government and sentenced to death. Protestant Ontario exploded when
Thomas Scott[1] was "murdered" by Riel's government. Unable to find a

political solution, the prime minister was eventually compelled to authorize an expeditionary force to go to the Red River area. This was Canada's
first major military test as a new nation after Confederation in 1867.

The force was put together to affirm Canadian sovereignty and to
restore order in the northwest. Macdonald knew that these Canadian
troops had to be sent through an all-Canadian route either via the Great
Lakes or through Hudson Bay. The use of a route through the United
States to the Red River was out of the question. Clearly, the Hudson
Bay route would be too slow and the logistics involved meant that soldiers would not be able to return until the year following.[2] Besides, this
timetable was unacceptable to the British government, which agreed to
send a contingent to accompany the Canadian expeditionary force provided it would be only a one-year commitment. By late April 1870, the
decision was made. Troops would be moved by rail from Toronto to
Collingwood and then by ship through the Great Lakes to Prince
Arthur's Landing and subsequently to the Red River.

Engineer and surveyor Simon J. Dawson, who had been working on
the overland route from the Lakehead to the Red River since 1868, was
now ordered to complete the road immediately. Dawson's road was a
particularly difficult construction job. The work in bug-infested north-
western Ontario was an extremely unpleasant experience. Not only were
there swamps, forests and hundreds of lakes in the way, there was the
proverbial plague – "the little blackfly." Millions of these pests gorged
on the necks and ears of the workers in May and June. Millions more
mosquitoes feasted on their blood in July and August.

To get the job done on the government's schedule, over one thousand
additional labourers had to be hired and sent west by steamer. Specially
built portage boats and road construction equipment were designed to
accompany these rough, tough "Dawson men." Tons of foodstuffs and
tools were to follow. The organization of the operation was impressive
for an emerging Canadian transportation network. Indeed, the lessons
learned were not lost on observant businessmen who realized the future
importance of a coordinated steamer and rail supply system to service
the northwest.

The diplomatically difficult part of the troop movement came when ships
had to pass through the locks on the St. Mary's River. The locks were on
the United States side of the border. No locks yet existed on the Canadian

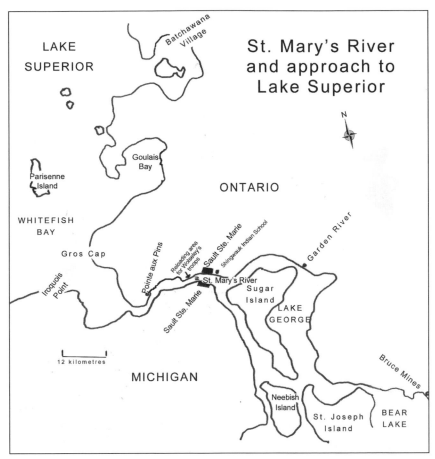

Map of the St. Mary's River and the approach to Lake Superior. The locks at Sault Ste. Marie, Michigan, were closed to Canadian vessels carrying military supplies in May 1870. Soldiers and supplies were unloaded at a location just above the Shingwauk Indian School and portaged five kilometres (about three miles) to a landing above the rapids on the Canadian side. There they were reloaded for shipment to the west, thereby avoiding the locks.

side. The Canadian actions were watched closely at the highest levels in the American cabinet. The ultimate issue, the passage of troops through United States territory, would not be resolved until after the *Frances Smith* became involved. While these national and international issues were speeding toward military action by the new government of Canada, Captain William H. Smith did not realize he would soon be involved.

Owen Sound harbour was clear of ice early in April 1870. However, on April 17 ice still clogged the outer reaches of Georgian Bay. Captain Smith was anxious to get his ship out of port as soon as possible to earn some money. He had worked hard over the winter making arrangements with shipping interests in Montreal and with the executives of the Northern Railway at Collingwood to blend his fares with theirs so he could offer "through rates" to Montreal and Toronto for his Georgian Bay clients (see Appendix D). Freight handling, pricing, billing, commissions and insurance issues had been resolved. The *Frances Smith* was ready to go, but the heavy ice beyond Cape Commodore and Vail's Point was not ready to loosen its heavy winter grip.

The *Smith*, as she became known, had been extensively remodelled over the winter to fit the demands of her potential customers. The whole interior was repainted and two new cabins were added. The forward cabin on the main deck was to be a gentlemen's cabin immediately in front of the ladies' quarters. Another passenger cabin was constructed aft. New and additional furniture were brought on board. New woodwork was installed. First-class passengers were the target customers. The lavishly fitted *Frances Smith* was the pride of the lakes and the Owen Sound papers sang her praises. The *Advertiser* claimed the *Frances Smith* "will be as handsome and commodious a craft as ever sailed the waters of a lake."[3] Captain Smith's strategy was to emulate the luxurious palace steamers that had plied the American waters prior to the Civil War. These were mothballed during the depression of 1857 and for the most part, never restored. Smith believed the concept could be resurrected on Georgian Bay in 1870. At the start of the season, Captain Smith assumed he would consolidate his vessel's primary position as Georgian Bay's best option for moving people and freight along the south shore of Georgian Bay.

By Monday, April 18, 1870, Captain Smith had his crew in place and was ready to sail despite the winter-like conditions on the bay. He ordered up steam, cast off the lines and left his winter berth in Owen Sound late in the evening, heading for Collingwood. Large ice pans lurked well offshore so Smith kept close to the east coast of the sound. He stayed away from the centre of the deep fiord-like body of water and steamed past Leith near rocky shores where large boulders left over from the last ice age lay just a few metres below the surface. He made his way on a course NNE. The occasional pan of slush ice brushed against the bow and small floating chunks were swept into the paddle box. At a speed of ten knots, even thin ice could be destructive. Its sharp edges acted like thousands of chisels on the waterline of the wooden hull.

Advertisement for the *Frances Smith, The Owen Sound Times* April 21, 1870. W.H. Smith developed the concept of "through rates" for freight from Owen Sound to Montreal after designing "through rates" for passengers from Toronto to Owen Sound. This novel pricing ploy made it easier for his customers. The concept was expanded later to include "through rates" from Montreal to Duluth and points west as far as Oregon. *Courtesy of the Owen Sound Union Library.*

STEAMER
FRANCES SMITH.'

THROUGH RATES FROM MONTREAL AND TORONTO.

GREAT REDUCTION!

I have arranged with the N. R. and with Jacques, Tracy & Co. to convey the under-mentioned Freight at the following rates :

MONTREAL TO OWEN SOUND.

	100℔s
Freight and General Merchandize	40c
Bar Iron and Nails in lots of 10 tons	30c
Pig Iron " "	25c

CLASSIFIED FREIGHT, TORONTO TO OWEN SOUND

First Class	40c per 100
Second Class	32c "
Third Class	25c "

Special—Owen Sound and Meaford to Toronto.

Wheat, Peas and Beans, in lots of 360 bushels, per 60 lbs	7c
Barley and Buckwheat, in lots of 450 bushels, per 48 lbs	6c
Oats and Malt, in lots of 600 bushels, per 34 lbs	4½c
Flour in barrels, lots of 100, per brl	30c
Flour in bags, in lots of 200, per bag	15c
Through Tickets to Toronto	$4.00
Return Tickets, good for 6 days	6 00

W. H. SMITH,
Master.
Owen Sound, April 21, 1870.   99

Becoming concerned, he steered cautiously even closer to the shore where there was more open water. At about 2 a.m. Tuesday, April 19, just off Vail's Point, he struck a sandbar and ran firmly aground.[4] It was less than a year and a half since he was last aground and surrounded by ice. It is said that Captain Smith behaved with the "bluntness of a sailor,"[5] so it is not hard to imagine the language in the pilothouse. At dawn several crew members rowed back to Owen Sound and dispatched an overland request for help to Collingwood. With the assistance of the steamers *Okonra* and *Waubuno*, the skill of the crew, hard work and a bit of luck, the *Frances Smith* backed off the bar without damage twenty-four hours later and made it to Collingwood by the next day.

The return trip of the *Frances Smith* to Owen Sound by way of Meaford on April 20 was every bit as difficult as her maiden trip of the season to Collingwood. Meaford's harbour was notoriously awkward because of the heavy discharge of springtime water flowing down the Big Head River. Strong currents pushed any approaching vessel away from Meaford's poorly situated wharf. In fact, plans were made in the early spring of that year to do a major renovation of what was called "Stevenson's Wharf."

This wharf was a straight pier extending about 130 metres (about 142 yards) directly north of Bayfield Street, at the foot of Collingwood Street on the west side of the river. Large deposits of sand and mud created bars across the river mouth and the occasional uprooted cedar tree from "up river" added additional hazards to an approach from the east. From the west the water was shallow and strewn with huge submerged boulders. The end of the wharf had less than three metres of water. To compound these difficulties, there was a heavy fog on April 20 as the cold air over the lake mixed with warm moist air over the lands of St. Vincent Township. Captain Smith had difficulty seeing the wharf, let alone docking. He manoeuvered, backed up, moved forward, then repeated the operation several times. When he finally rubbed the side of the wharf and lines were thrown, the assembled crowd on the dock gave a "rousing cheer."[6] The year 1870 had not started well despite the enthusiasm of Meaford's welcoming committee.

By Saturday, April 23, 1870, the *Frances Smith* was in full operation on her regular route from Owen Sound to Collingwood carrying mail, passengers, freight and through shipments to Montreal in concert with Smith's agents at Jacques Tracy & Company, a Montreal trading company.[7] At this point Captain Smith still did not realize he would be involved in the Red River expedition.

*   *   *

By the end of April 1870, Colonel Garnet J. Wolseley[8] was ready to move his forces to the northwest as quickly as possible. It was an ambitious and complex military project and the steamers on Georgian Bay were to play an important part in the logistics. They would have to transport road builders, horses, wagons, food, soldiers and material almost nine hundred kilometres (almost five hundred and sixty miles) from Collingwood to Prince Arthur's Landing at the western end of Lake Superior.

Colonel Garnet Joseph Wolseley (1833–1913), from a photograph by Notman. Colonel Wolseley, leader of the Canadian expedition to the Red River, had had experience in India, China and the Crimea as quartermaster general. His planning skills and background made the transportation of troops from Ontario to Manitoba a brilliant success. Taken from the *Canadian Illustrated News*, June 25, 1870. *Courtesy of the Toronto Reference Library.*

Colonel Wolseley commanded a combined force of British soldiers and Canadian militia. It was agreed that the British troops on the expedition would return to central Canada before the shipping season closed in late October. The Canadian militia would remain in the Red River as a garrison after the campaign was successfully concluded. The force consisted of the following:

Royal Artillery – 20 men with four 7-pounder bronze mountain guns
Royal Engineers – 20 men
1st Battalion 60th Rifles – 377 men
Army Service Corps – 12 men
Army Medical Corps – 8 men
1st Battalion Ontario Rifles (7 companies of 50 men each)
1st Battalion Quebec Rifles – (7 companies of 50 men each)
Staff Officers – 21[9]

In addition there were 120 workers and voyageurs including Native Peoples, principally Mohawks from Kahanwake near Montreal, required for road construction.[10] The support needed to keep the soldiers and workers fed and supplied was considerable. Georgian Bay steamers would be put to the test.

On May 5, 1870, a special train brought Lieutenant General, the Honourable James Lindsay, commanding officer of the Imperial forces in Canada; Colonel Wolseley, commanding officer of the military expedition;

Secretary of State for the United States, Hamilton
Fish, ordered that all Canadian ships carrying
military supplies attempting to press through the
locks at the Sault in 1870 be turned back. Both the
Chicora and the *Frances Smith* were caught up in the
diplomatic wrangle in May 1870. *Courtesy of the U.S.
Library of Congress, LC USZ 62-37517.*

Simon Dawson, road engineer; Frederic Cumberland, manager of the
Northern Railway, and scores of military planners to Collingwood. They
inspected the *Chicora* and the *Frances Smith* and returned to Toronto with
the captains of the two steamers, and an agent of the sidewheeler *Algoma*
to discuss contract arrangements.[11] The *Algoma* was under an initial contract and had already left Collingwood on May 3, fully loaded with "Dawson
men" and equipment. There were no troops on board.

To fully comprehend the broader political and economic scope of the
mission into which the steamers of the Great Lakes were about to be
drawn, it is necessary to turn the clock backwards and understand the
Riel issue in the context of some of the diplomatic pressures and political issues in the United States and Britain.

The proponents of the Northern Pacific Railroad in the States had
visions of a rail line from Minnesota to the Pacific and a spur line into
Canada in order to tap into the resources of the Canadian northwest. They
had powerful lobbyists operating in Washington who had the ear of President Ulysses S. Grant and Secretary of State Hamilton Fish.[12] Their
expansionist views were well-known by the government of Canada, however President Grant was not willing to publicly support the expansionist
position. The American administration was astute enough to realize that
construction of the Northern Pacific Railroad just south of the border
would make any attempt by Canadians to build a solely Canadian railway in the future an economically risky business. Thus the potential
growth of the Canadian West might simply fall into American hands
through economic expediency. Secretary of State Fish believed that

Young Canada: "Never mind, Uncle. I think we can go without your canal." Uncle Sam: "Do tell! Wal [sic] now, I never thought of that!" Taken from the *Canadian Illustrated News*, May 21, 1870. *Courtesy of the Toronto Reference Library.*

Britain wanted to get rid of the burden of Canada anyway because it was a drain on their treasury. Furthermore, he had reports that Confederation was weak and not functioning well. There was dissatisfaction with the new government in the Maritime Provinces and British Columbia was making overtures to join with the United States. In short, there was every reason to believe that Canada might implode on its own without running the risk of offending the British by provocative expansionist moves. The Canadian West might just happen to fall into American hands of its own accord.

In addition, the "Alabama Affair" was not yet resolved. Its future resolution might possibly be used as a lever to gain concessions in Canada from Britain. The United States claim against the British was that the *Alabama,* a commerce raider built in Britain, had caused considerable damage to Union commerce during the Civil War. President Grant's administration demanded compensation from Britain. Thus, when news leaked out that Canada was planning an expeditionary force to deal with Riel, the United States cabinet decided to play hardball. If the British requested permission to move troops and military equipment through the American-controlled Sault locks, permission would be denied. Access to the locks could be used as a bargaining tool for the eventual resolution of the *Alabama* dispute. Fish informed British Ambassador Sir Henry Thornton of the decision to deny troop movements through the Sault locks. He also informed Thornton, that shipping military supplies through the locks was out of the question.

Thornton responded by proposing several scenarios:

1 Allow ships to pass through the Sault locks with men and equipment
2 Allow ships to pass through the Sault locks with material only
3 Allow ships to pass through the Sault locks with neither.[13]

Thornton reminded Fish that Union ships had been allowed to pass through the Canadian Welland Canal between Lake Erie and Lake Ontario during the Civil War without impediment. Fish saw no parallel. Clearly the Canadian steamers were sailing into trouble.

The *Algoma* was the first ship to sail for the head of the lakes. The *Chicora* followed her on May 7. At the same time, on the American side of the border, customs officers were instructed to deny passage through the locks to all ships carrying military supplies. By May 10, the orders were implemented, but the *Algoma*, laden with a "chaos of military stores" had already slipped past the authorities at the American locks. She was now operating in Lake Superior where she would remain over the summer.

The *Chicora* was an iron-hulled, 220-foot blockade runner in the American Civil War, known as the *Let-Her-B*. In 1866, she was purchased by Canadians, cut in half at Sorel, Quebec, and welded together above the Welland Canal. The ship was a symbolic sore point for the Americans and was certain to attract attention when she tried to get through the locks at the Sault in 1870. *Courtesy of the Library and Archives Canada, PA 12446.*

The *Chicora* arrived at the Sault locks five days behind the *Algoma*. With her history as a blockade runner in the American Civil War, it was assumed by Canadian officials there would be trouble for her at the locks. The assumption was not that difficult to make. The Canadian government knew that the Americans did not want Canada to interfere in the events at Red River. What they did not know was that Hamilton Fish, as secretary of state, with the full knowledge of the president, had personally issued orders saying that no military forces would be allowed to pass through the locks without his government's approval.[14] The stage was set for a diplomatic imbroglio.

To avoid a confrontation, the Canadians had decided that *Chicora* would discharge her passengers and military stores on Canadian soil below the rapids.[15] The equipment and stores were then to be carried over a three-mile portage to a landing above the rapids.[16] There they would await the clearing of the "empty" *Chicora* through the American locks.[17] Once reloaded above the rapids, the *Chicora* would proceed to Fort William with her cargo.

In order to pave the way for this "empty" passage of the *Chicora,* the government of Canada went to great lengths to hide the fact that she had been chartered to move military men and stores. To pull off the ruse, the *Chicora* was given a mail contract for $4,900, an unheard of sum for a mail contract at the time. Ostensibly, the steamer was simply a well-paid mail carrier. The addendum to the contract stated the *Chicora* was to carry "such men and stores as the Government may desire to send."[18] The Americans, of course, were not aware of the addendum.

When the "empty" *Chicora* left the Canadian shore and proceeded to the locks, American officers were waiting. They inspected the ship and found several wooden boxes labelled "hardware." After inspection and a four-hour negotiation, passage was denied because the steamer was, in the opinion of the Americans, obviously carrying military supplies.[19] Captain D. McLean of the *Chicora* returned to the Canadian side, unloaded the remainder of his "hardware," and returned to Collingwood.

What happened next was a series of diplomatic moves initiated by Lieutenant-Colonel W.F. Boulton, commanding officer of Canadian forces in the Sault. He first presented himself in civilian clothing to the U.S. commander at the Sault to negotiate passage for the *Chicora*. When that failed, he contacted Ottawa. Canadian government officials let it be known to Secretary of State Fish that unless there was some positive resolution, they might in turn close off the Welland Canal. President Grant blinked. He ordered Governor Henry P. Baldwin of Michigan to henceforth allow vessels like the *Chicora* passage, as long as they carried no military troops or supplies

By May 17, the issue was resolved. Canadian ships with passengers and commercial cargo would be allowed to pass the locks. Military supplies and anything related to Wolseley's expedition on any vessel must be portaged from below the St. Mary's Rapids at the village of Sault Ste. Marie to the landing above the rapids. Once the results of the negotiations were telegraphed back to Collingwood, the 135-foot *Waubuno* immediately departed for the Sault with companies of soldiers under Major Wainright.[20] Piled high on the decks were 15 wagons. Below were hundreds of bags of flour and oats, hay, and nine yoke of oxen. The government of Canada then hired an American vessel, the propeller *Brooklyn,* to pass through the locks without any cargo into Lake Superior. She would work alongside the *Algoma*, moving portaged equipment and men to Fort William and Prince Arthur's Landing from above the Sault locks. Because of the *Brooklyn*'s U.S. registry and the captain's protestations that he was not in the employ of the Canadian government, she managed to get though the locks without American intervention and scrutiny.

With the resolution of this diplomatic issue, all seemed to be in order for the transfer of materials around the Sault locks to Lake Superior. Meanwhile, the *Frances Smith* completed her regular run from Parry Sound to Collingwood on May 20, and on to Owen Sound. Overnight, the ship's carpenter and eight workers built stalls for 40 head of livestock and outfitted the *Frances Smith* for her new job. On the morning of May 21 she returned to Collingwood ready to enter the service of the Canadian government. She would carry Colonel Wolseley's supplies for the looming conflict with Riel.

As the greening of spring spread over the Blue Mountains, Collingwood had been filled with excitement and life all week.[21] Visitors, children and residents swarmed around the wharf hoping to get a glimpse of the soldiers. Special freight trains arrived day and night, blowing their whistles as if to announce a holiday. As a result, the citizenry had very little sleep. The clatter of wagons and shouts of teamsters created a hubbub that transformed the town into a bustling seaport.[22] On the docks there was no time for idlers or spare talk. Workmen were busy hauling heavy bales, rolling barrels of provisions and packing cargo on board the *Frances Smith,* now tied up at the wharf. Hand trucks pushed by rain-drenched men clattered over planks and through the gangway, and onto the forward deck. The freight was dropped into the hold where it was stacked high along the sides. Only a few oil lanterns gave enough light to complete the tasks. The work was brutal and relentless.

Between 8 a.m., Saturday, May 21, and early evening, the *Frances Smith* was loaded with 200 half barrels of pork, 300 barrels of biscuits, 100 barrels of sugar, 300 half barrels of flour, enough tents for a battalion of 350 men, camp equipment, 300 bags of oats, 40 horses with their teamsters and tons of pressed hay. There were caskets of tobacco, bags of beans, and chests of tea crowded into the main deck. The *Chicora* tied, up a few metres away was similarly loaded.[23]

In spite of rain all day, a large throng met the troop train at the station. The first train arrived from Toronto two hours late with three hospital corps, a company of the 60th Rifles[24] and a contingent of staff officers. When the train pulled into Collingwood station with whistle blowing, the rain stopped and the sun appeared.[25] It was a moment of magic. Smart-looking officers, their brass buttons shining, marshalled onto the platform. After them, the soldiers fell into formation. Each soldier carried a bedroll over one shoulder and a rifle on the other. After inspection the soldiers marched to the pier with their kit and their new Bibles, donated by the Upper Canadian Bible Society. The crowd cheered. The soldiers elated by their enthusiastic send off, cheered and waved back to the crowds.

While they lined up to board the waiting ships, a heavy fog rolled in from the frigid bay, obscuring the horizon with a wall of low white clouds. As is common in the spring, heavy fog hunkered over the shoreline and the horizon, while inland warm temperatures and clear skies prevailed. The departures were delayed. By 5:30 p.m. the fog lifted slightly and the *Chicora,* taking advantage of the break in the weather, departed for Sault Ste. Marie, her decks overcrowded with barrels, wagons and soldiers. There was barely room to move about. The people of Collingwood witnessed a grand sight as Queen Victoria's forces sailed from the docks toward the distant fog bank.

Before the *Chicora* was out of sight a second troop train arrived, whistle blowing, with four more companies of the 60th Rifles from Ottawa. The soldiers marched to the wharf and waited until 9 o'clock before the *Frances Smith* was ready for boarding. On command, they filed through the gangway and to the upper saloons where they stowed their gear and then went out on deck. Officers and officials took the comfortable cabins. Along with the soldiers on deck there were regular passengers and some of Dawson's construction workers aboard, all adding to the excitement. By midnight the fog had returned, so the *Frances Smith* delayed sailing. The crowd stayed on the docks until late into the evening, shouting "God's speed" to the soldiers packed onto the decks. They waved and cheered back at the crowds. It was not until dawn the next morning that the *Smith* steamed out of Collingwood harbour toward the hazy horizon, leaving only the smudge of wood smoke behind.

Because of bad weather and Captain Smith's apparent unfamiliarity with the route, the *Frances Smith* arrived at the Sault two days late. The weather remained foggy and rainy, forcing Smith to pick his way slowly through the North Channel. It was later reported that he was lost among the islands and nearly wrecked the ship. An on-board accident in which a drover was gored by one of the oxen caused some concern, further distracting the captain from his duties.

At the Sault, Lieutenant Colonel Boulton was not pleased with Smith's late arrival. He was less pleased on hearing the report from Major Robertson, the commanding officer on the ship, that there were no life preservers on board, and there were only two lifeboats and these could not be lowered into the water because of equipment deficiencies. More damning, was his report that the ship's compasses did not work. And for the most damning information of all, Major Robertson reported that Captain Smith had been drunk during the entire voyage.[26]

While the cargo and troops were being unloaded for transport around the Sault portage, Boulton and Smith got into an argument. Although most of the material was on the dock, some still remained on board the ship. Smith refused to lock upbound through the canal to complete the trip to the Lakehead unless the government covered his vessel with $65,000 insurance against possible loss.[27] Captain Smith then stated, "In the event of your not complying with my request within two hours, I shall charge for the *Frances Smith* at the rate of Five hundred dollars for every twenty-

four hours after 10 p.m. tonight."[28] Smith further demanded a pilot for
the unfamiliar Lake Superior waters.[29] To this latter demand, Boulton
agreed. He refused all the others.

Captain Smith's position was stated clearly in his letter to Boulton:

Sir.

NOT having received any instructions before my departure from
Collingwood to proceed beyond the 'Sault,' I did not effect insurance
upon the 'Frances Smith' for Lake Superior, and the insurance now
held on the 'Frances Smith' only covers as far as this point, consequently I could not think of proceeding to Fort William without a
special guarantee of 65,000 dollars, and also a stipulated amount for
conveyance.[30]

A frustrated Boulton avowed that he would refuse to sign the manifest
when all the material had been unloaded. Smith, who by this time
decided in his own mind that he would not go beyond the Sault, threatened to hold the remaining freight and haul it back to Collingwood
unless Boulton certified his manifest.[31] It was a standoff on the dock
between two iron-willed personalities. In the end, Colonel Boulton
signed the manifest and ordered all passengers and their non-military
cargo off the *Frances Smith* at Sault Ste. Marie. Freight and passengers
were transferred to the *Algoma* and the *Brooklyn*, which awaited departure orders at the landing on the Lake Superior side of the rapids.

Within the week, Captain Smith was back on his regular route along
the east coast of Georgian Bay and Owen Sound. His service with Her
Majesty and the government of Canada had been short and acrimo-
nious. The single trip was enough. As for Colonel Boulton, he had seen
enough of Captain Smith.

*   *   *

By the end of 1870, Riel was on the run and the Red River was firmly
in Canadian control. With the success of Colonel Wolseley's expedition
to Upper Fort Garry and the Red River, there remained the necessity
of keeping order in the vast territories stretching a thousand additional
kilometres to the Rocky Mountains. Whisky traders ranged through
the Canadian prairies selling alcohol and rifles to the Natives in exchange
for buffalo hides. It was a deadly mix, and one that threatened to plunge

this huge part of the continent into a lawless quagmire. In order to meet the challenge, the Canadian government created the North West Mounted Police on May 23, 1873. To allay American fears of a Canadian military presence in the west, the term "police" was selected over the preferred name, North West Mounted Rifles. John A. Macdonald wanted no more "Chicora incidents" in moving the force through the Sault locks. Policemen were not soldiers.

In August, an Order-in-Council authorized the force to be assembled in the spring of 1874, but by September matters were spinning out of control at Fort Whoop-Up (Lethbridge) in the west. In addition, a gang of hunters from Montana had crossed the border and murdered many Natives in what is today southern Saskatchewan. The government's response was quick and decisive. Three detachments of about fifty men were recruited and given orders to proceed from Toronto to Collingwood, and thence by the same route to Red River as Wolseley had taken a few years earlier. They would sail to Prince Arthur's Landing and then haul their equipment over the Dawson Road to Fort Garry.

In 1873, the wharf at Collingwood again became a staging ground for armed forces. The first contingent of recruits and officers arrived by train on October 3 and prepared to sail on board the *Cumberland*. They were a ragtag collection of undisciplined men who had virtually no training and no issued equipment. There was a twenty-four hour delay in the sailing so the commanding officer, Inspector James Walsh, made arrangements to billet the men at the Railway Hotel overnight. They were warned to keep away from too much "intoxicating liquors" and to present themselves on parade the next morning for drill.

After being issued a basic kit of knife, fork, spoon, plate, cup, soap, towel and greatcoat, the men prepared to board the steamer.[32] Even after departure Walsh was so concerned about these recruits that he posted guards at the gangways each time the *Cumberland* arrived at a village along the way through the North Channel. He wanted no trouble. For five days his North West Mounted Police were virtual prisoners on board ship.

The second contingent arrived in Collingwood on October 8 and left aboard the *Chicora*. The third and final contingent of fifty-three men and their officers, (C.F. Young, James McLeod and John Colton), arrived two days later and boarded the waiting *Frances Smith*. Their

The *Cumberland* was a 205-foot steamer built at Port Robinson, Ontario, in 1871. Here, the *Cumberland* steams past the new Collingwood grain elevators heading out to Georgian Bay. In 1873, she carried scores of the North West Mounted Police from Collingwood to the Lakehead. The *Cumberland* was wrecked in Lake Superior in July 1877. Sketch taken from the 1875 "Bird's-eye view of Collingwood." *Courtesy of Scott Cameron.*

full kit with a blanket was issued as they prepared to head out onto Georgian Bay. A sense of adventure among the members of the detachment was evident as the men crowded onto the decks while the *Frances Smith* steamed into the bay past the fortress-like Collingwood grain elevator.

At the end of the voyage the officers wrote a public letter to Captain William Tate Robertson, who by this time had assumed command. Although passage had been rough and the men were seasick, they felt compelled to write this letter of appreciation:

Steamer Frances Smith
Thunder Bay, Oct. 15, 1873

Dear Captain Robertson:
We the undersigned officers in command of detachment of Mounted Police and artillery en route for Fort Garry, who have had the good fortune to sail in your fine steamer from Collingwood to Prince Arthur's Landing, desire, before leaving to express the deep obligations we are under to you for the very pleasant voyage we are just about finishing,

Nothing could exceed the attention and courtesy of every one connected with the vessel, to ourselves and men under our command, and we attribute in great measure the total absence of complaint and irregularity and the continual flow of good humor and heartiness amongst the men to the very perfect arrangements made for their comfort, and excellent food with which they have been supplied.

Wishing you and your obliging and courteous brother a long and prosperous career aboard the good ship Frances Smith, we beg leave to subscribe ourselves, dear Captain Robertson, your obedient servants

> C.F. Young, Capt.
> Superintendent MP
> Jas. F. MacLeod, Lt. Col.
> N.W.M. Police
> John Colton, Lt. C.A.[33]

The return trip of the *Frances Smith* was not so pleasant. A raging storm chased the heavily loaded steamer all the way downbound from Lake Superior back to Collingwood. For three days there was no let up from a full gale that sped the vessel on her final trip of the season, subjecting Robertson and his crew to long hours and dreadful conditions. It was almost impossible to keep a steady course as mountainous waves pushed the stern continually into the troughs of waves. The paddles were lifted out of the water with an attendant loss of power as each trough passed under the ship. Steering was a serious challenge even for a seasoned helmsman. But Captain Robertson was resolute. He wanted to go home. For fourteen hours he stood at his post without a break.

Meanwhile the *Cumberland* and several other steamers were safely at anchor in Waiska Bay on Lake Superior, waiting for the storm to subside.[33] In spite of the gale, a determined Robertson pressed on to Collingwood pushing the limits of his vessel's stability and seaworthiness. He was not waiting for fair weather.

Having arrived home safely, the *Smith* went into service along the south shore of the Georgian Bay for a few more weeks until being laid up for the winter at Owen Sound.

Aboard a Palace Steamer in the 1870s–80s

THE *Frances Smith* was one of several "palace steamers" on the Great Lakes in the mid-nineteenth century. These vessels were characterized as large sidewheel steamers with upper deck cabins, lavish appointments and spacious interiors. They were noted for their fine furnishings, artwork and carpets. While most ran out of ports in the United States, the *Frances Smith* was one of a few operating from Georgian Bay.

For the travelling public, a trip on the *Frances Smith* usually began with a departure from Collingwood or Owen Sound. Both towns in the 1870s were rough and tough places with bars, brothels and a seamy underbelly overlaid with a genteel exterior. Usually passengers arrived in town by rail a day or more before the ship's departure and found accommodation at one of several hotels. Immigrants and itinerant labourers sometimes slept out near the docks. Both towns persistently took swipes at each other, each attempting to present itself as better and more enterprising than the other. For example, *The Collingwood Enterprise* stated that Owen Sound, "Presents the appearance of a rough county town blessed with plenty of the bone and sinew of the nation but with none of the cosmopolitan elements of a city."[1] In response *The Owen Sound Advertiser* claimed that the *Enterprise* exercised "Sublime cheek and impudence" in its evaluation of their home town. Owen Sound, they bragged had "the best drydock, a complete water system and the finest public buildings and churches."[2] A few years later the *Advertiser* called Collingwood a "Forlorn and poverty-

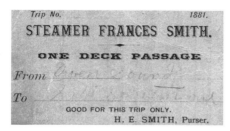

This deck passage ticket on the *Frances Smith* in 1881 from Owen Sound to the Sault, allowed the passenger to board the main deck only. The forward main deck was shared by animals and passengers when there were heavy loads. *Courtesy of Grey Roots Archival Collection.*

stricken hole, and nothing but a fishing village."[3] Prospective passengers on the *Frances Smith* remained aloof from the relentless battle between the two towns and focused on getting aboard quickly.

As the ship approached the dock, the forward gangway was opened by the deckhands in readiness to receive her waiting load of freight piled high on the dock. Just behind the paddlewheel a section of the bulwark was lifted out, revealing a two-metre gangway for passengers. While freight was wheeled through the forward cavity, passengers paraded to the after gangway. Often there was dockside confusion as passengers tried to connect with friends or acquaintances. Families with children attempted to keep everyone together, while businessmen, surveyors and farmers jostled one another to push their way to the purser's wicket. Boarding passengers showed their ticket to an agent or directly to the purser who validated their entry.

There were two classes of passengers on the *Frances Smith:* cabin passengers and deck passengers (steerage). Cabin passengers were given a key, then directed up an interior stairway to their assigned cabins. Deck passengers remained on the main deck. On the promenade deck cabin passengers were accommodated in berths, two or three to a room. These narrow cabins flanked the two forward open spaces or saloons, one of which doubled as a dining room. Cabins located aft of the central engine area at the stern were larger and were classified as staterooms.

By modern standards all cabins were small. There was running water to a small sink in the cabin, fed by gravity from a tank on the hurricane deck above. The entrance to the cabin was on the inside, facing the saloon. An outside window faced the narrow deck. For privacy, a moveable shutter could be pulled up from its wall pocket located below the deck window. Few passengers remained in their cramped cabin, preferring to lounge on the benches located in the saloons or, if the weather was fine, choosing to stroll around the upper decks. The saloons on the promenade deck had a raised ceiling with clerestory windows under a curved and panelled crown. The filtered light from these narrow coloured windows brightened the carpeted open areas below.

The ladies' saloon was essentially off limits to single men. In the forward gentlemen's saloon spittoons squatted in the corners. Cigar and stogie smoke hung in the air. The men played cards and swapped stories. At night there was always someone with a musical instrument to entertain. Dancing, singsongs and poetry renditions were normal late evening diversions.

The two large upper cabin saloons were well-maintained and often repainted. On the walls hung large mirrors with gilt detail superimposed on white walls. This gave cabin passengers a sense of something palatial while aboard. The coal-oil lamps flickering at night and the fluttering decorative bunting by day gave a festive air to every summer voyage. In the first few years, cabin arrangements and interior space were reconfigured to make better use of deck space and changing customer demands. The constant attention to customers insured that the quality of the accommodations aboard the *Frances Smith* was unequalled on the upper lakes in the 1870s.

Cabin passengers usually purchased their meals on board. The food was hearty, hot and sometimes served amidst the confusion of overcrowding in the narrow dining saloon. The boat was only 27 feet wide in total and the cabins on each side of the saloon seriously reduced the area available for dining. Despite the limited quarters, dining saloon passengers were recipients of the full public relations treatment at dinner. On passenger vessels plying the lakes it was customary for the captain to preside over the dining table, asking the Lord's blessing on the food, charming one and all with tales of the lakes and performing the role of host. He carved the roast, made small talk, and initiated toasts to one and all. He was in fact the entertainment steward. Newspaper accounts of voyages on the *Frances Smith* routinely gave Captain Smith and Captain Robertson high praise for "politeness," "gentlemanly conduct," "courtesy," "generosity" and "kindness" to all passengers. During rough conditions, the captain's role changed. He performed the opening rituals at the table and then returned to his post in the pilothouse. Then he was described as "competent," "a fine seaman" and "brave," while many passengers headed for their cabins, green with nausea. Some simply clutched the deck rail, so sick they wanted to die.

In the early years eating was "mess style." Passengers crowded shoulder to shoulder on benches pulled up to wooden plank tables. The chief steward and two waiters served meals on long tables set up on the upper cabin deck. He and his two waiters ran back and forth to the "dumb butler" galley service elevator, dispensing large bowls of steaming food prepared on the main deck below by the cooks, then hauled to the deck above. Perishable food was stored in a zinc-lined cold room where ice was packed in sawdust to keep the temperature low. Often one or two livestock were kept below to be slaughtered for meat en route.

Following one of the later interior design changes on the upper decks, individual tables and chairs were added. While this added a more sophisticated approach to mealtime, the manners of lumberjacks, farmers and miners continued to set the tone. After the meal, the men went out on deck or into the saloon to smoke cigars or stogies. Women returned to the ladies' saloon where they played cards. Sometimes they would promenade around the upper decks if the weather was fine.

One of the best descriptions of cabin meals on a Great Lakes steamer in the 1880s may be found on line at the Project Gutenberg Web site.[4] Mary Fitzgibbon's "A Trip to Manitoba" describes in wonderful detail her experiences on board the steamer *Manitoba* in 1880. The breakfast conditions were the same on the *Frances Smith*. Selected excerpts from her diary are printed below:

> Later the passengers appeared, grumbling at the cold, and at being obliged to turn out so early, and wishing breakfast were ready. ...the friendly steward warning most of us to secure our seats without delay, the cabin-walls being gradually lined with people on either side, each behind a chair. One of the "boys" strode ostentatiously down the long saloon, ringing a great hand-bell.
>
> It was amusing to watch the different expressions on the faces down the lines while waiting for breakfast. Men, chiefly surveyors, who during their annual trips to and from work had got used to "that sort of thing," took it coolly; judiciously choosing a seat directly opposite their state-room door, or standing in the background, but near enough to expel any intruder. New men, looking as uncomfortable as if they had been caught in petty larceny, twisted their youthful moustaches, put their hands in their pockets, or leant against the wall, trying to look

perfectly indifferent as to the event; some of their neighbours smiling satirically at their folly. Old farmer-looking bodies, grumbling at the crush, mingled with Yankees, toothpick in hand, ready for business; sturdy Englishmen...and dapper little Frenchmen, hungry yet polite. Here stood a bright-looking Irishwoman, who vainly tried to restrain the impatience of five or six children...there, an old woman, well-nigh double with age, who, rather than be separated from the two stalwart sons by her side, was going to end her days in a strange land. Here was a group of bright, chatty little French Canadians, with the usual superabundance of earrings and gay ribbons decorating their persons; there, a great raw-boned Scotchwoman, inwardly lamenting the porridge of her native land, frowned upon the company.

The bell ceased, and – "Presto!" all were seated, and turning over their plates as if for a wager. Then came a confused jumble of tongues, all talking at once; the rattle of dishes, the clatter of knives and forks, and the rushing about of the boy-waiters. It required quick wit to choose a breakfast dish, from the "White-fish – finanhaddy – beef-steak – cold roastbeef – muttonchop – bacon – potatoes – toast – roll – brown-bread-or-white – tea-or-coffee," shouted breathlessly by a youth on one side, while his comrade screamed the same...[4]

As went breakfast, so went dinner, but with the captain presiding and decorum more evident.

Steerage passengers often carried their own food and a blanket. Their passage was characteristically more uncomfortable. During heavily sold trips burly lumberjacks, immigrants and labourers competed for some-place to sleep on the floor of the main deck or on cushioned benches around the periphery of the stern parlour. If there was an overflow, they moved into the forward area where freight was stored. The smell of crowded men in heavy woollen clothing can only be imagined. Fami-lies staked out a corner in the large after saloon or on the main deck forward where they exercised territorial control for the trip. Some stayed on the open fantail at the stern for the entire passage, whether rain, shine or storm. They were not allowed into the upper cabin areas. That is not to say that their large communal parlour was shabby. It had large rectangular leaded glass windows with ornate scrollwork around the top and the room itself was well-finished inside. When the boat was not overloaded, the conditions in steerage were quite acceptable. Since the galley was located on the main deck, tea, hot water and simple food were available to these passengers.

Sundays were special days complete with the captain reading the lesson. There was usually a hymn sing and, if a priest or minister was aboard, a sermon was usually on the agenda.

Aboard ship were two "ladies' maids" whose role was to look after the female passengers, replace bed linens and to insure general tidiness. A porter looked after the luggage, the mailroom and the needs of passengers during the late evening. The purser handled all the money, tickets and administrative tasks, including payment of the crew, loading manifests and customs clearances. There were no lists of steerage passengers on board.[5] Being on board a ship was similar to riding the railway. Pay your money, get a ticket and climb aboard. Reserved and prepaid tickets were recorded by the purser, as were cabin allocations. Tickets were valid for thirty days and, for an extra small fee, a layover at any one of the small ports was possible.[6]

The chief engineer and a second engineer, who had the responsibility of making sure the pressure in the steam boilers remained up, were in the boiler room. The firemen and the wood-passers maintained the fires. The work of the engineer's crew down in the hold was hard, dirty and dangerous. They toiled in dark, hot conditions below the waterline, with their only the light coming from the glimmer of a few coal oil lanterns hanging on hooks and the boiler fires when the furnace doors were opened.

After 1888 first-class or cabin passengers could purchase a layover ticket, allowing them to break up a trip. This arrangement was convenient for sales people visiting several communities along the route of the north shore. *Courtesy of Gore Bay Museum.*

The deck crew (four to six men) was under the authority of the two mates. Their responsibility was to secure and caulk the gangway doors with oakum when heading out on the lake, to coil and splice heavy hemp ropes, to secure and release lines at the dock as well as doing routine maintenance. They loaded and unloaded freight, painted and did any manual labour required on board ship.

A wheelsman worked in an apprenticeship role in the pilothouse, steering on the long legs of the trip and assisting the mates and captain with navigation. A watchman assisted with work and made regular rounds of the vessel. In all, the *Frances Smith* carried a crew of twenty-four to thirty.

At intermediate destinations around the lake, the gangway doors were opened and the heavy gangplanks were pulled onto the wharf. Mail was off-loaded immediately. Passengers then disembarked at the stern gang-way. Package freight, and then food stuffs (eggs packed in barrels full of sawdust, apples and slabs of pork) were trucked from the main gang-way by the deck crew pushing two-wheeled trucks. Next came the heavy items: salt, bagged grain, stoves, ploughs and iron tanks. And finally the livestock were herded into pens at the dockside. When the lading and unloading were completed, the captain gave a warning blast on the whistle, calling passengers back to the boat, and they were off again.

*   *   *

Before the railway connected Collingwood and Meaford in November 1872, a steamer on the Owen Sound to Collingwood route was a valu-able link in a relatively efficient transportation system on southern Georgian Bay. Beginning with the *Oxford* in 1855, Captain W.H. Smith continued his daily service with the *Clifton*, the *Canadian* and the *Frances Smith* up until the early 1870s.[7]

After the spur of the Toronto to Collingwood railway (Ontario, Sim-coe & Georgian Bay Line) reached Thornbury in July 1872, a "stage" between Meaford and Thornbury expedited the mail where it was sent by rail through to Collingwood and then to Toronto by train.[8] Meaford ceased to be an important steamer stop. When the rail link between Owen Sound and Toronto was finally completed in 1873, there was no longer any need for steamers to carry mail exclusively between Owen Sound and Collingwood. The horizons of lake traffic were now much wider and there was little demand for the large capacity offered by the *Frances Smith* on

Sir Sandford Fleming C.M.G., Chancellor of Queen's University 1880–1915. Sandford Fleming and a group of friends travelled west on the *Frances Smith* in July 1872. His friend, Reverend George Grant, published a diary on the trip. He seems to have been critical of everything from the ship's food to the captain's behaviour. *Courtesy of Library and Archives Canada, C-014238.*

her usual mail runs. It was time for a change. Besides, the owners believed that the *Frances Smith* could make more money on the Collingwood/Lake Superior route running to Sault Ste. Marie and the Lakehead.

It was on one of these regular sailings between Collingwood and Port Arthur that Sandford Fleming[9] (later known as the father of standard time) and friends sailed in July 1872. By then the ship was owned by William H. Smith's estate. The former purser, William Tate Robertson, nephew of Frances Jane (Eberts) Smith, at only twenty-four years of age was her new captain.

It seems that in the first year of operation after William H. Smith's death, there were loose ends that didn't auger well for the ship. Reverend George Grant, a close friend and travelling companion of Sandford kept a diary of the voyage and was not complimentary about the operation of either the boat or her master. Robertson was a greenhorn and had yet to acquire the full set of skills and responsibilities of captain. Over time he certainly learned to run a tight ship with confidence and an iron hand, but in 1872 these attributes were not yet apparent.

Grant stated that, when he and Fleming arrived at Collingwood from Toronto by train on July 16, the *Frances Smith* was scheduled to depart at 2 p.m. Instead he found commotion and near chaos. Amid the hustle and bustle of loading the baggage, the gangway became dislodged and the porter fell into the harbour. Unable to swim, he had to be rescued by one of the passengers who jumped in to save him. The initial disorder was inauspicious. Reverend Grant reported that an announcement was made at 2 p.m. stipulating that departure would be delayed until 6 p.m. Then at 6 p.m. it was announced that they would not leave until midnight. The *Frances Smith,* in fact, did not leave until 5:30 a.m. the next morning. Other passengers, including Fleming, were annoyed at the delay, but said nothing.

At 11 a.m. on July 17, the *Frances Smith* arrived at Owen Sound. She was supposed to lie over only long enough to take on a few passengers and provisions. Five hours later she was still at the wharf without "getting up steam."[10] According to Grant, the baggage and freight could have been loaded in an hour. Yet the boat still sat unmoving at the dock.

"In despair, we went in a body to the captain to remonstrate," he wrote. Robertson frankly agreed that it was "too bad," but "disclaimed all responsibility, as the Government Inspector, on a number of trifling pleas, would not let him start, nor give him his certificate." The real reason, Robertson said to Fleming's party was "that he [Robertson] was too virtuous to bribe inspectors." The deputation at once hunted up the inspector, and heard the other side of the story. A month before, the steamboat inspector had ordered the owners to purchase new sails and to replace the safety valve on the boiler. But the captain had "humbugged" and "done nothing" to meet the inspector's demands. The upshot was that the *Frances Smith* was not allowed to sail until Robertson complied with his orders.

Grant concluded that Captain Robertson, not the inspector, was clearly responsible for the delays. The passengers told the captain so, and they were promised that the ship would be under way quickly. Robertson consulted with the inspector and after some negotiation the order to sail was given. About 6 p.m. that evening, the *Frances Smith* headed out of Owen Sound to Leith, a small community on the east side of "The Sound" where the ship was to take on cordwood for the long trip north. They arrived at 6:30 p.m. and tied up to the small wharf. Fleming and his friends went for a walk, had a swim and returned to the boat to discover that the loading of the wood was going very slowly. Reverend Grant observed, "...two or three men set to work leisurely to carry on board a few sticks of wood from eight or ten cords piled on the wharf."[11]

By 10 p.m. Captain Robertson was still not ready to start. A whole pile of wood was yet to be loaded and the labourers were lounging, talking and generally taking their time. For his part, Robertson, a bachelor, was having a wonderful time dancing with the ladies inside the main cabin. Eventually a half dozen passengers assisted in stowing the cordwood and Captain Robertson set sail for Killarney two hours after midnight.

Grant remarked in his diary, "...the subordinates seemed to have learned from their leader the trick of 'how not to do it.' " In addition to all the delay, Grant complained that the milk was sour, and there was no attempt at getting more while in Owen Sound; there was no cheese to eat with beer after dinner and nobody seemed to be able to figure out where to find it.

The remainder of the trip through the North Channel was uneventful and, by May 21, the *Frances Smith* was beyond Sault Ste. Marie at "Nepigon Bay." Along the north coast of Lake Superior, there seemed to be ample time for disembarking to look for botanical specimens and to do a bit of trout fishing. The trip seemed more like a leisurely excursion than a regular voyage.

Service, passenger entertainment and customer satisfaction apparently improved a year later when twenty-eight-year-old John Walter Harris, a land surveyor, sailed aboard the *Frances Smith* in mid-July 1873. In his diary he had nothing but praise for the trip from Owen Sound to Port Arthur. He wrote, "Some pleasant young ladies on the steamer, also a fair brass band."[12] Later Harris noted, "We had dancing every night and a very pleasant time all the way." The still unmarried Captain Robertson was still interested in the finer things of steamer service and made sure his scheduled trips were interesting. For him that meant there had to be dancing. Possibly the divergent opinions expressed by Grant and Harris may simply have been that the tastes of a young land surveyor differed from those of an older clergyman.

The satisfaction noted by Harris was confirmed in August 1874. Mr. A.A. Wright wrote a letter to *The Renfrew Mercury* with his flattering account of his voyage aboard the *Frances Smith*.[13] Excerpts of his letters, printed below, give us the best possible snapshot about life aboard a steamer sailing from Georgian Bay to Prince Arthur's Landing:

Little Current, August 5, 1874
...We left Toronto at 11:30 a.m. on Tuesday by the Northern Railway for Collingwood....

At 5 o'clock on Tuesday night all were safely on board the steamer

"Francis (sic) Smith," except one French Canadian…We had been fortunate enough to secure our staterooms at Toronto, and well for us was
it that we did, for the boat, large and commodious as it is, was crowded
to overflowing in every part with passengers alone. Two hundred and
fifty Mennonites who arrived at Collingwood a few days previous,
crowded the lower part of the vessel to such an extent that no freight
could be taken, except what cattle and sheep were carried by the vessel to be killed on the way to supply its tables. The captain spoke of
these immigrants in the highest terms. Although they had been in
Collingwood for several days previous to embarking, they were never
known to swear, quarrel among themselves, or taste a drop of spiritu-
ous liquors; and they appeared to be very cleanly, inoffensive and withal,
intelligent class of people. They came from the south of Russia…

The first place we touched after leaving Collingwood was Owen
Sound. Here we received on board the brass band of the 31st Battalion, who are going on their annual trip round Lake Superior, to Duluth
and back; consequently we will enjoy their company the whole way.
We next touched Presque Isle about 11 o'clock Tuesday night, when
all "turned in" to enjoy a good night's rest, the weather being all that
we could possibly desire for pleasure and comfort… Weather delightful, scarcely a ripple on the surface of the water. Passed Lonely Island
a little before noon, and with the aid of field glasses had an excellent
view of the shore next to us and the lighthouse. We next reached Killarney… The houses are chiefly wigwams, made of poles collected at
a point at the top, and spread out at the bottom, and covered with
mats woven of rushes. The inhabitants profess the Roman Catholic
religion, and speak the French language. They gathered in great numbers on the shore as we approached, attracted by the music of the band,
and appeared to enjoy it immensely…Leaving Little Current at dark
the passengers aboard the steamer arranged for a grand Concert and
Ball, which came off with great success, dancing being continued until
a pretty late hour, notwithstanding the presence on board of the Roman
Catholic Archbishop of Toronto, the Bishop of Algoma, and several
Roman Catholic priests and Protestant clergymen.

On Thursday morning we reached Bruce Mines where we
remained for about half-an-hour and all embarked on an exploring
expedition to the mines. None of them are now being worked except

one…At one time a very large business was done here, but now the
place is in a very dilapidated condition. All were anxious to procure
specimens of the ore but few, however, were successful…We succeeded
in procuring a few, when the whistle blew and there was a general
race for half-a-mile to the boat, at which we arrived just in time, and
no more, but with appetites sharpened and in good time for breakfast. Early in the forenoon we passed through Nebeeshe [Neebish
Rapids], and really more beautiful scenery is rarely to be found…On
several of the bold rocks which form the shore, were engraved by the
aborigines rough images of men, wild beasts, & c. After passing Garden River we came to the much talked of Sault Ste. Marie.

The boat called at the Canadian side to bury a child belonging to
one of the Mennonites which died early in the morning from disease
of the throat: and as we had to wait for a rough coffin to be made we
had ample time to get a good view of the place. It is not over half the
size of the village on the American side…In about an hour after leaving the Sault we reached White Fish Point, a place containing one
store, two dwelling houses and several wigwams. The principal occupation of the inhabitants being the curing of white fish and salmon
trout for the American and Canadian markets, large quantities of
which are shipped weekly during the season of navigation. A good
trade is done here in selling Indian bark and beadwork to tourists,
many of the articles being very neat and the mats in particular bringing a very high price. This is the last port at which we touch before
reaching Duluth, the captain having determined to proceed by the
south shore, so as to land the emigrants and then proceed to Thunder Bay. This will lengthen our trip by one day…[14]

From 1872 through into the 1880s the *Frances Smith* worked the Georgian Bay to Lake Superior route on a regular timetable. Advertisements
and travel writings found in Toronto papers in the mid-1870s sang the
praises of a trip along the North Channel and Lake Superior as an experience not to be missed for its leisurely pace along the world's most
spectacular shorelines. The natural beauty of the Laurentian Shield
around Lake Superior, the opportunity to visit an authentic Indian village, the prospect of fishing the prolific waters at Nipigon and the chance
to invest in one of the new mines at Michipicoten were simply too great

to miss. A passage on the splendid and commodious *Frances Smith* was offered both as an opportunity and a pleasure.

By the mid-1880s there was a more focused business approach to regular sailings. In the early days, strict adherence to timetables was not always front and centre on the lake steamer's agenda. Bad weather, loading delays and unforeseen events meant that the long distances over defined routes combined to make schedules more like suggested arrivals and departures rather than deadlines to be met. In spite of this it is surprising how closely the *Frances Smith* did meet her printed timetables. *The Port Arthur Weekly Sentinel* recorded the comings and goings of ships in and out of that port in the 1880s. On most occasions the steamer was within a few hours of the printed schedule. Recognizing that she was covering over a thousand kilometres (over six hundred and twenty miles) from Collingwood, the accomplishment is amazing.

It was common knowledge that the criteria (in order of importance) for making money with a steamer were to: 1) load as much freight as you can, 2) sell as many passenger tickets as possible, 3) secure a Royal Mail Contract. But there was little customer loyalty at the dockside. The first steamer to a wharf loaded the freight if it was on the route on a first-come, first-served basis. There was competition for passengers too, particularly for large groups. With this kind of rivalry for business, the pressure to arrive at the dockside as early as possible was intense.

When Captain Robertson and Captain Smith's widow decided to shift the *Frances Smith* to the Lake Superior route in 1872, competition was much more serious than plashing about from Owen Sound to Collingwood. Now Robertson faced the Northern Railway organization with its alliances to the old *Algoma,* the *Chicora* and their newly built *Cumberland.* Even though the railway spur reached Meaford in mid-November of 1872, causing a loss of passengers and freight, there was still enough commerce to justify a smaller ship on the south Georgian Bay route. So, with their eyes on the bottom line, they contracted the *Silver Spray,* owned by Packer and Company of St. Catharines, to service Owen Sound for the 1872 summer season.[15]

The arrangement worked well until late fall, when the *Silver Spray* had a serious breakdown just off Thornbury. The walking beam broke but the piston continued its up and down action. Pieces of iron were sent flying along the hurricane deck and a large chunk of metal crashed though the deck into the promenade deck. Fortunately no one was injured. The *Silver Spray*, left without power, drifted helplessly all night while the *Algoma* searched for her. It was not until the next morning that the vessel was found and towed to Owen Sound for repairs. The *Frances Smith* was quickly pulled off the Lake Superior route and returned to Georgian Bay for the remaining three weeks of the season.[16]

The *Frances Smith* ended the year on Sunday, December 1, 1872, and tied up to the Peel Street dock below the Smith's home. During the preparations to lay up for the winter, Isaiah Davis, the forty-three-year-old chief engineer, was concerned that the ship was not berthed properly. It was just before noon. He ordered his second engineer, Frank Young, to move the *Frances Smith* ahead by giving the paddles a couple of turns and immediately went down into the crank room. Davis apparently stuck his head inside the paddle box to look at the water levels. Young gave the engine a turn and a half and then stopped.

Meanwhile the bell was rung for dinner and the officers sat down for their noon meal. Chief Engineer Davis did not show up. After dinner, the second engineer went down to the crank room and looked in. To his horror, there was the bloodied body of Davis stretched out on the floor. Young ran forward to get Captain Robertson, who hurried back to the crank room with the crew. Davis had been almost decapitated when he looked into the hole and miscalculated the speed of the wheel in making a revolution.[17] It was a tragic way to end the season.

Over the winter of 1872–73, work began in earnest to repair and upgrade both the *Silver Spray* and the *Frances Smith* for regular steamer service in 1873. The Corbet Company of Owen Sound installed a new walking beam and cylinder in the *Silver Spray* and new staterooms and upper cabins were built. Major decking changes were undertaken to make the ship more seaworthy. The former mate of the *Canadian*, William Myers, was appointed captain of the *Silver Spray* for the new season.

At the Peel Street dock, painters, woodworkers and metalworkers did a major cosmetic job on the *Frances Smith* as well. New furniture was purchased for the saloons and the upper cabins and staterooms were hung with gold and crimson damask curtains. Stencils depicting floral bouquets were painted on the interior walls of the saloon between the doors leading to the cabins. Transfer pictures of floral arrangements were pasted to the walls of the ladies' saloon and mirrors were hung on the doors, giving the room a spacious appearance.[18] A large portrait of the late Captain William H. Smith was placed prominently for all to see. A number of planks were replaced in the hull and the engines were completely overhauled. By the time the ice went out of Owen Sound harbour in 1873, both vessels were shipshape.

That spring Captain Robertson hired a new chief engineer, John Lee, and brought his older brother James J. Robertson, a lawyer, on board as the purser. James remained only a short while and was soon replaced by a cousin, John W. Waddell. Duncan Macpherson was hired as the chief steward. The captain and his crew had their work cut out for them. Their client base was beginning to shift. Immigrants from Europe were flooding into Canada, and the railway with its labour demands was about to commence construction in the west. Robertson and his aunt, Frances Jane Smith, saw opportunity on the horizon if they could only tap into the stream of Canadian growth. It meant new alliances with railways, other steamer operators and politicians.

*   *   *

Sir John Douglas Sutherland Campbell, Marquis of Lorne, 9th Duke of Argyll, husband of Princess Louise Caroline Alberta, (the daughter of Queen Victoria), was appointed Governor General of Canada in 1878. The duke was a good-looking young man when appointed at the age of thirty-three and was an inveterate traveller. It has been speculated that his promiscuous trolling in the parks of London prompted this appointment so far away from wagging tongues in England. In July 1881, he travelled even farther away by touring the Canadian west.

Along with his small entourage, the Governor General of Canada, Lord Lorne, spent five days aboard the *Frances Smith* in July 1881. The summer weather on the trip was perfect. Along with formal visits to communities, he was able to spend time relaxing, drinking tea and reading while seated at the stern of the promenade deck. *Courtesy of Library and Archives Canada, C 52051.*

On the second leg of his tour, from Collingwood to Port Arthur, he and his entourage (without his wife) booked several suites aboard the *Frances Smith*.

Several members of the British press were given free passage in return for filing stories back home about the glories of Canada and the potential for investment in a land of unlimited possibilities.[19] The Canadian press complained bitterly about the expense of the trip and the fact that they had to pay their own way in order to cover the story.[20] The Governor General's office countered by stating that the four members of the British press were accompanying him as personal friends. That did not stop the griping by some of the Canadian press, especially Toronto's *Globe*.

Others, in addition to the members of the press, included: Lieutenant Colonel De Winton, who was responsible for making all arrangements and contracting the *Frances Smith*; Reverend Dr. McGregor, a personal chaplain, and Lord Lorne's doctor, Dr. Colin Sewell. In order to make sure there was appropriate staff available, three aides-de-camp were assigned to the trip.[21]

The entourage left Toronto on a special train decorated with evergreen wreaths interwoven with the Campbell tartan. They arrived in Collingwood late in the afternoon and, after a reception in town, boarded the *Frances Smith* just before 8 p.m. The viceregal party took the six larger staterooms at the stern of the *Frances Smith* where they had exclusive use of a curtained section of the aft saloon as well as the cabin deck area at the stern. The deck area was decorated with cedar boughs and lanterns so that the Governor General's party could lounge in private. Captain Robertson and his officers welcomed all on board and immediately sailed for Meaford just as the sun was setting over Cape Rich, arriving at their destination near midnight.

The town of Meaford was decked out with flags and bunting. Torches lined both sides of the wharf and the main street. As the *Frances Smith* touched the dock, a large crowd cheered the royal visitor and the band played marching music. Mayor Charles Burns, who had accompanied Lord Lorne from Collingwood, introduced him to his councillors and to the local gentlemen lined up on the dock. A parade of citizens formed at the foot of Stevenson's Wharf. Cyrus R. Sing, one of Meaford's high profile citizens and the reeve of St. Vincent Township, had his polished carriage at the ready and waiting. The

Governor General, with appropriate ceremony, climbed aboard and set off down the street while two bands fell in behind.[22] The dignitaries stopped at Raper's Hotel, and toasts were made all around. Lord Lorne then mounted the stairs to the hotel's exterior balcony, made a short speech and listened courteously to the cheers of the crowd that had by this time swollen to almost three thousand people. The throngs below the wooden balcony sang "God Save the Queen," and gave three cheers for the Marquis and the absent Princess Louise. With a salute, Lord Lorne returned to Sing's carriage and paraded once again through the town and back to the waiting *Frances Smith*. Now fully lit with lanterns on all decks, the ship must have looked like a Christmas tree.

Captain Robertson ordered his crew to cast off, and the steamer slipped out to the dark bay with the royal guest preparing for bed in his stateroom. Shortly thereafter the he was fast asleep. Naturally, upon arrival at Owen Sound at 4 a.m., Captain Robertson was careful not to disturb His Excellency. There were no speeches at the dock. No bands played. There were no blasts on the ship's whistle. Every attempt was made to minimize noise.

Unfortunately for the slumbering regal guest, just before 6 a.m. a load of fat cattle destined for the west, was loaded amidst great bawling and snorting. They stampeded onto the main deck of the *Frances Smith,* waking everybody on board.[23] Shortly thereafter, the steamer departed with the unhappy cattle and possibly an unhappy governor general. We do know that the ship left behind a disgruntled set of Owen Sound politicians who were unable to meet their royal visitor because of his need for a quiet night.

Under clear skies and a gently rolling sea, the *Frances Smith* headed for Killarney. As she neared Lonely Island, a veil of mist hovered on the horizon and turned into a rain shower as they steamed north.[24] On arriving at Killarney, the Governor General went ashore for an hour to meet some of the residents and to attend a church bazaar.[25] Next day, July 21, was a fine windless day as they headed for Little Current on Manitoulin Island. The passengers sat out on the fantail, reading, chatting, drinking tea and promenading around the decks and looking at the scenery. To the north the rounded quartzite La Cloche Mountains, clothed in white pine at their lower levels, glimmered in the morning sunshine. The sea was quiet as the *Frances Smith* cut leisurely through the blue North Channel water, casting her shining wake to the sides and causing waves to wash the shores of uninhabited islands. It was a perfect day for a boat ride.

On arriving at Little Current they found the village decked out with a huge arch of spruce branches with the motto "God Save the Queen – God Bless the Campbells." By the time the *Frances Smith* finally tied up, it was dark. Still, everyone on board including the other paying passengers walked through the village, holding lanterns to see the local church, meet with Ojibwe Chief Nahgahboh and exchange gifts. The governor general made a special effort to talk with several of the Native women at their wigwams.

Once again everyone returned to the *Frances Smith* tied to the dock, but the steamer stayed there for several hours. In the pre-dawn hours of July 22, while everyone was still asleep, she left for the Sault.

As they entered the lower St. Mary's River, the vessel worked her way through the difficult Neebish Rapids until she reached Lake George. There they passed the wreck of the *Asia*, that fateful ship which would, a year later, sink again in Georgian Bay with one hundred persons on board. In this incident, which had just occurred two weeks earlier while downbound from the Sault, the *Asia* had passed the upbound steam barge *Havana* towing another barge called the *Helena*. Somehow the *Asia* crossed the towline and crashed into the *Helena*. A huge hole was ripped in the bow of the *Asia*. Captain Birney managed to beach his ship and evacuate all passengers and crew to safety. When the *Frances Smith* passed by on July 22, the *Asia* was still resting with its bow high out of the water and the stern submerged so that water covered the hurricane deck.[26] Captain Robertson slowed the *Frances Smith* and moved in close to the wreck so that all could have a good look at the beached ship. Little did anyone realize that the repaired *Asia* would end her career so tragically in September 1882 when she sank near Lonely Island. Her sinking and the resulting inquiry resulted in tougher regulations for the *Frances Smith* and other passenger vessels on the upper lakes.

The *Frances Smith* made a special stop for formal ceremonies at the Indian village of Garden River, where Ojibwe chiefs from around the District of Algoma assembled. In full-feathered splendor, they greeted the Governor General at the wharf. As the crew opened the doors of the gangway, a row of burly Native marshals lined up to clear a path

Pow Wow at Garden River, Ontario, artist SP. Hall, dated
July 1881. Lord Lorne meets with Chief Augustin
Shingwauk at Garden River near Sault Ste. Marie.
Courtesy of Library and Archives Canada, C-012836.

so that Lord Lorne could meet the array of chiefs, dressed in elaborate
ceremonial regalia.[27] Chief Augustin Shingwauk[28] was resplendent with
his headdress made of a skunk hide adorned with eagle feathers. A large
disk of birchbark was slung around his neck over a scarlet vest orna-
mented with white, red and yellow beads. At this time, Shingwauk was
an imposing grey-haired older man, weighing over two hundred
pounds. The Governor General, accompanied by his entourage, the jour-
nalists and Captain Robertson, paraded past floral displays onto the sand
beach which had been layered in sawdust to protect His Excellency's
royal feet from the water-soaked ground.[29] Greetings and pleasantries
were exchanged. The chiefs then offered Lord Lorne a peace pipe but
it was noted that he refused to smoke.[30] At the end of the ceremonies,
the vice-regal entourage walked back to the wharf and reboarded for
the short trip to Sault Ste. Marie.

At the Sault, Robertson remained at the dock for several hours while
Lord Lorne was first taken to the Shingwauk School for Indian children and then rowed across the St. Mary's River to the Michigan side
where he was greeted by a number of local officials.[31] The *Smith* next
passed through the locks at the Sault just after dark. Once in Lake
Superior, Captain Robertson made a stop at Michipicoten Island[32] and

anchored a short distance offshore. When the steamer was secured, the tug *Mocking Bird* pulled alongside and the governor general climbed aboard along with the routine freight, mailbags and local passengers. As the tug neared the island, a small rowboat came alongside and he stepped aboard to be rowed to shore. He was met by the mine manger, Mr. W.W. Stuart, who gave him a tour of the copper mine. Later that day after Lord Lorne returned to the *Frances Smith,* the weather began to turn ugly. Fog and mist hung over Lake Superior and the wind picked up. Robertson weighed anchor and headed for Silver Islet[33] where they made a short stop the next day.

Early in the morning as they left Silver Islet it started to rain. Brooding Lake Superior heaved slate grey swells from the west, threatening to make the last leg of the voyage a very unpleasant experience for the royal party. An ominous bank of fog lurked on the horizon and the breeze stiffened. Captain Robertson, conscious of the fact that rolling seas in bad weather might upset the regal stomach, altered his pre-arranged arrival plans. He was supposed to round Pie Island from the lake at the entrance to the harbour. Instead he took an inside passage.[34] An hour or so out, Robertson ordered his crew to run up extra bunting, streamers and flags for the grand arrival at Port Arthur.

And arrive they did, complete with a seventeen-gun salute from the shore and cheering crowds on the docks. It didn't matter that their appearance around noon was two hours early. The *Frances Smith* was as splendidly decorated as a birthday cake and as welcomed as mail from the Hebrides for the many Scots inhabitants. The local dignitaries were ready, all dressed in their finest, with speeches in their hands. As the *Frances Smith* approached Prince Arthur's Landing on July 25, 1881, a red carpet was rolled out from the dock all the way to the Queen's Hotel where a reception had been arranged.[35]

Lord Lorne stayed on the *Frances Smith* for lunch and then, dressed in a blue hunting shirt and a woodsman's outfit, prepared to disembark.[36] Attired in this improbable garb, he thanked Captain Robertson and his crew for a pleasant journey, and then paraded with his small entourage under several spruce bough arches to the Queen's Hotel to meet the people of the town. Shortly thereafter he left by train, heading for Winnipeg. Since the railway track ended forty miles away from Prince Arthur's Landing, part of the trip had to be made by foot.

The motivation for the Duke's outfit for the day was clearly political. He wanted to impress upon the good citizens of Port Arthur that he was going to walk the route of the proposed new CPR line, which the residents believed to be the golden path to riches, linking the northwest to the east through integrated rail and steamer routes. The Governor General's public relations posturing was an affirmation of the government's will to complete a transcontinental railway. Meanwhile his luggage remained on board the *Frances Smith,* to be delivered by one of his officers to Duluth where it was to be transshipped to Winnipeg.[37] He could not be expected to carry his own luggage.

*   *   *

Mid-nineteenth century excursions were run to make money for event organizers and boat owners alike. Arrangements were normally made to share profits, so it was in the organizer's and shipowner's mutual interest to pack as many people on board as possible, with little regard for safety. When the Meaford Masonic Lodge chartered the *Frances Smith* for the 1869 Dominion Day excursion, the ship was seriously overloaded. *The Meaford Monitor* estimated that 1,100 people crowded into the *Frances Smith*, and also observed that some additional people did not get on board because they feared the consequences of overloading.[38] The decision to restrict boarding was not made by either Captain Smith or the Masons, rather it was option of potential passengers exercising good judgment.

The weather for the trip was perfect. There was little wind, the sky was clear and the lake was mirror smooth. As the passengers crowded aboard, the purser was somewhat overwhelmed with the swarm of people. Ticket-taking took longer than expected. Captain Smith did not pull away from the dock until well after the posted departure time, but that did not seem to matter. This was a carefree excursion on the finest ship on Georgian Bay, on one of the finest days of the season.

Well out into the bay, the effects of overloading soon became evident. The wooden hurricane deck above the cabin deck was supported by metal stanchions and, as the *Frances Smith* steamed ahead, several hundred merrymakers crowded the rail of this upper deck to get a better view of the passing scenery. Without warning, one of the stanchions at the stern snapped under the weight above, causing one corner to sag into the deck below. Planking broke and crashed on the passengers standing underneath. In giving way, several boards struck a young man by the name of

Gilray and injured his leg.[39] Fortunately, no one else appears to have been hurt in the incident and apparently few took serious notice.

The Meaford Monitor reported later that all the passengers had a wonderful time, and further reported that the crowd was "generally well-behaved." The newspaper's observation leaves enough ambiguity in the statement to imagine that some rowdiness occurred, as was normal on mid-19th century excursions. A few drinks consumed by a few boisterous, hard-working pioneers out for a good time was to be expected. Despite the growing Temperance Movement in Grey County, whisky was always at hand. This was a Masonic excursion and the Masons always arranged to build in opportunities to "retire for refreshments" during their meetings and on their excursions.

Accidents due to overcrowding on passenger boats of the time seldom brought about changes. Steamboat inspectors had a certain degree of power, but the underlying regulations were inadequate. While it was a regulation that all passenger boats carry lifeboats, there were never enough for full capacity excursion crowds.

*   *   *

When there was maintenance work to be done on the *Frances Smith* at a distant dry dock, William H. Smith, ever the opportunistic entrepreneur, developed an extended excursion for interested passengers. In 1871, Owen Sound had not yet constructed the community's first drydock, and the *Frances Smith* had to go to Detroit for a contracted refit during the last week of August. Smith, who possibly was not feeling well, promoted his purser and nephew, William Tate Robertson, to the post of captain. The trip was to be a shared command.

As Captain Smith was preparing to set sail, word came that the brand new paddlewheel steamer, the *Manitoba*, purchased by the Beatty family for $60,000, had run aground at Cove Island.[40] Although Captain James B. Symes aboard the *Manitoba* had slowed his 300-horsepower engines, the watchman had not been able to see the rocks in the heavy fog. The 187-foot vessel was hung up and unable to get off.

Smith postponed his excursion. Both the *Frances Smith* and the Beatty's passenger ship *Waubuno,* under the command of "Black Pete" Campbell, left for the Bruce Peninsula to assist in the rescue. Fortunately, the combined power of the two steamers was sufficient to pull the *Manitoba* from the rocks without damage. She was able to continue her

Captain James B. Symes of the steamer *Manitoba*. Symes had an illustrious career on the lakes. He began as a mate on the *Kaloolah* and later was the master of the *Algoma* that transported Colonel Wolseley to Port Arthur. He also had the distinction of hauling the first barrel of silver ore from Silver Islet. Taken from *Canadian Illustrated News*, October 21, 1871, from a photograph by J.H. Davis, Collingwood. *Courtesy of Library and Archives Canada, Record 2296.*

journey without incident, and Captain Smith returned to Owen Sound. By August 28, 1871, the *Frances Smith* was ready once again for the long-awaited excursion to Detroit.

Eventually, she left Owen Sound with over one hundred and fifty passengers and sailed north along the east coast of the Bruce Peninsula. The weather by now was clear, and the sharp white cliff face of the Niagara escarpment was spectacular on the port side all the way upbound. The trip past Cape Croker, Lion's Head and Cabot Head was uneventful in the lee of a strong west wind. As the boat approached the tip of the peninsula and headed west toward Lake Huron, there were huge waves surging though the relatively narrow passageways around Flowerpot Island, Russell Island and Cove Island. Even today these narrow stretches of water are notorious for unpredictable currents, capricious wave action and recurring tragedies. The rocky bottom at the tip of the Bruce Peninsula is littered with dozens of wrecks and is the location of Canada's Fathom Five National Underwater Park where divers from around the world explore the wrecks in the park's crystal clear and frigid water.

Captain Smith wisely decided to turn back for the shelter of "Tobermoura," a perfect small harbour that is today the point of departure for the ferry *Chi-Cheemaun* from southern Ontario to Manitoulin Island.[41] In 1871, Tobermory was little more than a fishing station in the summer and home to one or two permanent settlers who had pushed the forest back far enough to erect a small log dwelling. Tucked into the enclosed deep harbour, the *Frances Smith* "laid over for two days," waiting for Lake Huron to settle down.

The passengers spent their time singing, dancing and listening to a
concert given by the 31st Battalion band of Owen Sound, hired for the
trip. A playful auction was organized in which old shoes, pots, and pans
were offered up for bidding. According to reporters, everyone had a
wonderful time despite the lack of amenities.[42]

On August 31, the *Frances Smith* left Tobermory and sailed downbound through Lake Huron to Sarnia, down the St. Clair River, through
the St. Clair flats and eventually arrived at Windsor where passengers
disembarked. Captain Smith and his newly appointed captain, William
Tate Robertson, sailed across the river to Detroit where the ship was
put into drydock for two days.

The owners of the drydock claimed the *Frances Smith* to be the finest
vessel to ever enter their premises. A large number of shipowners and
local spectators came to see the wonderful ship that was praised so highly
by *The Detroit Daily Post*.[43] This was a sophisticated audience, as these
professional sailors regularly saw large numbers of American vessels
running from Buffalo, Cleveland and Lake Erie ports en route to
Chicago and Milwaukee. They had seen dozens of steamers shuttling
emigrants to the west and moving wheat, pork and beef back to the
east. The audience was impressed with the graceful lines of the *Frances
Smith,* sitting high and dry.

Once the drydock work was completed, the *Frances Smith* returned
to Windsor, picked up her passengers and made a short "value-added"
trip to Amherstburg before returning to Sarnia. As she left Sarnia for
her return trip, the large crowd on the Sarnia dock gave three cheers
to Captain Smith while the band played "God Save the Queen."[44] Upon
arrival back in Owen Sound, the passengers joined together to thank
both captains for their "utmost endeavors to promote the comfort of
their guests" and for their "unceasing kindness and politeness."[45]

The excursion and the drydock repairs were a huge success. Unfortunately, it was Captain Smith's last excursion. Within two months he
was dead at age forty-five, from acute gastritis and general internal hem-
orrhage.[46] He died at home. As a measure of his statue in the community,
schools closed early the day of the funeral. It was Owen Sound's largest
funeral to date.[47] A man revered by children and adults alike had died.
Two decades later, a large commemorative stained glass window displayed at the Chicago World Fair was purchased by William Smith's

Left: This imposing gray stone monument in Greenwood Cemetery in Owen Sound marks the final resting place of Captain William H. Smith and his wife Frances. *Right:* Memorial window at St. George's Anglican Church, Owen Sound. This stained glass window was purchased by the son of W.H. Smith, Horace, at the Chicago World's Fair where it won a prize in 1893. The triptych had the bottom three panels added when installed at the church, the left-hand section dedicated to W.H. Smith and the centre section to Frances Jane Smith. *Photos by Scott Cameron.*

son, Horace, and installed in St. George's Church in Owen Sound as a family memorial. This richly coloured triptych Gothic window is located in the apse of the church, just a few blocks away from the original Smith home. The window shows Christ reaching towards a sailing ship under which is the quotation from Matthew 19: " And he saith unto them, Follow me, and I will make you fishers of men." Captain Smith was buried in Owen Sound's Greenwood Cemetery where a three-metre gray granite obelisk marks the family plot.

*   *   *

Between 1872 and 1887 one day excursions were well-advertised in local papers. There was always positive press coverage encouraging people to enjoy the on-board pleasures. Both Captain William H. Smith and his successor Captain William Tate Robertson were excellent public relations specialists, always mingling with their passengers and making everyone aboard feel welcome.

The main deck, with its open space and wooden flooring, provided opportunities for dancing and socializing. A piano with a caller, a quadrille band or a brass band from one of several militia units in Collingwood, Meaford or Owen Sound "discoursed sweet music" for the enjoyment of everybody Often there would be combinations of bands on board. Excursions were normally well-attended when the weather was good, the average participation being in the neighbourhood of 500 people. In bad weather when few passengers showed up, everyone lost money, including the sponsors of the trip.

Over the course of her lengthy career, thousands of people took excursions on the *Frances Smith*. Orangemen, "Sabbath Schools," Masonic Lodges, the Sons of Scotland, firemen and just plain folks paid their fifty or seventy-five cents for a day's entertainment on board. An excursion was a wonderful respite from the routine of daily work representing

The Sons of Scotland (note the tartan dress on the hurricane deck), crowd onto the *Frances Smith (Baltic)* for an excursion from Collingwood to Owen Sound, circa 1890–91. At times there were more than a thousand persons on board for an excursion. *Courtesy of the Collingwood Museum X969.491.1.*

a genuine holiday for the members of the community. In the early days schoolchildren were treated to "free" voyages on special occasions. Teachers and parents paid to accompany the children. William H. Smith began his tradition of free trips for children long before he owned the *Frances Smith* – a common feature on his earlier ship the *Clifton*. Consequently, Smith was seen as a generous, kind, and affable shipmaster who spared no effort to ensure the comfort of his young "guests." His adult guests were effusive in their praises. In time Captain Robertson would receive his share of applause from passengers also, but not the enthusiastic commendation normally given to Smith.

Special events like boat launchings, regattas, the Queen's Birthday and moonlight cruises prompted short trips out onto Georgian Bay by upwards of seven hundred people at a time. On full day excursions from Meaford to Wiarton there would be time for picnics ashore and spectator events like lacrosse games and foot races. The excursion schedule for 1878 was particularly busy. The Owen Sound Masonic Lodge had an excursion to McGregor Harbour and Cape Croker on June 20, the Loyal Orange Order of Owen Sound went to Meaford on July 12 and, on July 22 and August 22, the Oddfellows chartered two cruises, to Griffith Island and Christian Island respectively.[48]

The largest excursion of 1878 was one organized by the Pythagoras Lodge #137 of Meaford on Dominion Day, Monday, July 1. On that day, "the brethren of the mystic tie" chartered a trip from Meaford to Penetanguishene starting at 8 a.m. sharp.[49] At dawn, a hot summer sun rose over Christian Island, forty kilometres (twenty-five miles) to the northeast. There had been no rain for several days and this day was to be a scorcher. The bay was without a ripple.[50] By 7 a.m. the crew had loaded a small amount of freight on board and shortly thereafter, crowds arrived at the dock. Women with lunches in cloth satchels, clutching the hands of children, stood shoulder to shoulder on the wharf with burly farm men and townsfolk. The "worshipful brethren" met at the lodge early in the morning and donned their regalia, then organized themselves in a "cloud of flags"[51] for a march to the dock. With the band leading, they paraded through the streets of Meaford to the dock on Bayfield Street. The purser signalled passengers to enter the gangway and present their tickets. Advertisements in the Meaford weekly paper made it clear that "No one would be

GRAND EXCURSION
TO
MEAFORD

An Excursion under the auspices of the

ORANGEMEN

Of Owen Sound and vicinity, will be given on board the Steamer

FRANCES SMITH,

To Meaford, on

FRIDAY, JULY 12, 1878.

The Steamer will leave her Dock, foot of Peel Street, at 8 o'clock sharp, calling at Leith and Presque Isle, arriving in Meaford about noon; returning same evening. No pains will be spared by the Committee of Management to make this the Best Excursion of the Season.

The Band of the 31st Battalion

Will accompany the Excursion.

FARE—Single Ticket, 75c.; Lady and Gent, $1; Children under 12 years of age, 25 cents.
Tickets can be procured at H. Jackman's, Hoath & Hall's, Thos. Frizzell's and on the Dock on the morning of the Excursion.   No person will be admitted on board the Boat without a Ticket.
Owen Sound, June 22, 1878.

Advertisement for the Orange Day Excursion, 1878. Not to be outdone by the Masonic Lodge of Meaford, the Orange Lodge of Owen Sound planned their "Grand Excursion" to celebrate King Billy on the "Glorious" 12th of July, 1878. They had the added attraction of the 31st Battalion on board to help with the party. Taken from *The Owen Sound Times*, June 28, 1878. *Courtesy of the Owen Sound Union Library.*

allowed on board without a ticket." The heavy crush of holiday makers squeezed two by two through the gangway displaying their tickets, while the purser simply waved them on. When all were aboard, the whistle sounded and they were away.

Captain Robertson steered well offshore to avoid the treacherous shallow water beyond the Claybanks and Thornbury. He skirted the shoals beyond Craigleith at the foot of the Blue Mountains where the 1872 wreck of the *Mary Ward* rested on a ledge just a few kilometres offshore, and sailed into Collingwood to pick up extra passengers. Around noon, the overburdened *Frances Smith* staggered away from the Northern Railway's wharf in a full glare of sunshine. Close to one thousand people had pushed their way on board, well beyond the safety limits of the steamer. Photographs of the ship in 1878 clearly show that she had fewer than four lifeboats on the hurricane deck. It is apparent from newspaper accounts of the event that the "pleasure seekers" gave no thought for their own safety.

Once away from Collingwood, thirty-cent warm meals[52] were served at long tables set up in the saloons. Many passengers picnicked with their families on the crowded decks. Elbow to elbow, they ate bread, cheese and fruit, throwing the refuse overboard.

Five kilometres (three miles) from Penetanguishene, the *Frances Smith* nudged her way up to the small dock at the reformatory for boys. By prior arrangement the warden met the officials of the Masonic Order, and most of the passengers tramped up the hill to view the interior of the prison. For over an hour the excursionists were guided about the grounds by the guards. Passengers chatted with some of the young inmates who had been given special dispensation to assemble and to meet the curious. In the late afternoon the *Smith* cast off from the dock and steamed into the shallow waters of Penetanguishene Bay.

When the *Frances Smith* eventually docked at the village of Penetanguishene, the members of the lodge assembled on the main deck with flags at the ready. In front of them was the two-dozen member Cornet Band of Meaford led by "Professor" Miller.[53] With horns blatting and a drum pounding, they marched off the boat and up the dusty main street, followed by flag-carrying Masons with aprons and regalia shining in the hot afternoon sun. Passengers trudged behind, heading for the village shops. Meanwhile the crew unloaded the small cargo from Meaford and piled it on the dock.

By early evening the band again assembled and started its march back to the waiting ship, followed by all the passengers, ready to head for home. As soon as the vessel cast off and set course for the narrows between Beckwith Island and Pinery Point, William Russell, a popular musician from Thornbury hired especially for the occasion, struck up his quadrille band. Immediately couples squared off and started dancing to the music of the fiddles and piano. The dancing had hardly begun when the *Frances Smith* ran aground.[54] It took two hours to get the overloaded vessel off the sandbar. Apparently no one was concerned and no one abandoned ship. Upon arrival back in Meaford it was reported that passengers had a pleasurable trip. The event was pure Stephen Leacock. His delightful 1912 story about the Knights of Pythias aboard the "Mariposa Belle" gently satirizes excursions like this one organized by the worshipful brethren of Meaford.[55]

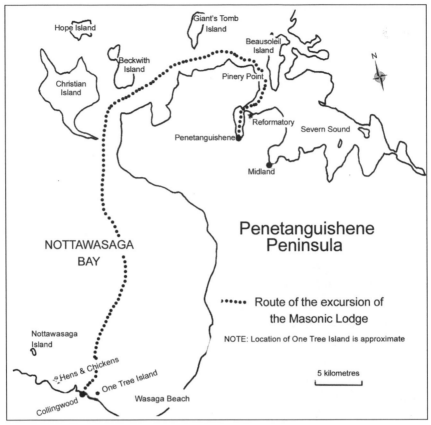

Map of the Penetanguishene Peninsula.

As time passed, larger iron propeller-driven luxury vessels replaced wooden sidewheelers on regular routes. They sometimes cut into the excursion trade as well. In response, the owners of the *Frances Smith* created a niche excursion business under the new corporate name, Collingwood Lake Superior Line. They designed specialty excursions much like those offered by cruise operators of today. Even after the aging *Frances Smith* had been renamed the *Baltic* in 1888 and placed under the flag of the Great Northern Transit Company (White Line), her last days were filled with excursions. One of these niche excursions was a round trip to Mackinac Island. A special excursion price of $12 (meals included) to Sault Ste. Marie and Mackinac Island was initiated in June 1886 and continued into 1892.

The Collingwood Board of Trade was so enthusiastic about the excursions that they bragged that a month-long excursion on the White Line was equal to a full year college course. Indeed, they claimed it was more beneficial to your health than a thousand visits to the physician or to the drug store.

In the spring of 1893, the Great Northern Transit Company withdrew the *Baltic* (*Frances Smith*) from regular service to concentrate solely on the excursion business. On June 14, she began her last series of excursions. These were two-week extended trips to the Chicago World's Fair. The competing company, the North Shore Navigation Company (Black Line), set up their own Chicago runs over the summer.[56] A fierce advertising battle ensued, each line claiming special services and attractions. Both appear to have been successful.

The *Baltic* ran every two weeks in 1893 from Collingwood, Meaford, Owen Sound and Wiarton to a private south Chicago pier where she tied up for six days while passengers visited the fair and toured Chicago. Prices for the full excursion, including admissions, berth and meals, varied from $40.00 to $50.00 per person. Passengers remained on the vessel during the entire visit and were treated with all the amenities of a floating hotel. For five cents, passengers caught the Electric Railway that ran every five minutes from the dock to the Chicago fairgrounds. They returned to the *Baltic* for supper and an evening of dancing, singing and socialization. It was the last great season for the steamer. After the excursion season of 1893, the *Baltic* was tied up in Collingwood and never sailed again. Time was almost up for the twenty-six-year-old palace steamer.

8

The Great Storm of '75

O N SATURDAY, OCTOBER 23, 1875, the *Frances Smith* spent all day loading at the wharf in Owen Sound. She was to be one of the last supply ships upbound that year. The weather had been like Indian summer the previous week but turned cloudy and wet a few days before departure.[1] Neither passengers nor crew had a premonition that they were embarking on what would become a harrowing voyage. Although the ultimate destination was Prince Arthur's Landing, most of the freight was destined for Silver Islet, a mining town on Lake Superior.

Today Silver Islet is a ghost town, but in 1875 it was a rough and ready, productive silver mine, with hundreds of miners, a company store, two churches, a bank, an assay office and a good solid jail. The rich silver ore created the allure of the California gold rush except that it was almost impossible to get at the veins submerged below the cold waters of Lake Superior. Mining here under such difficult conditions was considered a nineteenth century engineering wonder.

The silver deposit was located on a small shoal under the submerged rock of Sibley Peninsula. Thunder Cape towered like a colossus over the lake behind the shoal. The land mass behind the cape was given the name the Sleeping Giant. Indian legend had it that the mountain was indeed the sleeping body of the giant Nanabijou, who, if awakened, would roll over and crush those nearby.[2] When the fury of a Lake Superior storm beat upon the jagged coast, it was easy to imagine the potential

Left: Silver Islet Landing on the Collingwood Lake Superior Line. Located along the north shore of Lake Superior, Silver Islet was the location of the silver mother lode. During the 1870s, the village was a major stopping point for Canadian passenger steamers. *Courtesy of the Archives of Ontario, F1132-2-2, #192. Right:* Miners at Silver Islet, many of whom were of Cornish ancestry, pose for a photo circa 1875. The *Frances Smith* carried a heavy load of food to the miners on the remote island located off the coast of Thunder Cape in October 1875. It was to be the last trip of the season when the steamer was caught in a fierce gale and almost sank. *Courtesy of the Archives of Ontario, F1132-2-1-2 #198.*

danger if Nanabijou was aroused. Late fall tempests, born in the black sky over Lake Superior, sent massive breakers to the broken shores of the giant's frame. These great waves from a hundred kilometres (sixty miles) out in the lake crashed against Thunder Cape's mesa. From its steep shoreline walls, the breakers surged back into Superior, amplifying their size into lethal standing waves. Howling winds swept over the offshore islands. This dangerous place was in the path on the last trip of the season for Captain W. Tate Robertson and the *Frances Smith*. It was a trip that tested a provoked Nanabijou.[3]

Large breakwalls were built to protect the entrances to the mine shafts at Silver Islet. These were constantly smashed by Superior's relentless waves. Supply ships, heading for the village a short way off, were dangerously exposed to heavy surf. Far out in the lake it was sometimes possible to hide in the lee of Isle Royale or even the Slate Islands, but when a gale was blowing from the northeast this part of Superior was a truly terrifying place. Low-lying islands and shoals were scattered off shore, their sharp edges ready to tear a wooden hull apart.

In 1875, forecasting the weather was a hit-and-miss affair. Sailors' folklore, aching arthritic joints and insight were essential forecasting tools, with atmospheric observations and intuition being important predictors of weather for sailors. The notions of weather systems, warm and cold fronts, jet streams and coordinated weather observations were still fifty years into the future.[4] In fact, there was no such thing as standard time yet[5] so it was impossible to synchronize any observations that might have been made and communicated through the newly developed telegraph systems. There were no weather stations anywhere on Lake Superior until 1881, although some existed in the lower lakes.[6] Weather systems developing over the plains of Kansas or the Canadian North were unobserved because there were so few people there to monitor them. David Brown's book about the 1913 storms on the Great Lakes says that, "Meteorologists describe the Great Lakes as a climatological battleground where cold polar air and warm tropical air wrestle for control of the North American atmosphere."[7] The gales of November are legendary when low pressure cells form between the sharply divided cold and warm fronts above the earth. Hundreds of ships resting on the lake bottom are silent testament to this struggle.

Captain Robertson did have a barometer.[8] Certainly he must have noted the falling pressure. Certainly he knew this to be an indicator of bad weather. However, Robertson also knew that the navigation period was almost over and he had important cargo to move before winter closed

Lake Superior for the season. His crew continued loading as normal. Although the weather conditions were not good on loading day at Owen Sound, there was no possibility that ships' captains on the lakes could have known about the magnitude of the impending storm brewing in the west.

The barometer from the *Frances Smith* is part of the Grey Roots Museum Collection. *Photo by Scott Cameron.*

Loads of supplies were carted onto the wooden floor of the main deck and given that there were so few passengers that day, freight was placed on the upper decks as well. First Mate J. Wood and Second Mate Alex McLeod supervised as deckhands moved huge piles of freight from the dock into the hold. First Engineer James Johnson and Second Engineer Frank Young double-checked the fuel supply for the long trip. Extra wood was required to battle adverse winds and late October seas.

Dozens of barrels of southern Georgian Bay apples were packed into the *Frances Smith* for points along the route, along with boxes of bacon, turkey and butter. There was a special consignment of ninety-six chairs, assorted furniture and candles. D.C. Davis of Little Current had a case of tobacco, two-and-one-half chests of tea, one box of plums and a box of soap aboard. There were cases of raisins, cheese, sugar and peas destined for Prince Arthur's Landing. John Cameron, a sawmill owner in Batchawana, an Indian village sixty kilometres (some thirty-seven miles) beyond Sault Ste. Marie, had several bars of iron on board. In the hold were several hundred bags of oats, spring wheat and potatoes. In addition, the loading crew piled in 72 quarters of beef, 40 dressed lambs, 21 dressed hogs and several barrels of lard destined for the mining camp at Silver Islet.[9] But by far the largest part of the load was livestock.

Livestock belonging to Messers Alexander Speers, butcher, and Henry Kennedy, a trader from Owen Sound, were herded onto the dock and into pens to prepare them for loading through a chute and onto the main deck. Mr. Speers would accompany his cattle to oversee their delivery at Silver Islet. The 54 steaming beasts were driven into the ship, bawling and wild-eyed, alarmed by the uncertainty of their surroundings. Then 84 sheep and 21 hogs, even more terrified than the cattle, were herded into frame pens. Hay and feed sufficient for several weeks followed. Next came hundreds of chickens in coops. Extra cordwood for the boiler was squeezed onto the deck. Food for a fortnight was carried into the galley under the direction of Chief Steward D. MacPherson. Finally, passengers with heavy trunks presented their tickets to the purser, W. Campbell. They picked up cabin keys and parked their trunks and large parcels in the baggage room, then hauled their personal luggage up the stairway, past the portrait of William H. Smith and through the freshly cleaned saloons to their staterooms. Men without cabin assignments staked out a comfortable bench in a corner of the deck saloon.

About 4 p.m. Captain Robertson pulled the cord on the steam whistle, ordered the gangplanks pulled aboard and commanded the lines cast off.

He signalled James Johnson in the engine room to engage the starting bar. Johnson opened the steam throttle valve about half way and twisted the valve wheel to inject water into the condenser. As the piston gained momentum, the walking beam was engaged. The paddles turned slowly at first, gradually picking up speed as the *Frances Smith* moved into deep water. They were heading first for Killarney and eventually Thunder Bay.[10]

The body of water, originally known as Owen's Sound,[11] was formed millions of years ago when pre-glacial rivers cut deeply into the land formation known to-day as the Niagara Escarpment. The melt waters left over from the ice age, a scant eleven thousand years ago, flooded the ancient river bottom. It is this water that created the Great Lakes. The sound itself is cradled between two steep-sided arms of the limestone escarpment. On the western arm is Cape Commodore, on the eastern arm is Cape Rich. Beyond the capes, steamer routes lead to the more exposed Georgian Bay. Even although this part of the bay is in the lee of the Bruce Peninsula, the waves can be threatening, as they sometimes seem to come from all directions, particularly when there is an easterly wind. These were the conditions that greeted the *Frances Smith* on the night of October 24, 1875.

It was late Monday, October 25, before the *Frances Smith* completed her trip across the bay to Killarney. Captain Robertson reported later that it was a rough trip. He did not realize that the east-northeast winds were the leading edge of a larger and rougher weather system he would confront in a few days time on Lake Superior. A layover in the shelter of Killarney's narrow channel, protected on all sides by islands and promontories thrust into Georgian Bay, allowed livestock, passengers and crew a chance to recover before Captain Robertson set out along the winding "Turkey Trail" among the islands of the North Channel.

Out on Lake Superior several hundred kilometres away, the 205-foot passenger steamer *Cumberland*, belonging to the Collingwood Lake Superior Line and with Captain James Orr at the helm, was having her own problems battling the leading edge of the storm. Like the *Frances Smith* she was a sidewheeler built by the Simpson family of boat builders. Although three years newer than the *Frances Smith*, for all intents and purposes she could be called a sister ship.

At 2 a.m., on the 25th the *Cumberland* was on her way from Michipicoten to Thunder Bay when the blizzard struck. Heavy seas rolled in from

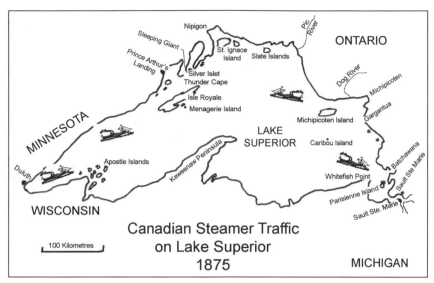

Map showing Canadian Steamer Traffic on Lake Superior 1875. The *Frances Smith* along with a dozen other passenger and packet freighters supplied Hudson's Bay Company posts and mining communities around Lake Superior with supplies and mail from May until November.

the northeast.[12] The brutal gale and swirling snow reduced visibility to less than a few metres beyond the pilothouse. Determinedly plunging ahead all day, Captain Orr made Silver Islet lighthouse by midnight,[13] but because of the intensity of the storm he was unable to reach the dock. Once past the light he stopped all engines. Then he ordered his wheelsman, Alexander Ross, and Second Mate Herbert Harris to make sure that they stayed in the centre of the channel by engaging in a series of manoeuvres in which they backed up and moved ahead, reversing and going forward over and over again. In doing this he hoped to keep his position until the weather cleared enough to allow him to see Thunder Cape.

The crew was directed to look for the newly constructed Thunder Cape lighthouse, built in 1874, but all they could see was snow, spray, and the blackness of the dark lake. While maintaining this strategy, Orr spotted land to leeward, and, thinking it to be a small island outside Thunder Cape, started ahead in order to clear it. He had not proceeded more than two boat lengths when he saw land dead ahead and Thunder Cape bluff towering above him.[14] He quickly realized that he was in a small bay called Tee Harbour and was being pushed onto the rocky shore. At this point the *Cumberland* struck bottom. Finding it impossible to budge

Thunder Cape 1867, William Armstrong, artist. The sheer cliffs at Thunder Cape make this a very dangerous spot in a storm. Armstrong's painting captures the mystery and power of this place. *Courtesy of the Archives of Ontario, C 33.0.0.0.4.*

off the sandbar, Orr made a critical decision. He opened the seacocks, letting about a metre of water into the hold, hoping to stabilize the ship firmly on the bar.[15] This was a difficult act for him; although a standard strategic course of action to save the boat, it was not always successful. The vessel had been put through this test under a previous captain, Captain McGregor. In 1872, he had run the *Cumberland* aground at Bear Lake near St. Joseph Island and left her stranded for the entire winter with only a skeleton crew aboard.[16] The situation was identical to the grounding of the *Frances Smith* at Key Harbour in 1867. Orr was well aware of the potentially disastrous consequences of the action – experiences he did not wish to repeat.

All night long the sea outside the tiny harbour threw monster waves inland, threatening to push the *Cumberland* onto shore. Light from the kerosene lanterns was barely visible from the bow to the stern. Captain Orr came to the realization that he could not stay where he was and at dawn he dispatched one of the lifeboats to sail back to Silver Islet, about four kilometres (two-and-a-half miles) away, for help. Before assistance could arrive, Captain Orr abandoned his initial plan. As the weather cleared somewhat the next morning, he decided the best tactic was to refloat his vessel and make a run for it. He commanded his crew to close the seacocks and pump the water from his vessel. Knowing that his exposed position on Lake Superior this time around would be fatal if winter closed

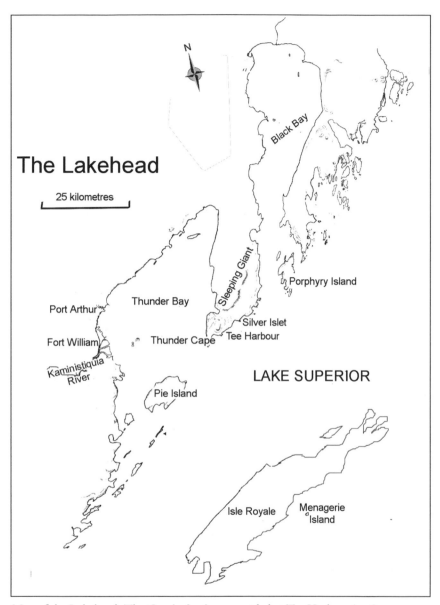

The Lakehead

25 kilometres

Black Bay

Sleeping Giant

Porphyry Island

Thunder Bay

Port Arthur

Silver Islet

Fort William

Thunder Cape

Tee Harbour

Kaministiquia River

LAKE SUPERIOR

Pie Island

Isle Royale

Menagerie Island

Map of the Lakehead. The *Cumberland* was scuttled at Tee Harbour in 1875.

in early, he decided to seize the opportunity presented by the break in the storm. Within a few hours the *Cumberland* was ready to attempt her escape from potential disaster. With courage and full steam ahead, Captain Orr pointed the steamer back into the lake. He arrived at Thunder Bay just before the tail end of the storm struck western Lake Superior.

Meanwhile on board the *Frances Smith* at 1 p.m., Captain Robertson left Killarney bound for Sault Ste. Marie on Tuesday, October 26.[17] Blowing snow and high winds from the northeast creating choppy seas met Robertson as he ploughed west through the North Channel. He stopped at the regular ports along the way: Little Current, Spanish Mills, Algoma Mills, Thessalon, Bruce Mines and Garden River. Headwinds were so strong that he did not arrive at Sault Ste. Marie until 5 p.m. on Thursday, October 28. By 8 a.m. the next morning the *Frances Smith* cleared the Sault Ste. Marie locks and headed upbound on Lake Superior. She sailed past Pointe aux Pins just a dozen kilometres (about eight miles) above the Sault where, in 1734, Louis Denis de la Ronde built the first wooden vessel to sail Lake Superior. Staying well off the north shore, he sailed between Iroquois Point and Gros Cap at the entrance to Whitefish Bay. By noon the *Frances Smith* steered north into the Indian village at Batchawana Bay where she dropped supplies and the iron bars for Mr. Cameron. She then sailed on to the small Canadian trading post at Michipicoten. It was a rough but uneventful trip and the *Frances Smith* arrived late in the afternoon that Friday. She left Michipcoten with a fresh breeze and what seemed like normal weather.[18] But unknowingly, Captain Robertson was sailing his boat into a lull before the devastating gale swept in from the northwest. This same kind of calm lured several Great Lakes ships to their end in the hurricane of November 1913.[19]

Little did the passengers and crew know what was in store for them over the next few days. Like the storms that sank the *Edmund Fitzgerald* in 1975, and literally scores of others over the years in the eastern end of Superior, a full November gale was approaching from the west. It was the back end of the storm, which the *Cumberland* had narrowly escaped.

At the newly constructed Menagerie Island lighthouse just to the south of Isle Royale, the lighthouse keeper Will Stevens[20] and his wife had just settled in a few weeks before. His log entry for October 26, 1875, describing the weather, gives an indication of what was in store for the *Frances Smith*:

> Damp and cloudy. The East-northeast gale increased almost to hurricane. At 6 a.m. the sea went clear over tower, rocks and broke the window sashes on south side of the house. Washed away everything loose, lumber, wood, rocks off the island.[21]

The weather became worse on Lake Superior as the eye of the storm passed through and the wind shifted. Elsewhere on the Great Lakes other ships were about to run into foul weather as well. Schooners ran for cover at ports all along Lake Erie and Lake Ontario. Not all made the right decision.

The 131-foot *Hubbard*, a two-masted schooner, left Buffalo a few days after the *Frances Smith* sailed from Owen Sound. The *Hubbard* carried coal and was heading for Chicago at the foot of Lake Michigan. About the same time, the 135-foot schooner *Minnie Williams* with a crew of eight, left Cleveland, also loaded with coal and likewise headed for Chicago. When the storm stuck Lake Superior on Friday, October 29, they were both battling their way up Lake Huron and through the Straits of Mackinac. Both sank a day later on Lake Michigan. The *Minnie Williams* was lost with all hands. The *Hubbard's* crew was saved. A few days later, the same weather disturbance sent two other schooners, the *Sutler Girl* and the *Conrad Reid,* to the bottom with all hands on Lake Erie. Dozens of other ships had sails ripped and masts snapped as they fled for safety.

The Menagerie Island Lighthouse. On October 25, 1875, spray and waves on Lake Superior went over the top of this lighthouse. The *Frances Smith* was not far away, battling for her life. *Photo by Jason Funkey.*

Within an hour of leaving Michipicoten on October 29, the *Frances Smith* encountered trouble. The winds picked up. The temperature plunged and mountainous rollers swept down the length of Lake Superior. As the ship ploughed into the heavy weather, the rain on the decks turned to ice. Spray from huge waves splashed onto the rigging and over the pilothouse, freezing instantly.

The steamer was soon entirely encased in ice. At this critical point Captain Robertson became aware that his vessel was not responding to the wheel. The *Frances Smith* slipped into a trough and, despite full power to turn her back into the sea, nothing happened. Here was a clear emergency that, if not resolved quickly, would result in the ship being swamped.

Huge combers smashed into the bulwarks and destroyed them. Solid water exploded as it smashed onto her side, heaving the *Frances Smith* over on her beam ends. For endless minutes the ship hung there, apparently unable to recover. When she did right herself, the waves stove in the gangway on the seaward side and "burst it out the other [gangway] sweeping overboard a considerable amount of freight and listing the vessel severely."[22] Cattle on the main deck were knocked down and piled against the port wall. As soon as the terrified beasts attempted to stand, they were immediately washed back to the starboard wall. In the confusion, chicken coops slid about, freight broke the lashings, and the *Frances Smith* listed even more seriously. Mr. Speers, one of the owners of the livestock, talked with Captain Robertson and agreed to have his cattle pushed overboard through the gaping gangway in an attempt to stabilize the ship. The crew drove the panicked cattle into the raging water. As the ship pitched and rolled, one of the unfortunate beasts was picked up by a massive surge and thrown back onto the deck. It was immediately swept away again to disappear in the foam. Chicken coops were tossed overboard from the promenade deck, smacking the water and bursting on impact. The sheep remained on board in their crowded pens, however all eventually drowned.

Gradually the *Frances Smith* began to correct her list, but she still refused to answer to her helm. In desperation, Captain Robertson left the pilothouse and crawled, rolling and tumbling, until he reached the deck opposite one of the smashed open gangways. At that moment, a huge sea washed though the boat and swept him toward the gaping gangway opposite. As he was about to be washed overboard, he desperately clutched one of the secured hencoops with his free hand. One of his legs was in the water outside the ship.[23] After pulling himself back onto the deck, he continued working his way aft, half swimming, half crawling and then wading through water awash on the deck. Robertson discovered that the chain from the wheelhouse to the rudder was fouled. He ordered his crew to secure the tiller, located at the stern, while he worked to restore the steering system. Once this task was successfully finished, he inched his way back to the pilothouse with waves, spray and torrents of rain washing over him. Back in the wheelhouse, the intrepid Robertson again took over direct control of navigation and the handling of the vessel.

Captain Robertson remained on duty Friday night and Saturday without sleep. He was on duty again Sunday and Monday without food or drink while winds lashed the ship with gale force. Waves continued to crash over the bow, swamping the ship with water. Spray immediately froze on the railings, the masts and the paddle boxes. Swirling snow streamers enveloped the ship, reducing visibility to zero. Despite the efforts of the crew to chip the ice away, by Saturday evening the ship was encased in over ten centimetres of ice.

In the upper cabin saloons, one hundred terrified and seasick passengers discussed their imminent death. Some huddled in prayer. When Captain Robertson got wind of their desperate talk and their bleak appeals to the Almighty, he marched to the saloon and ordered them to be quiet. His authority cowed them into submission and they stopped all supplications. Robertson returned to his post in the pilothouse, steering blindly to the shelter of the islands that studded the north shore of Lake Superior. It was a calculated but dangerous move, one that could throw the vessel on the rocks where everyone would perish.

Around 3 a.m. Sunday, October 31, the snow stopped and the wind shifted again to the northwest. At daylight when Robertson realized he was just off the Pic River, he altered course to the Slate Islands. By then his boots were frozen to the floor of the pilothouse, and he had to be chipped away when at last the danger subsided. The crew carried him, exhausted, to his berth.

By this time the *Frances Smith* was almost out of fuel. Only three cords of wood remained, not enough to reach the village at Silver Islet. Robertson returned to his post and assumed personal control once more. As he approached the inhospitable north coast of Lake Superior, he stopped engines and anchored close to the shore in the lee of the Slate Islands. He dispatched some of the crew and passengers into the bush with axes to gather more wood for the boilers. Others were put to work repairing some of the damage to the boat. After several hours, the whistle blew and the *Frances Smith* was on her way again. Robertson assessed the damage. The kitchen was gone except for the stove. The bar room was demolished. Glassware was smashed. Broken furniture littered the saloons. Cabin windows and shutters were demolished. The port quarter was gone and the planks on the starboard quarter were raised. The *Frances Smith* was described as a "badly beaten pugilist" when she arrived at Prince Arthur's Landing at 9:30 a.m. Wednesday, November 3.[24]

The Thunder Bay Sentinel of November 4 reported the address made to Captain Robertson by grateful passengers on their safe arrival at the wharf. They commended the "heroic and noble courage" of the captain and crew. The passengers went on to say, "You were the instruments in the hands of Almighty God for saving our lives on that momentous occasion – more particularly do we remember your dauntless courage and presence of mind at that trying moment when the rudder became unmanageable and we lay in the trough of the sea; in the very jaws of death, when the thoughts of the bravest could look only to his God for mercy and pardon."[25]

On their return to Georgian Bay ports, the passengers wrote letters of appreciation to local newspapers, praising the leadership of Robertson in delivering them from what many believed was certain death. Robertson's reputation was at its peak.

Alex Speers, the owner of the drowned cattle, wrote a bit of doggerel in *The Owen Sound Advertiser*. He took advantage of public interest in the heroic voyage to advertise his Christmas meat sale. The poem is pure marketing genius before the advent of modern sales sophistication. The first and last stanzas of his verse are shown here:

CHRISTMAS ADDRESS (To His Friends and Patrons)
On Lake Superior's stormy wave,
The Frances Smith was toss'd,
Her timbers creaked, her decks gave way,
And all gave up for lost...

And when around your board,
At Christmas and New Years,
Please don't forget your thanks to give,
And still remember Speers.[26]

During the 1875–76 winter lay up in Owen Sound, extensive interior repairs had to be made to the *Frances Smith*. In anticipation of a large number of immigrants heading for the west, the promenade deck was opened up to hold more passengers. The main mast, which ran though the ship from below, was clad in mirrors where it pierced the upper saloon, in order to give the appearance of a larger space. Additional mirrors were placed on the interior walls beside the cabin doors. Potted plants were hung from hooks around the saloon, further enhancing the commodious feeling of the interior.

The new decor featured patriotic symbols. At the forward end of the saloon was a painting of the royal coat of arms with the legend *Dieu et mon droit* written below. The rose, thistle, and shamrock — symbolizing England, Scotland and Ireland were painted on the lower corners. The maple leaf of Canada was painted above. Below the royal coat of arms were several framed photographs depicting scenery from around Lake Superior, including pictures of Indians and the wild shore near Thunder Cape. The aft saloon (drawing room) on the promenade deck, which was for cabin passengers, was entirely refitted with new paint and carpets. The larger staterooms off the drawing room were refurnished and repainted. The redecorated drawing room opened onto the private stern deck.[27]

Expectations were high that 1876 would be profitable. The *Frances Smith* and the *Cumberland* were to be the only Georgian Bay steamers out of Collingwood on the through routes to the Canadian Lakehead.[28] Their trials on Lake Superior during the previous fall solidified their owners' resolve to turn the year into one of financial gain.

9

Serious Challenges

BOOM AND BUST cycles in the North American economy were recurrent themes in the shipping industry of the late nineteenth century. The cycles were also recurrent for railways. Since the shipping industry depended upon the railways, the fortunes of individual steamers depended on the railways and their ability to meet the demands of huge capital investments and revenue cash flows. Railways were seen as the driving force in the new industrial economy and were the recipient of huge government subsidies. Municipal and county governments joined provincial/state and federal governments in financing rail lines in both the United States and Canada. Steamboats, however, did not get the same public support. Visionaries saw that the most efficient method of trade between the east and the west in North America was a system of interlocking rail and steamboat systems. Although this concept was not fully understood when the *Frances Smith* was launched in 1867, it was crystal clear seventeen years later in 1884 when the CPR developed its magnificent steamship fleet sailing from the Owen Sound terminal. The three sisters, the *Athabasca*, the *Alberta* and the new *Algoma,* provided thrice weekly connections to Port Arthur and the new transcontinental railway to the west. The realization that transcontinental service was the way to grow business had a significant impact on Georgian Bay shipping and the *Frances Smith*. For the transportation business, the 1870s represent a transition from small tightly held company operations to larger coordinated corporate systems with powerful financial and political connections.

Events in Canada were not isolated from those in the United States. There, huge sums of money were invested in railroads, shipping and new technologies. Boiler and engine advancements followed year after year from 1870 onwards. There, passenger ships grew larger and larger with every new launching. In the United States the sheer volume of trade from Buffalo, Chicago and Cleveland pushed the limits of the locks at Welland and Sault Ste. Marie. Governments were forced to spend millions on infrastructure to support the booming trade in the upper lakes. Monopolies controlled coal prices and squeezed shipowners for all they could manage. Concerns about immigration caused governments to continually adjust their quotas. The result was that the economics of passenger shipping were at times lucrative and at other times quite shaky.

Captain Smith first took advantage of the opportunities in Georgian Bay by initiating service with the *Oxford* when the Northern Railway set tracks from Toronto to Collingwood in 1854. The railway, then known as the Ontario, Simcoe & Huron Union Railway (OS&HUR), had even bigger visions of trade to Chicago from the new port of Collingwood. Under the leadership of Frederic William Cumberland,[1] the original railway chartered five steamships to run from Collingwood to Chicago, Illinois, and Green Bay, Wisconsin. The *Lady Elgin, Niagara, Hunter, Montgomery* and *Ontonagon* were engaged, but the scheme was not profitable. Loss mounted upon loss and by 1859 the railway was in receivership.[2]

During the 1860s, with his own connection to the railway terminal at Collingwood, William Smith was making money with the *Canadian* and the *Clifton* on the local service from Owen Sound. Government reorganization of the OS&HUR ensured that the rail line at Collingwood remained operational and thus Smith's steamers continued to be profitable. The construction of the *Frances Smith* in 1867 was part of the plan to make even more money on this southern Georgian Bay route.

By early 1871 W.H. Smith saw that his stranglehold on the southern shore of Georgian Bay was about to end. A railway line from Collingwood to Meaford was on the drawing boards, and Owen Sound was negotiating to create the Toronto, Grey & Bruce Railway for its own direct connection to Toronto. Direct railway lines joining all the communities along the south shore of Georgian Bay would reduce the need

First Train to Meaford, the Canadian Northern of Canada. When this train chugged into Meaford from Collingwood in November 1872, the *Frances Smith* had already repositioned itself to sail from Collingwood to Fort William. She would only make visits to Meaford and Owen Sound once a week instead of running a daily schedule. *Courtesy of Library and Archives Canada C-035485, Canadian National Railways Collection.*

for a local steamer. With railways, passengers could rely on daily service, the Royal Mail could be delivered on time both winter and summer, and, besides, everyone embraced railways as the way of the future. A steamer service along the south shore of the bay could become an unnecessary and unprofitable enterprise.

Heavy freight haulage, transportation of immigrants and supply delivery to the new settlements on Manitoulin Island and Lake Superior were possible new opportunities for Captain Smith if he were to extended his operations to the northwest. As he contemplated his options, he was invited by James Beatty of Sarnia and the Collingwood Lake Superior Line to join their syndicate. Initially, the syndicate had been set up in the mid-1860s by Captain E.M. Carruthers and given a contract with the Northern Railway through the efforts of Barlow Cumberland, son of Frederic W. Cumberland, who as one of the founders of the Northern Railway, was well-connected to the emerging service.

William Tate Robertson, Smith's successor, began discussions with Barlow Cumberland about augmenting the Collingwood/Lake Superior route with the services of the *Frances Smith*. Some sort of agreement was made, but whatever it was, there was tension between Robertson and railway officials. One of the side issues related to home port services. Would the *Frances Smith* be based in Collingwood or Owen Sound? The bitter rivalry between the two towns coloured their initial negotiations. In late July 1873, Robertson met with the directors of the railway in Toronto and finally convinced them that the *Frances Smith* should continue regular service on the Lake Superior route along with the *Algoma, Chicora* and *Cumberland* and that the *Frances Smith* would still be based in Owen Sound.[3]

By the summer of 1873 increasing numbers of immigrants were using the regular services of steamers to get to the promised lands of Manitoba and the northwest. It was clear to shipowners that there could be a boom in passenger lake traffic if conditions were right. Robertson knew that in order to cash in on the expected boom, he had to cooperate with Frederic Cumberland and the Northern Railway. Thus began an alliance that was to shape the future of the *Frances Smith*. However, 1873 marked the beginning of a depression in Canada. It also marked the beginning of Alexander Mackenzie's Liberal government, which had just defeated John A. Macdonald and his party. Meanwhile, to woo Canadians back to their side, the Macdonald Conservatives developed their National Policy.[4] A major plank in that policy was settlement of the west – a sure-fire attraction for shipowners and those in the transportation business. Robertson hoped for the return of Conservative governments, but he had to wait until 1878. Meanwhile the tide of western migration was building, even without the National Policy.

Letters from settlers in the local newspapers filled heads and hearts with dreams of quick riches out west. Prospective western settlers from Ontario swelled the ranks of immigrants following Horace Greeley's command in the United States to "Go west."[5] Here was a double-barreled opportunity for Canadian steamships. Ontarians and immigrants seeking a fortune in the golden lands of the west became the key to prosperity. The only way to get "out west" at the time was by boat or by rail though the United States, and that latter alternative was distasteful to many Canadians. Not only was it politically distasteful, it was circuitous, uncomfortable and time consuming. Thus, upper lakes shipping interests began a period of expansion, alliance building and fierce competition.

By the mid-1870s the Canadian exit points for all this western traffic were Sarnia and Collingwood. Each port was a terminus for a railway. The Beattys ran the North West Transportation Company from Sarnia in connection with the Grand Trunk Railway, while the several steamer lines from Collingwood had connections to the Northern Railroad and the Cumberland family. Frederic Cumberland was concerned

Telegram from Frederic Cumberland to John Lowe, Minister of Agriculture, July 25, 1876. In the late 1870s there was fierce competition for the business of transporting immigrant Mennonites to the west. Cumberland wanted to be sure that the *Frances Smith* got its share of the business. He was concerned that the government was favouring the Sarnia terminal of the Grand Trunk Railway over the Collingwood terminal of the Northern Railway. *Courtesy of Library and Archives Canada,*

that he was losing business to the Beattys at Sarnia so he appealled directly to the Liberal government. It is clear from Cumberland's telegram of July 25, 1876, to John Lowe of the Department of Agriculture, that he wanted his share of the seven hundred Mennonites arriving by transatlantic steamer in Quebec that month and destined to settle in Canada's northwest.[6] The *Frances Smith* shared in Cumberland's contract arrangements with the government to use Collingwood as the departure point for settlers. Through that provision, the ship became an important factor in the movement of thousands of immigrants to Manitoba over the next decade. In addition, Cumberland took measures to ticket passengers from Toronto, through Collingwood to Duluth, and then by means of the newly constructed Northern Pacific Railroad to the American west. In this way the steamer *Frances Smith* participated in the settlement of Minnesota, Washington and Oregon.[7]

Now that the *Frances Smith* had joined the *Cumberland, Algoma,* and the *Chicora* on the Collingwood to Lake Superior route there were her

Advertisement For Royal Mail Line. The *Frances Smith* was forced to shift its route to the Lakehead when the railway pushed westward from Collingwood. She joined a loose syndicate with the *Cumberland* and *Chicora*. Together they pioneered an integrated passenger/rail service from Ontario to Fort William and Duluth. Taken from *The Owen Sound Advertiser*, July 18, 1872. *Courtesy of the Owen Sound Union Library.*

former mail contracts to consider. The *Frances Smith* held a mail contract from Collingwood to the west.[8] To cover the portion of the contract from Owen Sound to Collingwood, as noted earlier, Robertson chartered the much smaller *Silver Spray* in 1872 to take the place of the repositioned *Frances Smith*.

By 1873 the Collingwood Lake Superior Line's fleet of ships, *Algoma, Cumberland, Chicora* and now the *Frances Smith*, was one of the most powerful in the Canadian upper lakes service. Unfortunately, the aging *Algoma* lasted only one more year in service and was retired at Collingwood in 1874, leaving the remaining steamers to do the company's business.

Meaford was left out of the economic loop, while the growing competition and animosity between Owen Sound and Collingwood was about to spill over in bad feelings that would last for more than half a century. If Owen Sound had a dry dock, Collingwood needed one also. If Collingwood had a large grain elevator, Owen Sound had to have one larger. These two towns were bitter competitors for the Lake Superior trade. The bitterness was reflected in the ongoing editorial mudslinging in their respective newspapers.

Advertisements in 1874 indicate that the *Frances Smith* was still in some sort of an alliance with the syndicate Collingwood Lake Superior Line, but arrangements were not always harmonious. *The Owen Sound Advertiser* of 20 May, 1875, stated:

> The steamer Frances Smith arrived here last night from Collingwood with a large number of passengers and some freight which was loaded at the Northern Railway Wharf on receipt of special and peremptory orders of the owners. We are informed that the Frances Smith being unwilling to submit to the dictation of the Northern Railway and the owners of the Chicora and Cumberland have determined to compete with the Collingwood and Lake Superior Line for passengers and freight to Thunder Bay, Fort William and Duluth. On the first trip of the season every obstacle possible was thrown in her way at the Northern Railway Wharf. Even the conveyance by cars of passenger's baggage was refused. This fact becoming known in Toronto, a large number of passengers including the Canadian Pacific survey party under Mr. Hazelwood took the one o'clock p.m., train per Toronto, Grey and Bruce Railway and received here the attention which was refused them in Collingwood.

The paper continued, "We are glad that Captain Robertson has shown the pluck to defy the dictators and are sure that the travelling public, having appreciated in the past the comforts and conveyances of this favourite vessel, will second his efforts, and by generous and liberal support prove that overbearing despotism will not meet with the approbation of the public."

By early June 1875 the *Frances Smith* was again advertising itself as part of the Collingwood Lake Superior Line. Whatever differences there were appear to have been resolved. At this point an old competitor became more aggressive. It was the Beatty line of ships running from Sarnia to Fort William which, according to *The Northern Advance of Barrie*, "...by connivance of the Government, get the cream of the trade, Collingwood is justly indignant thereat."[9]

In 1876, Captain "Black Pete" Campbell left Beatty's ship, the *Waubuno*, and, with the participation of the Dodge family lumber interests from Byng Inlet, plus several others including Charles Cameron and John Long of Collingwood, created the Georgian Bay Transportation Company. They purchased the steamer *Northern Belle* and two years later added the *Northern Queen*. The Dodge/Campbell/Cameron/Long group targeted business along the east coast of Georgian Bay as far as Manitoulin Island. At this point the group was not yet a serious rival to the Collingwood Lake Superior Line which was more interested in the long distance trade beyond Manitoulin Island. However there was an overlap in service and cutthroat competition for freight, passengers and Royal Mail contracts.

During the economic downturn in 1877, the Collingwood Lake Superior Line found itself in financial trouble. They also faced serious problems with the fleet. On July 26, the *Cumberland* slammed onto an unmarked shoal near Rock of Ages at the western tip of Isle Royale in Lake Superior. Attempts to pull her off the shoal were unsuccessful and the ship was abandoned. The *Frances Smith* anchored offshore and transferred officers, crew, furniture and everything moveable on board.[10] She then sailed to Collingwood, abandoning the *Cumberland* to the battering seas of Lake Superior. By mid-August the *Cumberland* was a complete wreck. The aged *Algoma* was still mothballed at the dock in Collingwood. The *Chicora*, a notoriously inefficient wood burner, was sold to the Niagara Navigation Company because she was deemed unprofitable.[11] It became expedient for the Line to reorganize under a new name, the Canada Transit Company, which later became the Canada Lake Superior Transit Company with the *Frances Smith* the only remaining vessel. The earlier owners of the company had by then departed for other ventures, and the company was now in the hands of two Toronto businessmen, Alexander M. Smith and grocer William Keighley.[12] Alexander Smith had money and political influence. He had

The propeller-driven steamer, *City of Owen Sound* tied up at the
town dock sometime between 1875 and 1879. The small steamer
on the right is believed to be the ill-fated *Waubuno* which sank
in November 1879 with all hands and passengers. *Courtesy of
Grey Roots, Archival Collection, 978.6.9.1.*

been a member of the legislature in the Canada West (Ontario) government before Confederation and was vice-president of the Ontario
Bank. With his considerable financial and political clout, he planned to
build on the reliability of the *Frances Smith*.

The new company subsequently added the 184-foot propeller-driven
City of Winnipeg and the 172-foot *City of Owen Sound* to the syndicate.
The *City of Winnipeg*, originally built in Michigan in 1870 as the *Annie
L. Craig*, was purchased in the United States. The new owners, upgraded
the passenger accommodation and added several cabins on the main
deck before putting the ship into service. The *City of Owen Sound* was
a "Simpson-built" propeller steamer constructed at the shipyards of
Owen Sound in 1875, and was designed for service in the upper lakes.
She initially sailed for John Pridgeon's Sarnia Line but was sold to Smith
and Keighley in 1876. After a thorough remodelling job in the winter
of 1876–77, the *City of Owen Sound* made regular trips to the Lakehead.
Together, the three ships made solid business sense and offered good
service to the Georgian Bay/Lake Superior communities. Although the
service was regularized, it was not quite systematized. The boats still
ran on a kind of "wildcat" service, visiting ports as the need arose rather
than a scheduled predetermined service to each port.

Although the company controlled the ship operations, the *Frances
Smith* remained in the ownership of W.H. Smith's widow, Frances, until

Timetable of the Collingwood Lake Superior Line of steamers, circa 1878, produced by the Northern Railway Company of Canada. *Courtesy of the Toronto Reference Library, Baldwin Room, BR 385.20971 N59.*

1882. Registry documents show that ownership was then transferred to Captain William T. Robertson, and Henry Eberts Smith, her son, sometime in 1883 or 1884

At the beginning of 1878 the three ships made irregular trips from Collingwood via Meaford and Owen Sound to the Sault and Port Arthur. There was criticism of the irregularity so Smith and Keighley decided that it would be good business to define schedules to serve these two southern Georgian Bay ports. They therefore promised on August 9, 1878, to have one of the ships stop at Meaford every Tuesday and Friday evening.[13] The *Frances Smith* was designated to ply the route because she was well-equipped to carry livestock as well as first-class passengers. Once again she became one of the most regular visitors to Meaford and Owen Sound. The other two vessels were propeller ships and focused on carrying passengers and package freight directly from Collingwood to Fort William and Duluth.

Cheap land in Manitoba continued to attract thousands to the west. Some were legitimate farmers, others were land speculators. The newspapers were full of letters from settlers and land agents extolling the potential riches in the west. In order to get started, farmers needed breeding livestock. The Frances Smith carried heavy loads of cattle, sheep, and pigs from southern Georgian Bay on consignment to be sold in the west. George Brown, a grocer, and Thomas Brown, a butcher from St. Vincent Township, sent dozens of cattle every week during the latter months of the shipping season in 1878.

By 1878 the depressed economy during the final year of Prime Minster Alexander Mackenzie's Liberal government turned around and became a boom for the shipping companies. John A. Macdonald's Conservative party was swept into office that year on their protectionist, manufacturing-friendly National Policy. They advocated trade policies aimed at settlement in the west and cheap transportation of Canadian wheat to Montreal. They initiated their policy of railway building through the prairies, aggressive settlement for immigrants beyond the head of the lakes and a standardized canal system to move these new Canadians through the lakes efficiently. They developed plans to move Canadian grain to the port of Montreal as cheaply as possible.[14] This meant an integrated Canadian canal network from Sault Ste. Marie through to the St. Lawrence. It was good news for the shipping companies and everyone in the transportation business. Prosperous times returned to the steamer business. The Smith family and the Robertson family were, and remained, rock solid Conservatives for good reason.

In order to understand the Robertson/Smith family dynamics, it is important to retrace the timeline above, but this time with a focus on family affairs. National politics and regional economic considerations acted to bond the families together, but interpersonal relations and immediate family financial matters were more complex. In the 1860s and early 1870s, the Ebert's family roots melded the Smiths and the Robertsons into a cohesive force in the transportation business then evolving in Owen Sound. After the death of W.H. Smith, his widow

Frances, affectionately known in the family as "Frank," assumed ownership of the *Frances Smith*. By then her young nephew, William Tate Robertson, known as Tate, had been promoted from purser to captain. He was full of ambitious dreams despite his inexperience. He managed the operational side of the business with Frances controlling the financial side and her son Henry serving as business advisor. During the winters of 1871 to 1877, Tate, an eligible bachelor, lived with his Aunt Frank in her Owen Sound home. He saw first hand that a good living could be had running a steamer. Besides, there were all those ladies – the young ladies, who admired a young cigar-smoking commander.[15] He began to dream of owning a steamer.

By 1874 although profits were down, Tate appeared pleased with the fact that he had not had an accident on the lake and that there were solid profits in the three years of his command. He toyed with the idea of running for the House of Commons in Algoma but was dissuaded by his brother, Alexander Rocke Robertson.[16] That winter he attempted several times to purchase the steamer *Cumberland* from the Lake Superior Navigation Company. This was a clear case of ambitious opportunism.

The *Cumberland* was designed along the lines of the *Frances Smith*. She was a sidewheeler built by the Simpson's, the same family that built the *Frances Smith*. After its launch in 1871, the ship worked the Collingwood Lake Superior route. Unfortunately in November 1872, both she and the *Chicora* ran aground during a snowstorm at Bear Lake near St. Joseph Island. The *Chicora* got off but the *Cumberland* was scuttled and remained there until the spring of 1873.[17] The *Cumberland*'s 1874 season started badly. With heavy repair bills, the owners seemed ready to sell out at a discount. Tate offered $35,000 for a ship that had originally cost $95,000. He was unable to make the deal, but when his Aunt Frank purchased the *Silver Spray*, he decided to put money into the operations side of that account. His younger brother James, a fresh young lawyer, also put in a small amount and was appointed as purser "to look after our mutual interests" in 1875.[18]

There appear to have been some unresolved financial questions between Tate and his Aunt Frank in 1877. His brother James was somehow in the middle and was accused of "playing double" in the affair.[19] In an effort to smooth things over, Tate put extra money into the operation in order to cover some financial shortfalls associated with the *Silver Spray*.

In March of 1878, the *Silver Spray* burned to the waterline while tied to the wharf at Division Street in Owen Sound.[20] In the resulting insurance settlement, tensions between Frances and Tate reached the breaking point. Aunt Frank was the registered owner of the *Spray* and therefore was the person to whom the Royal Insurance Company intended to pay the insurance money. Tate assumed that he had an agreement providing coverage for his portion of the investment in the operations (the management/pilot account). Despite the fact that some negotiations had led him to belief, it was not so. Tate found himself out of pocket by $11,000, while at the same time Frances collected $10,000 and even accused him of trying to rob her. Tate believed that his younger brother James was out to make sure his own $4,000 investment would be covered, while Tate was left holding all the debts of the management/pilot account. He felt financially "pushed."

On top of that, the insurance company changed the account manager for the claim, and the new person refused to acknowledge any previous negotiations between the company and Tate. The company refused to hand over the contract books, while at the same time his Aunt Frank refused to let him see the financial accounts.

During the season of 1879, the family relations remained strained. By December, Tate was unsure whether his aunt and his cousin Henry Smith would appoint him once again as captain of the *Frances Smith* for the upcoming season. It might be time to purchase his own ship so that he could at least have some control.[21]

Despite the fact that family relations were tense, Tate wanted to sail for the firm in 1880. By the time he was appointed, the stress arising from his financial difficulties and family situation had affected his health. Although he found the cold and freezing temperatures out on the lake particularly difficult that year, he took his responsibilities as captain very seriously, staying on deck all night during storms and getting very little sleep when his officers took their regular watches. He was lonely and still without prospects of a wife. His overall apprehension increased in 1881 when once again he was appointed commander of the *Frances Smith*. The glamour of being captain was now gone, replaced with an increasing fretfulness and disquiet. During a fierce blow in the middle of Lake Superior he reflected bleakly on the fact that there were eight new widows in Collingwood that week. He wrote, " I am so anxious tonight. I can hardly write."[22] Three days later while off Cape Rich in a rolling sea that knocked the *Frances Smith* about so much he could barely hold his pen, he confided to his brother Alex, "We have 4 more trips to make yet. I dread them very much indeed."[23]

By the spring of 1882 many of the unresolved differences between the Robertsons and the Smiths had been put aside. Both Tate and James acted as groomsmen at the marriage of Cornelia Smith, the little girl who had launched the *Frances Smith* fifteen years before. Shortly after the wedding, the Robertson brothers took leave from their shipping careers and went to Manitoba for two years. Time and death appear to have healed the family quarrel, because Tate assumed command of the *Frances Smith* again in 1884. Aunt Frank died in her 58th year in May of that year and Henry Eberts Smith became his purser and friend. The feud was over.

* * *

The evils of liquor in pioneer communities in Canada are well-documented. The Temperance Movement in Canada was a direct reaction to the drunkenness and abuse of alcohol in these early communities. Political pressure on the federal government to take some sort of initiative resulted in a classic Canadian political resolution for difficult issues. The government decided not to make a decision. Instead, the responsibility was passed to each local community. The choice, whether to be "wet" or "dry," was called a "local option" in the Dunkin Act of 1864. As a result some towns voted wet, others dry, while the tendency was for rural communities to choose to be dry. Thus, Ontario became a patchwork of wet and dry communities in the 1870s.

The Crooks Act of 1876 made it harder to obtain a tavern license, and a number of taverns and bars were closed. The Scott Act of 1878 extended the option of the Dunkin Act so that if one-quarter of the electorate presented a petition to vote "dry," the sale of liquor would be banned in that community. Many more rural communities presented these petitions. The rules, of course, did not apply on board ships sailing outside the jurisdiction of land-based local government. Except for ships owned by the Beattys, who were teetotallers, most lake steamers sold whisky, beer and wine. The topic of liquor vs. temperance was a populist one and arguments raged in small town newspapers during that decade.

By 1876 the federal government, in genuine concern for First Nations people, took the initiative and passed the Indian Act.[24] The law prohibited the sale of alcohol in any form to Indians. This included everything from fermented malt, wine and anything that could be considered intoxicating in a drinkable form. Because the topic was another populist one, magistrates and policemen were pressured to be on the lookout for people who violated the law.

Captain Tate Robertson was caught up in this debate and charged as the master of a vessel that allowed liquor to be sold to Indians. While on an excursion to Nipigon Bay in the fall of 1880, a number of his American passengers apparently sold illicit alcohol to the local Natives there. Robertson was charged on two counts of breaking the law. He was released, pending his sentencing. This was a serious offence and punishable by a large fine or a jail term or both. Robertson was so concerned that, on October 12, he sailed the *Frances Smith* without passengers or freight from Collingwood to the Sault where he faced the charges. *The Manitoulin Expositor* claimed that Robertson was fined about $500 including costs.[25]

Robertson believed that he was wrongfully convicted and engaged two solicitors from Toronto to appeal his conviction. By May 1881 Judge John Hawkins Hagarty, an Ontario chief justice, heard the case and reversed the lower court decision, much to Robertson's relief. This issue, added to his ongoing family feud, was one more distraction from the allure of being a steamboat commander. It also made him less respectful of the law and government officials.

At Michipicoten on the Lake Superior route, demon liquor was out of control in 1884. The CPR, in the process of constructing the railway through Northern Ontario, outlawed the use of alcohol in their work camps. The prohibition did not stop bootleggers. Whisky and prostitutes flooded into the town from the United States and from Canadian ports. All visiting vessels were suspected of taking part in the illicit trade. Indeed, it was reported that the crew of the *City of Owen Sound* openly sold whisky directly from the ship.

By late in the season of 1884 things were so out of control that an armed confrontation erupted with the Wallace gang (led by the former chief of police, Charlie Wallace) taking over Michipicoten for several weeks.[26] In order to restore order, a force of Toronto policemen was dispatched to Lake Superior. They arrived after a stormy passage on October 23 and, within a few days, had several ringleaders in jail. Two of the Toronto policemen, John Cuddy and David McKee, got wind of

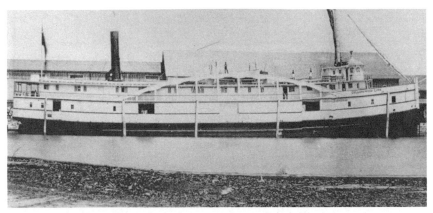

The steamer, *City of Winnipeg*, circa 1880. When the vessel burned at Duluth in 1881, it was rumoured that there were 150 barrels of whisky on board. Over the next decade and a half several attempts were made to find this treasure. Only five barrels were recovered. *Courtesy of Father Edward J. Dowling S.J., Marine Historical Collection, University of Detroit Mercy.*

a possible escape attempt by some of the gang. They thought the outlaws had managed to stow away on the *Frances Smith* which had anchored just off the wharf. The policemen decided to board the *Smith* accompanied by their informant, a local constable, to conduct a search. They rowed out to the anchored sidewheeler and climbed in the open gangway. The first place they looked was in the hold. While they were below, the *Frances Smith* quietly weighed anchor and sailed into the lake.[27] By the time the police officers ran back to the main deck, the steamer was well offshore, steaming for the Sault. They claimed that they were not put off until they reached Gros Cap where they were forced to spend overnight on board and then had to walk back to Michipicoten, a walk through the bush that took three hours.[28] Their account of the walk back is highly unlikely, as Gros Cap is over a hundred kilometres (sixty miles) from Michipcoten, However, the story of their being shanghaied fits with the character of Robertson whose respect for the law, by now, was grudging at best.

*　　*　　*

The *Frances Smith* was laid up for the winter of 1880–81 at Collingwood. Heavy ice in the spring of 1881 meant that the opening of navigation did not begin until after the 5th of May. Her first port of call was Owen Sound where she went into dry dock for minor repairs while the other ships of the Lake Superior Line, the *City of Winnipeg* and the

City of Owen Sound, commenced their regular schedules to the Lakehead. It was not until May 14 that the *Frances Smith* was out of dry dock and back in service, getting a late season start.

Unfortunately for the company, events turned for the worse in 1881. The *City of Winnipeg* left Port Arthur for Duluth at the same time as her main competitor, the *Manitoba*, on July 18. As it was an overnight trip to Duluth, the evening meal was served. After sunset most passengers settled down for the night voyage. Although Second Mate Alexander Brown later denied it, the ships reportedly raced to their destination that evening, with all the steam they could muster. Rumors later claimed that the firemen used wood soaked in oil to add extra heat to the boilers.[29] Brown was supposed to go off watch at 1 a.m., but realizing they were well past Two Harbours, and just a half hour from Duluth, he did not awaken the first mate, who did not take his watch until 3 a.m. after the ship was secured at the wharf. At 4 a.m. he saw flames pouring from the hurricane deck half way between the smokestack and the wheelhouse, directly above the port side boilers. He immediately raised the alarm. Purser Crawford ran though the ship, knocking on cabin doors to rouse the sleeping passengers. Amid the confusion and frantic attempts to save lives, members of the crew threw their clothing to the dock below, ahead of the women who were then lowered with ropes over the side. Suitcases, handbags and valuables were tossed to the dock as men scrambled to safety.

The Duluth fire brigade arrived, as did local opportunists who gathered the scattered valuables and valises from the dock and made off with them. A pillar of smoke and fire arched into the night sky as the flames swept to the stern of the *City of Winnipeg*. The fire brigade was able to contain the fire to the ship, while saving the freight sheds and other buildings on the wharf.

By this time, the lines of the vessel were burning and the bow drifted into the harbour. Escape from the forward part of the main deck became impossible. Six members of the steward's crew were trapped in their room beside the kitchen. They managed to break a hole in the starboard side of the ship facing the lake. In a panic, three of the men jumped into the water and swam to safety. The remaining three, a porter, William Harvey of Collingwood, Head Waiter James Branscombe of Owen Sound and an unidentified pantryman refused to jump for fear of drowning, preferring death by fire.[30]

In the boiler room the engineer scrambled up the iron ladder just in time to reach the deck safely. Collingwood resident Joseph Smith, the fireman on duty, did not escape. He burned to death in the engine room as the flames consumed the *City of Winnipeg*, burning her to the waterline.[31] Although the ship was insured for eighty percent of its value, its loss represented a serious loss to the fleet and to the company's reputation.

The later advertisements of the *Frances Smith* and the *City of Owen Sound* reflect a change in the company's business attitude after the tragic loss. The demoralized ads of mid-1881 stated that the Lake Superior Line had "The best route for Live Stock" and the vessels had "New cabins on deck for steerage passengers." This approach was a long way from the appeal to first-class passenger traffic of just a few years earlier. In late September 1881, the *Frances Smith* arrived in Collingwood in a "leaky condition" and was again sent the to drydock in Owen Sound for repairs.[32] On Sunday, October 16, 1881, at about five o'clock in the morning, the *City of Owen Sound* ran aground on a rock at full speed about fifteen kilometres (about ten miles) from Gore Bay.[33] The steamer *Manitoulin* responded to the whistles of distress and went immediately to the wrecked steamer. They transshipped about six thousand bushels of grain by hand into the *Manitoulin*'s hold over the next day. When the *Owen Sound* still did not budge from the rock, an additional two thousand bushels of wheat were pitched overboard to release her.[34] She was towed to Gore Bay for repairs to the damaged rudder.

In late November, for the third time in 1881, the aging *Frances Smith* was sent to drydock at Owen Sound for more repairs that required another two weeks.[35] She was then anchored at Harrison's dock in the Owen Sound harbour for the winter while workmen rebuilt her bulwarks and restored her above deck structures.[36] Clearly, this was a difficult period for the company.

In a bold move to reinstate the position of the company, the newly organized Canada Lake Superior Line purchased a new ship in England in late 1881. This was no ordinary Great Lakes ship. Originally built in 1873, and operating in Argentina and South Africa under the name *Campana*, she had twin-screw propulsion, an iron hull and, at over 240 feet in length, she was bigger and more powerful than anything west of Montreal.[37] The *Campana* had cabins for 200 passengers on the upper deck and sleeping cabins for 400 steerage passengers on the main deck.[38] She sailed across the Atlantic, was cut in half, and rejoined at Port Dalhousie after being moved up the St. Lawrence River in two pieces. The *Campana* under Captain E. Anderson defined a new standard in Canadian passenger shipping on the Great Lakes.[39] Working alongside the *Frances Smith* and the repaired *City of Owen Sound*, the *Campana* enabled the company to meet all competitors in 1882.

As noted earlier, Tate Robertson decided to seek his fortune in Manitoba in 1882. Along with his brother James, they headed west with their heads full of the wonderful stories about the potential wealth to be had in this new frontier. The company replaced him with Captain A.M. McGregor for two seasons. Under McGregor, the *Frances Smith* was back in business in 1882 with fresh paint, new bulwarks and upgrades to her interior. McGregor kept an old tradition by ensuring that the *Frances Smith* was one of the first ships out of the Owen Sound harbour en route to Collingwood. He arrived there within a few days of the clearing of ice on the bay.[40] With tradition sustained, McGregor made sure the *Frances Smith* remained a favourite on the lakes.[41]

The serious challenges during the years from 1879 to 1881 were clearly not the best for the aging *Frances Smith* and her captain. Nor were they good for the syndicate. Worse was yet to come for the whole Georgian Bay steamboat industry.

10

Delivering the Royal Mail

CONTRACTS FOR THE delivery of mail from Collingwood to Sault Ste. Marie in the early 1860s were handled by a succession of steamers including the *Kaloolah*, the *Ploughboy* and the *Algoma*.[1] Captain Smith with the *Clifton*, and later the *Frances Smith*, controlled the daily mail contracts in southern Georgian Bay except during freeze-up. During the winter months the mail was conveyed by stage, sleigh and horseback from Owen Sound to Collingwood. In these early years in the dead of winter, Native men carried mail by dogsled on a three-week trip from Penetanguishene to Sault Ste. Marie.[2] As communities grew around Georgian Bay and Lake Superior, a number of small businesses became established The post office department in Ottawa was pressured to create more outlets, establish more scheduled services beyond the south shore and generally provide more reliable deliveries. Railways, as they developed, were a partial answer to this demand, but until the late 1880s, it was steamers like the *Frances Smith* that provided essential mail service in spring, summer and fall.

The Royal Mail was used for the transfer of cash, the conveyance of money orders, the distribution of newspapers from the city, the transaction of business and the delivery of personal letters. Steamers delivered the mail to the dock where it was picked up and transferred to the local post office. There, patrons waited for the postmaster to do the sorting and finally hand the mail to them directly. The steamer's whistle as she

Mail Contract.

TENDERS' addressed to the Postmaster General, will be received at Ottawa, until Noon,

ON FRIDAY, 1st MARCH,

For the conveyance of Her Majesty's Mails, on a proposed Contract for Four Years, six times per week each way,

Between Collingwood and Owen Sound,

During close of Navigation, from the close of Navigation, 1867.

Conveyance to be made in a Waggon, Sleigh, Cutter or Passenger Stage.

The Mails to leave Owen Sound daily, Sundays excepted, at such an hour as will secure a delivery of Mails at Collingwood in time for their despatch by afternoon train going to Toronto. To leave Collingwood as soon as possible after the arrival of the morning train from Toronto, and to arrive at Owen Sound in nine hours afterwards.

Printed notices containing further information as to conditions of proposed Contract may be seen, and blank forms of Tender may be obtained at the Post Offices of Collingwood and Owen Sound.

J. DEWE,
Post Office Inspector.

Post Office Inspector's Office,
Toronto, 19th January, 1867.   421-3in.

Advertisement for mail contract, 1867, calling for tenders for winter mail delivery between Collingwood and Owen Sound. During the winter months it was difficult to move mail overland. Summer mail was contracted to steamers like the *Clifton* and the *Frances Smith*. Taken from *The Owen Sound Comet*, February 1867. *Courtesy of the Owen Sound Union Library.*

approached the village dock was the signal for a community event, especially for those with an interest beyond their small world. Those expecting cash through registered mail from faraway relatives were often the first in line. For those who did not pick up their mail, local newspapers carried long lists of undelivered mail about once per month. This mail was of both personal and commercial importance to thousands of people on the upper lakes.[3] Farmers, lumbermen, professionals and businessmen alike depended on a regular delivery service.

Not all post offices were created equally. Some simply acted as delivery points for hinterland outposts. Some became the central distribution point of pioneer settlements. Some offered the added service of a money order office where nascent businesses struggled for survival. In large communities sometimes a banking service was also provided, causing

The Mail Train, Mohawks, Penetanguishene, March 1853, pencil, watercolour and gouache, B.A.W. artist. The mail for "Saulte de Ste Marie" is carried across Lake Huron on ice. Then the delivery time from Penetanguishene to the Sault was about three weeks. Steamers moved the mail in two days during the summer. *Courtesy of Library and Archives Canada, Acc. No. R9266-422 Peter Winkworth Collection of Canadiana.*

the post office to become the focal point for growing villages and towns.

Given the fact that steamers also stopped at locations where no post office had yet been set up, the captain or purser would act as a postmaster. They took mail on board, cancelled stamps and sorted letters into bags. In reality the vessels became floating post offices. In the modern philatelic community, sales catalogues sell cancelled stamps from several Georgian Bay and Lake Superior steamers: the *Clifton*, the *City of Owen Sound*, the *City of Winnipeg*, the *Asia* and the *Northern Belle*, to name just a few. None of these stamps are known for the *Frances Smith*, but she too participated in the business. No doubt a cancelled stamp with markings from this steamer is hiding in a forgotten box in someone's attic.

When the *Frances Smith* moved to the Collingwood/Lake Superior route after 1872, she seems to have secured a portion of the contract delivering mail along the "Turkey Trail," so named because of the meandering route through the islands and bays of the North Channel from Killarney to Sault Ste. Marie. At the same time, the Northern Railway steamers *Chicora* and *Algoma* held contracts

Postal cancellation stamp from the steamer *Clifton*. *Courtesy of Bill Longley Auctions.*

Envelope on stationary from the *Frances Smith*. To date no
cancellation marks have been found with the *Frances Smith*
imprint. It is suspected that mail was cancelled aboard the
ship as it was on the *Clifton. Courtesy of Stuart Robertson.*

to deliver mail from Collingwood to the Lakehead.[4] In 1872, the Postmaster General (PMG) requested that the Privy Council renew the
railway's contract for two years at a cost of $12,500. The newly created
Beatty Line of steamers, sailing out of Sarnia,[5] also wanted a share of the
contract but their request was turned down, partly because there was concern about their proximity to the United States.[6] The government wished
to encourage connections to the west through Collingwood only.

The *Frances Smith* continued to hold post office contracts in 1873 and
1874.[7] These contracts were shared with the Northern Railway Company's ships, the *Cumberland*[8] and the *Chicora*, on the Collingwood to
Fort William run.[9] In 1874, tenders were called for the next year's season. The Beatty Line of Sarnia finally landed a contract for $8,000, while
the Northern Railway with the *Chicora* and the *Cumberland* renewed
theirs for a reduced rate of $10,000. For some reason, the *Smith*, sailing
under the banner of the Collingwood Lake Superior Line, did not have
a contract at the beginning of 1875, while her former two running mates,
Chicora and *Cumberland* did.[10]

That spring the ice did not retreat from the lakes until late, and drift
ice impeded the sailing of vessels in Lake Superior right up until May
25. Ships travelling north through Lake Huron had a very difficult time
of it in mid-May, especially in the lower St. Mary's River. In fact, the
first mail ship to the Sault did not arrive until after May 14. Unfortunately for post office customers around the lakes, the winter contracts
to deliver mail overland via Detroit had been terminated at the end of

April. As a result, Sault Ste. Marie residents did not receive mail from late April until the latter part of May, which was particularly upsetting to the business community and the local customs officer. But Fort William customers did not receive mail until June. Several grieved community leaders complained to the Postmaster General.[11] Likewise, the postmaster at Killarney was upset. Overland transport from Penetanguishene was always slow, but, in 1875, Killarney's mail and everyone else's along the north shore was especially late. Matthew Sweetham, the postal inspector for the region, was a target for the grievances as well.

Sweetham replied to the PMG about the complaints, suspecting that the owners of the *Frances Smith* were orchestrating the criticisms of the services in order to secure leverage for an 1875 contract. He stated, " I have good reason to believe that a good deal of the complaining this season has been prompted by the owners of the steamer *Frances Smith* which boat formed one of the Collingwood Line of mail steamers during the season of 1873 and 1874 – but [is] not this year connected therewith."[12]

Sweetham was probably correct in his assumptions about skullduggery on the part of Captain Robertson of the *Smith*, a man not afraid to use his connections to get what he wanted. Reading between the lines of Sweetham's correspondence, it is clear that there was pressure being placed on him to accommodate the *Frances Smith* in the roster of mail steamers in 1875. That pressure was coming from both Georgian Bay's community leaders and from the PMG himself. In his response to the latter, Sweetham implied that a contract with the *Frances Smith* could possibly be "arranged" as long as the steamer in question commenced mail deliveries on a "day other than the present mail days, namely Tuesday or Friday for leaving Collingwood for Fort William."[13]

The upshot was that an arrangement was made. By mid-August 1875 Captain Robertson placed his bid for a mail contract from Collingwood to all ports on the route to Thunder Bay for the balance of the year. He offered to do the work for $2,323.00.[14] Sweetham looked over the bid and told Captain Robertson that to win a contract he had to call at each of the following ports: Killarney, Little Current, Spanish River, Bruce Mines, Garden River, Sault Ste. Marie, Pointe Aux Pins, Batchawana, Michipicoten, Red Rock, Silver Islet and Thunder Bay.[15] Robertson replied that requiring him to stop at Michipicoten and Red Rock would make it impossible complete the round trip every week. These ports,

Robertson stated, were too far out of the way to service regularly. As advantageous as a mail contract was, the steamer's main source of income was moving freight between southern Ontario localities and the already established towns like the Sault and Prince Arthur's Landing, not to wildcat mining villages like Michipicoten. Robertson counter-offered to visit Red Rock fortnightly on the up and down trip if the weather and safety considerations were to his satisfaction.

Sweetham finally accepted Robertson's conditions. To appease the people at Michipicoten, Sweetham extended the existing contract with Beatty's steamer *Manitoba* out of Sarnia to include calling there every ten days. He negotiated with Robertson to change his sailing date from Friday to Thursday so that the Collingwood Lake Superior Line could fill in with Monday departures from Collingwood to the north. Thus, the lakehead communities would have guaranteed trice weekly mail service.

Such was the give and take in establishing a complex web of mail service to Ontario's growing northlands. Clearly, the long-term solution was to abandon steamers, which were useful for only seven months of the year anyway, and shift delivery to railways. Sweetham had to wait a decade for that to happen. Meanwhile, the post office arranged to divert some mail from the contentious steamers and send some mail through the American railroad system to Winnipeg. Mail was then rerouted overland back to the Lakehead, but Port Arthur customers remained unhappy as this method took several days. Steamer service remained the fastest way to move the mails during navigation season, even though the post office considered it to be too expensive. Matthew Sweetham and the residents of Port Arthur and Fort William wanted a speedy, reliable all-Canadian railway route to the west. It was a card that played directly into the Conservative Party's National Policy and the plans for the Canadian Pacific Railway.

John A. Macdonald's promise to build a transcontinental railway was important to more than just the lakehead communities and British Columbia. Inspector Sweetham saw railways as a solution to the complicated schedules he was required to create, balance and juggle each year. In 1884, he negotiated contracts with four Ontario steamer companies to deliver mail. The system was so complicated and expensive that by the end of the season, he was given directions to get a better deal from the steamers.[16]

Meanwhile, in late 1881, the CPR had developed plans to use Algoma Mills on the north shore of Lake Huron, near present-day Blind River, as their Georgian Bay railway terminal for heavy freight and passenger service to Toronto. This decision meant bypassing Collingwood and Owen Sound and creating a new transportation hub under its direct control. The CPR wanted to build luxury steamers to service the upper lakes until a full transcontinental rail service was built. To accomplish this it commissioned a company in Glasgow, Aitken & Mansell, to build the propellers, *Algoma*, *Athabasca* and *Alberta*. A railway line between Algoma Mills and Sault Ste. Marie commenced the same year and was completed by 1884, although not needed until 1888. Then, in mid-1884, the CPR changed its mind and decided to locate at Owen Sound. This new decision doomed any further growth for Algoma Mills. Today there is little evidence of the dreamed grandeur that was to bring recognition and prosperity to the Algoma site. The proposed 300-room hotel was redesigned and relocated, and became the Banff Springs Hotel.

The decision also had a profound effect on the *Frances Smith*. The future of mail delivery contracts by boat to all the communities along the north shore of Lake Huron was now in jeopardy as the railway was extended beyond Algoma Mills to the Sault, with stops at almost every community the *Frances Smith* had once served along the North Channel. "Through" mail from Toronto to the Lakehead via Owen Sound and the Sault could be better served by the CPR's faster and larger luxury steamers, but these ships would not stop at the small ports that were now expecting regular mail delivery. This service was left to the small steamer operators who had only a few years left as mail carriers.

Increased costs to the post office for the delivery of mail to outposts on the upper lakes annoyed the PMG and Inspector Sweetham. In 1883, Postal Inspector Sweetham was directed to review all contracts. The *Frances Smith*, then sailing under the flag of the Canada Transit Company, received $500 in 1883 for a short-term contract and $3,000 in 1884 for a full year. The total cost for all steam mail services out of Collingwood rose from $9,500 to $12,000 in the same period. Costs were spiralling out of control. Realizing they had a window of advantage before the rail lines were completed, the Long and Cameron group[17] with their Great Northern Transit Company (GNT) upped their demand in 1885 to $5,000 from the previous season's $3,500. They argued that the contracts were not worth their while because their main competitor, the *Frances Smith*, did not have to stop at out of the way locations like Cockburn Island[18] and, therefore, was able to beat their ships to the docks in larger communities to pick up passengers and acquire the more lucrative freight loads. It was still first-come, first-served in the competitive world of steamer traffic. A third company, the Owen Sound Transport Company tried to get in on the bidding, but Sweetham had no confidence in the line.

Sweetham wrote to the Deputy Postmaster General, William Henry Griffin, stating, " It is annoying because the company [Great Northern Transit] has the Department in a tight place."[19] Eventually Sweetham went to Collingwood and met with James Beatty, John Long and Charles Cameron and negotiated a price (to deliver mail to Lake Superior) of $4,000 for each of two seasons, a price Sweetham considered a "liberal remuneration."[20] This meant that the steamers of the Great Northern Transit Company, (the *Atlantic* and the *Pacific*) held the contract to deliver mail from Sault Ste. Marie to Collingwood in 1885 and 1886. The *Pacific* left Collingwood at 1 p.m. each Wednesday and the *Atlantic* at the same hour Saturday on the arrival of the Northern Railway train from Toronto and the arrival of the North Western Railway train from Hamilton. Both the *Pacific* and the *Atlantic* stopped each way at most of the small communities along the North Channel and Manitoulin Island. They also called at Meaford and Owen Sound twice each week. Robertson and the *Frances Smith* seemed to be out-manoeuvered by the competition. As well, Sweetham's long-standing distaste for Robertson's manipulative behaviour in gaining contracts worked against future deals.

This arrangement to exclude the *Frances Smith* was unsatisfactory to the people of Owen Sound who claimed they needed a third trip to and from the north. As real as their need may have been, Robertson was unmistakably involved in the protests to the government and the post office.

The gist of Owen Sound's argument was twofold. Firstly, registered letters from the west remained in an unopened special "through bag" to Collingwood. When sorted, the mail had to be shipped from there back to Owen Sound by way of Meaford or Toronto. Although the steamer stopped at Owen Sound on the way downbound, the "through bag" could not be opened. The time involved in this second step put Owen Sound enterprises doing business with ports along the north shore at a commercial disadvantage to Collingwood businesses. Secondly, the *Frances Smith* of the Lake Superior Line was scheduled to leave each Friday and would be able to augment the existing service for very little extra cost. She could carry registered mail directly to Owen Sound, as well as broadening the regular service offered by the *Atlantic* and the *Pacific*.

Tate Robertson of the *Frances Smith* this time orchestrated the Owen Sound town fathers, the Owen Sound Board of Trade and *The Owen Sound Times* to attempt to reopen the bidding and support his application to extend the mail service directly to Owen Sound from all points, including Lake Superior. In conversations with Inspector Sweetham, Robertson offered to deliver mail to and from Owen Sound to the Sault (not including the intermediate points) for the sum of $1,000.[21] He also stated it was his plan to run on Thursday each week to connect with the CPR steamers at Sault Ste. Marie and points west.[22] The Great Northern Transit Company countered by offering the same service for $600. With cut-throat competition like this, the end of steamer mail was near.

Post Office Inspector Sweetham saw through Robertson's orchestration and dismissed Owen Sound's need for faster service and objections that businesses were suffering. "There is clearly little weight in this objection; it is probably put forward as an argument in favour of using the *Frances Smith*," he stated. Sweetham, in fact, favoured using the new CPR rail line through Northern Ontario to service Port Arthur.[23] Sweetham eventually tempered his final letter to the PMG, stating that if mail delivery was to be increased to three times per week, then the proposal by the *Frances Smith* was "reasonable" even though the concern about delays in receipt of registered mail at Owen Sound was, in his opinion, "trifling."

In the end, the *Frances Smith* did not get a contract in 1886. However, in 1887, an arrangement was made to share the mail delivery with the Great Northern Transit Company. The relations between the owners and operators of the *Frances Smith* and the GNT were less than cordial that year. When the *Frances Smith* had to go into drydock for repairs in November 1887, Captain Robert D. Foote of the *Atlantic*, one of the GNT's vessels, refused to take up the slack in mail delivery from Owen Sound to points north. At the time, the *Atlantic* and the *Smith* took the mails on alternate weeks. Captain Foote claimed that it was not his responsibility to fill in for the unfulfilled obligations of the *Frances Smith*. Besides, he claimed that he had no authority to deliver mail every week.[24] Postmaster Robert

MAIL CONTRACTS.

Oontraots for Mails, by Steamer, on Georgian Bay and Lake Huron.

Sealed tenders, addressed to the Postmaster-General, will be received at Ottawa until noon on MONDAY, 13TH MAY, 1889, for the conveyance of her Majesty's mails, semi-weekly, on a proposed contract for the season of navigation 1889, in each case, viz :

1. COLLINGWOOD AND SAULT STE. MARIE, and 2. OWEN SOUND AND SAULT STE. MARIE.

The ports at which mails are to be exchanged will be the same as during last season.

The service will include the conveyance of the mails between the steamers and the post-office, as heretofore.

The steamers employed in this service must be good and sufficient, with a speed of not less than ten miles per hour, and must be at all times subject to the inspection and approval of the Postmaster-General.

Each tender must state the names of the steamers, the ports of call, and the days and hours of departure from each end of the route.

The entire service must be performed subject to the usual conditions governing mail contracts in Canada.

Each tender to state the price asked for the season of navigation 1889, in words at length.

The Postmaster-General will not bind himself to accept the lowest or any tender.

Blank forms of tender may be obtained at the post-offices at Collingwood and Owen Sound, and at this office.

MATTHEW SWEETNAM,
Post-office Inspector.

Post-office Inspector's Office, }
Toronto, 29th April, 1889. }

By 1889 mail contracts like this one to deliver mail from Collingwood to the Sault were about to end. Steamers were effectively put out of business except for service to small villages and island communities.
From *The Owen Sound Comet*, April 1867. *Courtesy of the Owen Sound Union Library.*

Crawford of Owen Sound prevailed upon Foote and, in the end, he agreed to carry the mails until the end of the shipping season.

Meanwhile Great Northern Transit Company purchased the *Frances Smith* from Smith and Keighley that winter, renaming her the *Baltic*. In 1888, now with three steamers, Long and Cameron once again secured a mail contract – this time for an additional $1,000 for the use of three steamers (*Baltic*, *Pacific* and *Atlantic*) and thrice weekly delivery to Lake Superior.

By 1889, the rail line to the Sault was fully operational and Sweetham recommended it as the mail delivery method for year-round service. The Great Northern Transit Company's victory was sweet but short. Except for the islands and a few remote villages, the days of steamer mail service were over.

11

Troubles on the Lakes

SCARCELY HAD THE shipping season opened in 1882, when a major tragedy struck Georgian Bay. The steamer *Manitoulin* of the rival Great Northern Transit Company caught fire on May 18, in a dramatic disaster six kilometres (about four miles) offshore from the village of Manitowaning. In an heroic attempt to save the ship and her passengers Captain "Black Pete" Campbell ordered up full steam and pointed the bow toward land. At an estimated speed of thirteen miles per hour, the *Manitoulin* slammed into the shore and burned to the waterline. Over a dozen deaths were recorded in the accident. The reaction of the government to the calamity was to clamp down on the steamship lines and pass regulations to limit the number of passengers and crew on all steam vessels on the upper lakes as shown:

STEAMER	PASSENGERS	CREW
Frances Smith	370	30
City of Owen Sound	400	25
Campana	600	30
Northern Belle	60	18
Asia	40	20
Africa	40	20[1]

These new regulations dampened the enthusiasm for high volume trips for a while, but within months the rules were simply ignored. There were reports of 1,000 excursionists on board the *Campana* in July 1885. The *Frances Smith* regularly carried 600 or more excursionists after 1882, and the sad case of the sinking of the *Asia* in mid-September 1882 gives the lie to the effectiveness of regulations. In that tragedy about 100 persons drowned. Indeed, Captain Scott, the chief investigator in the *Asia* disaster observed a year later that the *Africa* sailed with 150 passengers yet had only a license for 40. He stated that all he could do was to warn passengers of the danger of overcrowding.[2]

On September 14, 1882, one of the most brutal storms in the history of 19th century sailing sent the *Asia* to the bottom. The *Frances Smith* was safely tucked into Collingwood harbour when the gale swept across the lakes.[3] Captain Alexander Murray McGregor, her new master, was cautious. He had taken note of the way the sky looked and the way the sheering wind bent the trees on shore, so he remained in port. It was not until two days later that he nosed the *Frances Smith* out into Georgian Bay, arriving in Owen Sound later that day. A personal family tragedy related to the sinking of the *Asia*, delayed him and he did not arrive at Duluth until September 22.[4] This next day he sailed to Prince Arthur's Landing.[5] Captain McGregor remarked that the crossing of Georgian Bay earlier in the week was the worst he had ever encountered. And that was after the storm had passed!

Other lake vessels were not so fortunate. The North West Transportation Company's *Manitoba* left Southampton with two hundred persons aboard at 2 a.m. on the 14th of September. At exactly the same time, the Great Northern Transit Company's *Asia* left Presqu'ile bound for Killarney with about one hundred on board.

By dawn of September 14, the *Manitoba* was in serious trouble, pounding her way west of the Bruce Peninsula. The captain, A.E. McGregor (not to be confused with Captain A.M. McGregor of the *Frances Smith*), turned toward the shelter of Cove Island just off the tip of the peninsula. He found it impossible to keep the ship on course and there was a real danger that she would be smashed on the coast. Waves crashed over the side of the vessel, smashing doors, windows and even the skylights on the top deck. Everyone was exhausted from lack of sleep and all were violently seasick. Not even the crew were able to stand upright

Bill of lading Marks' Wharf, Prince Arthur's Landing, 1881, the first trip down-bound for the *Frances Smith*. Nineteenth century bookkeepers carefully recorded freight items in journals and logbooks. Passengers were not so carefully recorded. When ships sank it was often difficult to identify those lost, particularly if they were immigrants. *Courtesy of Captain Gerry Outerkirk.*

on the pitching decks. Down below in the engine room, the iron rod that braced the walls of the ship snapped, and the steering chain gave indications that it too was about to break. The terrified women passengers "wailed" and "God Himself would not quell the storm" despite the prayers of all.[6] Fortunately, the *Manitoba* made safe harbour at Tobermory at the tip of the peninsula.

A few miles to the east, the schooner *Nellie Sherwood* was fighting for her life. Loaded with block stone for Algoma Mills in the North Channel, the vessel was last spotted running before the wind, flying a distress flag near Cabot Head. She sank with all hands. Captain Thomas Blanchard and a crew of five, including his son, perished.

Meanwhile, the overburdened *Asia* under the command of Captain J.N. Savage, battled her way along the east coast of the Bruce Peninsula towards Lonely Island in the centre of Georgian Bay. About 11 a.m. the top-heavy, poorly loaded vessel rolled on her side in a trough between two waves. Many people leapt into the frigid water from the upper decks. Terrified passengers grasped the ship rails in a desperate bid for security just as the *Asia* shuddered and sank stern first. The hissing boilers sent up clouds of steam and smoke as the boat plunged to the bottom. People in the water groped for the gunwales of lifeboats that somehow broke away from the sinking ship. As they were hauled aboard one by one, they fell exhausted into the bottom of the lifeboats, only to have huge waves lift the crafts out of the water and flip them over. Time after time the lifeboats spilled their cargo, exhausting even the strongest. The injured simply slipped away to drown. Only two of about one hundred people on board survived.

On Lake Ontario the *Mystic Star* lost her masts and the *Mary Ann Lydon* dumped her entire load of lumber. In Lake Huron the *Admiral* lost her after masts. From all around the lakes were reports of wreckage, but Georgian Bay was the most severely hit. It was only the prudence and good judgment of Captain A.M. McGregor that kept the *Frances Smith* away from the fury of the hurricane offshore from Collingwood.

In an era when storm warnings were not standardized and the weather patterns were unknown, it is a wonder more people did not perish on the lakes. Safety was apparently not the prime consideration. All Great Lakes ships violated the regulations in an attempt to make profits. Money was clearly more important than safety[7] After the violent September 1882 storm and the investigations that followed, there was ample evidence to continue to condemn the practices of the lake-carrier operators. The captain of the *Frances Smith* was not above condemnation both before and after 1882.

In 1882, the Canadian Pacific Railway (CPR) hired an experienced and talented steamboat businessman, Henry Beatty (from the North West Transportation Company of Sarnia) to develop a strategy for the company whereby their existing railway system in Ontario could be linked to the newly constructed rail line from Fort William to the west.[8] In order to make an inspection of the territory, Canada's Minister of Railways, Charles Tupper, made a personal visit to the west. On his return trip he arrived in Prince Arthur's Landing from Winnipeg and boarded the *Frances Smith* for his return trip. While waiting for departure, a committee from the community arrived and presented Tupper with a petition in support of the railway and the National Policy.[9]

Tupper responded positively to the committee before sailing and, by 1883, the CPR made arrangements, through one of its subsidiaries, to lease the Toronto, Grey & Bruce Railway, which had a terminus in Owen Sound. Beatty contracted the *Frances Smith* and the *Campana* to carry passengers and freight between the two disparate ends of the rail lines during 1883. The *Frances Smith* adjusted her schedule to include Duluth in order to connect with American railroads moving immigrants to

Dakota and points west. This was a boom year for the *Frances Smith* with Captain McGregor still at the helm. There were times when she was so well-laden with freight that she did not even stop in Owen Sound on her return trip to Collingwood.[10] This raised the ire of Owen Sound citizens and the local press alike. The construction of the railway in the west was so aggressive that by late summer Beatty was using two additional steamers to transport labourers for work on the CPR line out west.

The arrival of the Canadian Pacific Railway steamers in Owen Sound in April 1884 meant trouble for the *Frances Smith* and the Collingwood Lake Superior Line. The CPR's brand new Glasgow-built 262-foot steamers, *Algoma*, *Alberta* and *Athabasca*, were state of the art, steel, propeller-driven luxury liners.[11] They were faster, larger and full of technologies unknown by other great lakes steamers, including the *Frances Smith*. For the first time on the lakes, the Chadburn telegraph[12] replaced bells and whistles as a signalling device between the pilothouse and the engine room. An electrical generator on board provided running lights and interior illumination at night. The Thompson compass

Canada Pacific Steamship Line poster. Faced with competition from the luxury liners of the CPR, the *Frances Smith* and other steamers focused on supplying the smaller ports on Manitoulin Island, the North Channel and Lake Superior after 1885. *Courtesy of the Owen Sound Marine Museum.*

made steering easier and more accurate. Clearly, the *Frances Smith* was out-classed when the first of these exceptional vessels reached Owen Sound. She also lacked the capacity, the glamour and the integrated transportation schedules of the Canadian Pacific Railway.

Interlocking transportation systems between rail and steamships put enormous economic pressures on relatively small stand-alone steamer companies. Even before the CPR arrived on the scene, the Grand Trunk Railway had developed its own interlocking system though Montreal, Sarnia and Duluth with the North West Transportation Company. As well, in 1879, the Hamilton & North Western Railway amalgamated with the Northern Railway to provide service links between Collingwood and southwestern Ontario.[13] The *Frances Smith* made the most of this new market along with the *City of Owen Sound*. The company's railway schedules were published and departures timed to link directly with the new railway system. But in the long run, a more heavily financed and integrated system would be needed to compete effectively with the CPR's strength.

The CPR now had a rail line now from Montreal through Toronto to Owen Sound, and it had a new rail line from Port Arthur to Manitoba. The port of Collingwood found itself squeezed out of the booming trade to the west and was left with only the Georgian Bay routes to Sault Ste. Marie. However, that is not to say that there was no steamer traffic out of Collingwood. The Great Northern Transportation Company of Collingwood was aggressively adding ships to its roster. The Owen Sound-built, 179-foot *Pacific* and the rebuilt *Manitoulin*, now renamed the *Atlantic*, were put into service by 1883. The company added the 209-foot *Majestic* in 1885, but they remained outclassed by the CPR. They also faced fierce competition from the Collingwood Lake Superior Line. Despite the heartbreaking total wreck of the CPR's new *Algoma* with 38 deaths on Lake Superior in November of 1885, smaller companies were competitively at a disadvantage.

To bolster income to compensate for her very competitive pricing, the *Frances Smith* ran excursions in 1884 at the head of the lakes while she awaited turn around time for her return trip to Collingwood. Agents sold tickets for a full two weeks before she took an excursion with two bands aboard for a May 31 cruise from Port Arthur and out into Lake Superior and back to the Kaministiquia River.[14] A few extra dollars at each

The three CPR sisters: *Algoma, Athabaska* and *Alberta* came to Owen Sound in 1884. These luxury ships were built in Scotland, sailed across the Atlantic, cut in half to be towed through the lower Great Lakes, then welded together. The *Algoma* was wrecked in a November 1885 storm at Isle Royale. In the photo above taken at Owen Sound Harbour, the *Athabaska* is at the dock, the *Alberta* is turning, preparing to dock. *Courtesy of Grey Roots Archival Collection.*

end of routine trips was a strategy for economic survival. The vessel took on any kind of freight, including the transportation of the dead. A surveyor by the name of Peter Beveridge drowned while canoeing on the Serpent River at the end of June 1882. His body was taken to the Sault by the *Northern Belle* and then transshipped from there to the Lakehead on the *Frances Smith*.[15] Dead or alive, paying passengers were accepted.

The weather on Lake Superior on Sunday, June 21, 1885, was bitterly cold. Gale force winds were blowing from the west when the *Frances Smith* left Sault Ste. Marie at midnight. All night long the ship ploughed through heavy seas in Whitefish Bay. By Monday afternoon she approached Cape Brule just east of Michipicoten when the officer on deck spotted a fishing smack in the distance. It had obviously been swamped in the open lake. There was a man calling and waving frantically for help from the water-logged boat. The officer ordered the wheelsman to bring the *Frances Smith* about and to go to the rescue.

After turning a full circle and bringing the steamer back into the wind, Captain Robertson, who was now in the pilothouse, called for the

Lake Superior fishermen circa 1880. Men from small fishing villages around Lake Superior in open fishing boats like this ventured several miles offshore to catch lake trout and whitefish. It was a craft similar to this that was rescued at Dog River by the crew of the *Frances Smith. Courtesy of Archives of Ontario, F1132-2-1-2, #183.*

engines to be stopped. The yawl was drawn up to the gangway and dispatched with several crew members to get close to the half-submerged smack. It was too dangerous to manoeuvre the paddlewheel steamer any nearer. With a great deal of effort, the exhausted fisherman was pulled into the yawl and then hauled on board the *Frances Smith* through the open gangway doors.

The fisherman had been in the swamped boat since Sunday afternoon when his smack had overturned then righted itself. In order to keep from being washed overboard, he had lashed himself to the tiller. Inside his small boat were two dead bodies. One was the fisherman's fourteen-year-old son, Antoine Boyer. The other was a twenty-year-old friend by the name of Sourier from Sault Ste. Marie. He had offered to help with the fishing chores when Boyer set sail from the mouth of the Dog River early Sunday morning. When the wind came up in the afternoon, the boat was driven toward Gargantua at which point the wind veered to the southwest and blew the small craft out into the lake where it capsized. Both Sourier and young Boyer died from hypothermia on Monday morning. By the time the old man was pulled aboard the *Frances Smith*, he too was almost dead.

Robertson gave orders for his ship to alter course for the Dog River where he delivered the surviving elder Boyer and the two bodies to Boyer's wife and five children.[16] Robertson did not stay long at the dock before he returned to his scheduled route to the Lakehead. There was nothing else he could do.

In early September of 1885 there were rumours in Port Arthur that the *Frances Smith* herself had sunk in Georgian Bay. Word had it that the ship had gone down and was out of sight. Other rumours declared that the *Frances Smith* had struck a rock and that the hull was pierced. *The Meaford Monitor* on August 28, 1885, stated, "The vessel lies on a rocky bottom in ten feet of water." *The Chicago Times* on September 26, 1885, and *The Duluth Tribune*, two days later, echoed the same story.

Water, it was said, flooded the boat, dooming her to the scrapyard. In fact, the *Frances Smith* did hit a rock on August 23, 1885. After arriving late in Port Arthur. Captain Robertson and Henry E. Smith, (Robertson's cousin and partner) secretary-treasurer of the company and also the ship's purser, stated in no uncertain terms that the damage to the ship was minimal and not worth discussing. To prove their point, the *Frances Smith* sailed directly back to Collingwood without repairs. On arrival there, the ship did go to dry dock for the necessary inspection and repairs. *The Cleveland Leader* casualty list (December 7, 1885) for the Great Lakes notes that the damage was more than minimal and that the cost of repairs at the Collingwood drydock was $3,900.00. Neither Robertson nor Smith was willing to recognize any problems with their vessel. Henry Smith, especially, became agitated at any suggestion that the *Frances Smith* was anything but perfectly sound.

12

Confrontation with United States Customs

In 1886, Captain Tate Robertson removed the *Frances Smith* from the run to Lake Superior and placed her back on a Georgian Bay route terminating at Sault Ste. Marie. He and his partner, Henry Eberts Smith, brokered an arrangement with the CPR to develop the tourist trade around Georgian Bay by running excursions commencing on July 15, 1886. These cruises were run in conjunction with their routine trips. In all, five excursions were to be made to Mackinac Island in addition to the weekly Sault Ste. Marie sailings.[1] The *Frances Smith* left Collingwood each Wednesday following the arrival of the Toronto train, and then stopped at Meaford and Owen Sound, arriving in Wiarton by evening. It was then an overnight passage to Killarney, arriving early Thursday morning. While freight was off-loaded and cordwood stacked below, passengers were given the morning to walk about the village and buy blueberries and crafts from the resident Indians. The *Smith* sailed Thursday afternoon and, after stopping briefly at Little Current, Gore Bay, Kagawong, Spanish River, Thessalon, Bruce Mines and Garden River, she arrived in Sault Ste. Marie on Friday. She stayed there all day Saturday and Sunday while passengers visited the Shingwauk Indian School, the locks, the St. Mary's Rapids and local churches. The ship finally sailed to Mackinac Island early Monday morning and left for the return trip to Collingwood that evening about 6 p.m. The whole package including meals cost twelve dollars.

The *Frances Smith* inaugurated excursions to Mackinac Island on July 16, 1886. This marked the beginning of a year of struggle with the United States customs. From *The Meaford Monitor* July 1, 1886. *Courtesy of the Meaford Public Library.*

At the time, Mackinac Island was billed as a "tourist's paradise."[2] There were several American vessels that sailed to the island from Buffalo, Chicago and Detroit. These excursionists would land at the main pier below the town and walk around the historic island fort and take wagon rides to view the island's natural features. Mackinac was becoming a summer tourist destination for wealthy Americans. Her trademark Grand Hotel was under construction, due to open in 1887. Canadians too regarded this gem on the upper lakes as an important destination. The problem was that the *Frances Smith* sailed under the Canadian flag and, as a foreign vessel, had to clear customs whenever she docked at any American port. But there was no customs house on Mackinac Island. Therefore no passengers could disembark, no baggage could be discharged, no freight unloaded and no supplies purchased at that port.

In 1886, international borders were not as carefully monitored as they are today. However, local circumstances conspired to cause trouble for the owners of the *Frances Smith* when they stopped at Mackinac. William Tate Robertson believed he was on safe ground by stating in his clearance at the U.S. customs office in Collingwood, that he would pass into American waters and stop at Mackinac Island. At Grand Haven, Michigan, the head customs officer for Michigan, Dudley O. Watson, knew nothing of Robertson's arrangements.

The docks at Mackinac Island circa 1889. The *Frances Smith* was
seized in 1886 at these docks by U.S. customs officers for failing to
report to St. Ignace, a small village on the mainland of Upper
Michigan. At the dock in this photo are the *City of London* and the
India. *From the Thunder Bay Research Collection, courtesy of the
Alpena County George N. Fletch Public Library, Alpena, Michigan.*

A rivalry for tourist trade existed between Mackinac Island and the
village of St. Ignace, just six kilometres (about four miles) across the
strait in Michigan's upper peninsula. St. Ignace did have a customs office
and a newly appointed Deputy Customs Officer Jesse Warren, who
seemed determined to make things difficult for the Canadian vessel.
He wanted to force the *Smith* to dock at St. Ignace. Warren apparently
also worked in a bar beside the customs office and, when the court eventually heard the case, the purser of the *Frances Smith*, Robert Parrot,
implied that Warren had ulterior motives in wanting the steamer to
report to St. Ignace.[3] The bar was very handy to the dock and excursionists were potential customers.

On her first excursion to Mackinac, the *Frances Smith* landed on July
19, 1886. Purser Robert Parrott asked for directions to the custom's office.
The people crowded along the pier at Mackinac stated there was no customs house there, nor did they know where one was. Unaware of the
one at St. Ignace, Captain Robertson sailed back to Canada that evening
without reporting and without proper clearance.[4] Although this was an
innocent enough mistake, Captain Robertson knew the rules about entry
to the United States and knew he was in clear violation of U.S. law.

On the second trip, August 2, Parrott discovered the location of the customs office and took a ferry to St. Ignace. There he made a verbal report
to the deputy customs officer. Jesse Warren in turn declared that this
approach was not acceptable and demanded to see the vessel's manifest
and other papers. When none were produced, he refused to grant entry

to and clearance from the United States. Parrott later claimed that Warren told him that if he brought clearances from Collingwood for these first two trips and for subsequent trips, the letter of the law would be met.[5] This claim Parrot subsequently withdrew at the inquiry that followed.

When Parrott returned to the *Frances Smith*, still docked at Mackinac Island, Captain Robertson received his report and made a decision. He had a schedule to follow and a timetable to meet. He decided to sail back to Collingwood with his crew of twenty-five and several hundred passengers. For a second time he proceeded without the formalities of documenting entry and exit to and from a U.S. port.

Four days later on August 6, the rookie customs officer, Jesse Warren, contacted the Customs Inspector Dudley Watson at Grand Haven, Michigan, for advice and assistance. Watson immediately saw that the violations by Robertson had the makings of an international incident. He went up the chain of command and sent an urgent telegraph to the acting secretary of the treasury in Washington D.C., seeking direction. The telegraph stated:

> The Canadian steamer "Frances Smith" has been to Mackinac Island with two excursion parties and returned to Collingwood without reporting or clearing. She will be at Mackinac Island again on the 9th instant.
>
> Shall I enforce the penalty prescribed by section 3109? [Revised statutes]
>
> Please wire answer.
>
> D.O. Watson
> Collector of Customs Dist. of Michigan[6]

Washington's telegraphic response on August 7 was quick and unequivocal:

> If Canadian steamer "Frances Smith" has violated a section thirty one hundred twice by landing excursion parties within your district without reporting, hold the vessel wherever in your district.
>
> Hugh L.S. Thompson
> Acting Secretary[7]

As if the first telegram was not clear, Thompson sent a second telegram on August 7, reiterating his direction to seize the *Frances Smith* if she landed again at an American port. The fuse for a major confrontation had been lit for the third trip to Mackinac Island on August 9. Robertson docked his steamer as usual at the main pier and dispatched his purser, Parrot, to St. Ignace with three sets of papers from Collingwood. Each set contained clearances from the U.S. customs office in Collingwood. Two were for the two previous visits and a third was for his current visit. Warren refused to accept any of the documents. He further refused to deal with anyone except the master of the vessel. He demanded that Captain Robertson sail the *Frances Smith* to his dock at St. Ignace for clearance. This he later admitted was for his personal convenience because it was near his home. He further admitted that he planned to seize the ship at St. Ignace where he could keep an eye on it. Parrott informed him that he would carry the message back to Captain Robertson. By the time Parrot returned to Mackinac Island it was getting late, so Robertson decided to disregard Warren's demands and, for the third time, he left for Canadian waters without further communication with U.S. customs.

A frustrated and angry Jesse Warren immediately advised his superior, Dudley Watson, that the *Frances Smith* had failed to clear customs once again. He was instructed by Watson to intercept the vessel at Mackinac on her next scheduled excursion, on the 16th of August. In order to make sure things were done correctly, Watson himself arrived from Grand Haven to add authority to the seizure. Watson and Warren then gathered a few men and went to Mackinac on the Sunday evening preceding the anticipated arrival of the Canadian steamer. There they stayed in a hotel where they plotted their strategy to carry out the seizure. The *Frances Smith* arrived at 6 a.m. Monday morning and Parrot once again headed for St. Ignace with customs documents, this time obtained from the Sault Ste. Marie, Michigan, customs office, unaware that Warren was not there but rather with Watson and his men right on Mackinac Island and planning their seizure.

Warren and his crew boarded the *Smith* in mid-morning and went directly to the engine room where they dismantled the engine, thus rendering the boat without power. Captain Robertson was furious. He protested, saying these formalities of clearance were unwarranted.[8] Warren and Watson had no official court papers to serve the *Frances Smith*.

From his perspective, they seemed to be acting arbitrarily and outside the law. Captain Robertson, a man not noted for adhering to formalities in general, apparently became "badly worked up." [9] Despite this show of temper, his ship was impounded. The passengers on board were upset as well, since they expected to be home in Canada the next day. Eventually, the disgruntled excursionists managed to catch another steamer back to Collingwood.

With the *Frances Smith* disabled and a tug, the *Peter Coates*, at the ready, the U.S. customs agents put the steamer under tow to a small coal and lumber dock owned by George Arnold. There they made her fast to the dock while Robertson fumed. He was additionally agitated about the safety of the vessel should a wind get up from the east, claiming there was no protection for his ship from either the east or the southwest.

At this point the story becomes complicated. Warren was instructed by the U.S. Treasury Department that if Robertson was prepared to put up a bond then and there, he could be released. The amount of the bond would have to be $25,000, the estimated value of the *Frances Smith*. This bond would be held until the courts could determine what to do about the customs violations by this foreign vessel and her master. Warren claimed Robertson never offered to put up the bond. Robertson said he did but it was refused. Whatever the truth, Robertson got in touch with Mr. Stuart, the deputy custom's collector in Sault Ste. Marie, with whom he had had some earlier dealings. The result was that the customs collector there agreed to take a $16,000 bond. Stuart sent Warren a telegraph and told him to release the *Frances Smith* on August 21. After five days in custody, the much agitated Robertson sailed away from Mackinac Island.

The *Frances Smith* returned to her regular run from Collingwood to Sault Ste. Marie and took four trips in the next four weeks in Canadian waters. Meanwhile on September 9, back in the United States, the U.S. treasury department lawyer, Gilman Chase Godwin, appeared before district judge Henry F. Severns, to have the $16,000 bond declared void and illegal. The next day Judge Severns made his decision. He found in favour of Godwin and the Treasury Department and ordered that the *Frances Smith*, and everything on board, be forfeited. The vessel was to be seized and sold in accordance with the United States law. On September 10, 1886, a court order was issued under the authority of the

President of the United States to the U.S. Marshal of the Western District of Michigan:

> You are therefore hereby commanded, to attach the said Steamer "Frances Smith" her tackle, &c, and to herein detain the same in your custody, until the further order of the Court respecting the same, and to give due notice to all persons claiming the same, or knowing or having anything to say why the same should not be condemned and sold, pursuant to the prayer of the said libel, that they be and appear before the said Court, on the Rule Day of the next session to be held at the City of Marquette, in and for the Western District of Michigan, Northern Division, on the first Tuesday in October next, at ten o'clock in the forenoon of the same day…. Then and there to interpose a claim for same, and to make their allegations in that behalf.[10]

Early Monday morning, September 20, the *Frances Smith* sailed into American waters at Sault Ste. Marie, Michigan. On orders from Watson in Grand Haven, the Deputy Customs Collector Charles Stuart seized the vessel and telegraphed Jesse Warren in St. Ignace who immediately left by steamer for the Sault. He and Stuart once again supervised the disabling of the ship's machinery. The next day a U.S. marshal arrived

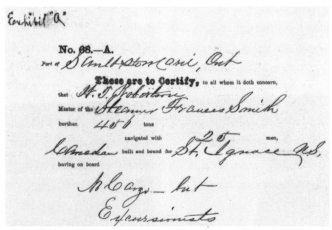

Exhibit A: The clearance papers issued at Sault Ste. Marie, Michigan, for the *Frances Smith* to enter the U.S. port of St. Ignace. Captain Robertson did not report there. He believed he could report directly to the Mackinac docks, seven miles away. *Courtesy of the U.S. National Archives and Records Administration, Chicago, Illinois.*

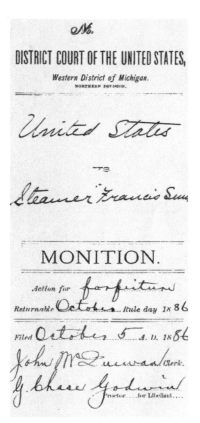

District Court Order to seize the Frances Smith, October 5, 1886. An application for forfeiture against the Frances Smith for failing to meet the court demands was issued under the signature of G. Chase Goodwin who represented the District Court. Courtesy of the U.S. National Archives and Records Administration, Chicago, Illinois.

and the *Frances Smith* was placed in his custody. A contract was let to a marine construction company, Hickler & Green, to secure the vessel with heavy chains to make sure Roberson would not run back to Canada. The bond was set at $25,000 until Watson arrived. Robertson at this point was in serious danger of losing his boat.

Through a process of negotiation, Robertson persuaded Watson to accept a reduced bond of $12,500. The agreement was acceptable to the U.S. marshal, so once again the *Frances Smith* was released. On September 27, 1886, after seven days in custody, Robertson sailed back to Owen Sound.

Robertson was supposed to appear in court on October 3. In the meantime he hired the respected Michigan law firm, Norris and Uhl, to represent him and plead for more time. He contacted his partner Henry Eberts Smith back in Owen Sound who then consulted John Creasor, a friend and highly respected local lawyer. Together they worked out their defence strategy. They decided that the best defence was to go on the offensive using the retained firm of Norris and Uhl.

Once the problem of entering American waters was resolved in 1887, Captain Robertson ran several excursions to Mackinac in 1888–90. By then the *Frances Smith* had been renamed the *Baltic*. This photo was taken at the dock in Sault Ste. Marie in 1888 as the steamer was about to leave the wharf. *Courtesy of the Sault Ste. Marie Public Library.*

When the lawyers, (Chase Godwin for the U.S. Government and Norris for the owners of the *Frances Smith*) appeared before Judge Severns on December 11, Norris argued that the owners had done nothing to forfeit their vessel. In fact, they were the aggrieved party. They had lost income for two weeks. They had incurred sizeable costs. They had lost significant unrecoverable revenue. Finally, Norris demanded that the owners be released from their bond and be paid costs by the government of the United States as compensation for the aggravation.

In the face of all this confusion, the judge ordered his clerk, James McQuewan, to take depositions from all those involved and to sort out truth from fiction. McQuewan was to present his findings in February. The case dragged on until April, when McQuewan finally tabled his report. By May 4, 1887, G. Chase Godwin declared that the U.S. Department of Justice would drop the case and rescind the bond if the ship's owners would pay the expenses of the seizures.

The total cost was $500. On Creasor's advice, Smith and Robertson paid. By mid-July 1887 they were once again running the *Frances Smith* on excursions to Mackinac Island. This time they checked in at St. Ignace around dinner time every Monday on their way back to Collingwood. Case closed.[11]

13

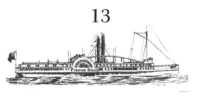

Changing Fortunes

THE YEAR 1887 was a turning point for the *Frances Smith*. Her owners continued with the business plan of 1886, making regular trips
to the Sault, and adding excursions to Mackinac in the summer. Until
the first of September, the year was an uneventful one for the company.

On Wednesday night August 31, 1887, there was a light drizzle in
the air. The *Frances Smith* had just returned from the Sault according
to schedule and was tied up at the foot of Hurontario Street in Collingwood. The wharf, as usual, had a number of ships on hand awaiting
freight and cargo to be loaded from the Northern Railway sheds that
lined the dock. Several railway cars sat on the siding ready to be unloaded
next morning into the holds of the *Campana* and *Niagara*. The *Frances
Smith* was also scheduled to receive package freight from the railway
sheds early in the morning in preparation for a noon sailing the next
day. All the passengers had disembarked and gone their various ways.

At 3:30 a.m. a fire alarm was raised. One of the sheds was on fire.
Within minutes the whole wharf was ablaze. There was little wind, but
flames raced through the wooden storage structures and ignited the
standing boxcars. Fearing that the large grain elevator at the far end of
the wharf would catch fire, the Collingwood fire brigade quickly hauled
their steam fire engine onto the docks. Water was pumped over the railway sheds without effect. They quickly burned to the ground in a
blazing inferno.

Frances Smith at the Collingwood dock circa 1885. A fire at the dock in 1887 threatened to burn both the *Frances Smith* and the Collingwood grain elevator, which had been built by the Northern Railway in 1871. Amazingly this elevator survived several wharfside fires and windstorms. *Courtesy of the Library and Archives Canada, PA 139086.*

Aboard the *Campana*, the roused captain immediately ordered steam from the engine room where first engineer A.J. Cameron (from the original crew of the *Frances Smith*) was waiting for instructions. The deck crew cast off from the wharf and the *Campana* sailed to safety out to Georgian Bay, her forward cabins scorched and smoldering from the intense heat generated while she had been tied up at the blazing dock. Aboard the *Frances Smith*, the officers were fast asleep until several of the local citizens let loose the ropes and hauled the ship out of harm's way. Only then did the bleary-eyed officers appear on deck.

The Globe in Toronto implied that the fire began on the side of the dock where the *Frances Smith* was tied. They further stated, " It is supposed she has a watchman on board but he was either asleep or neglecting his duty, for he gave no alarm...."[1] The bow of the steamer was severely charred, her white paint blistered and checked from the intense heat. It was a premonition of things to come at the same dock almost a decade later.

In the end, five of the loaded boxcars were destroyed, as were two empty cars. Merchandise in the sheds worth an estimated $25,000 and railway property worth $18,000 were lost. The damage to the *Frances Smith* was mainly cosmetic and easily repaired with a few planks and a bucket of paint.

If the fire was a near miss for the *Frances Smith*, a major storm in mid-October was a direct hit to the company's owners. The running mate of the *Frances Smith*, the *City of Owen Sound*, sailed from Duluth on October 19, 1887, and faced very heavy seas all the way down Lake Superior. On arrival at Sault Ste. Marie, her master, Captain Francis Xavier LaFrance, waited for the weather to clear. When conditions did not improve, he decided to press on regardless and left the Sault on the morning of October 23 despite a snowstorm with high winds. Threading her way through the North Channel, the vessel eventually approached the north side of Clapperton Island. At 4 a.m. she slammed into Robertson Rock just to the east of the island.[2] The impact caused the wooden hull to cave in and water poured into the ship, flooding the hold faster than pumps could remove the inundation. Within thirty minutes the *City of Owen Sound*, weighted down with 24,500 bushels of water-logged corn, slid into the deep water and sank. Fortunately, there were no passengers aboard and the crew managed to escape to the island. The *Campana* passed Clapperton Island five hours later and was hailed by the stranded crew. Anchoring close to shore, she picked up the survivors and returned everyone safely to port in Collingwood.[3]

When the *City of Owen Sound* went to the bottom in 1887, Alexander Smith and William Keighley, the owners, had to make a difficult business decision. Faced with losses and serious competition, they sold the *Frances Smith* in December to their competitor, the Collingwood Beattys of the Great Northern Transportation Line. Smith and Keighley then turned around and purchased the 131-foot *Cambria* (formerly the *Champion*) and the 173-foot *Carmona* (formerly the *Manitoba* from the Beattys of Sarnia). They were still in business but without the *Frances Smith* and the Robertson interests.

After the *Frances Smith* went to dry dock for major repairs that winter, she emerged in the spring of 1888 with a $36,000 refit, and was renamed the *Baltic*. The newly named steamer was now part of the Great Northern's fleet of ships: the *Pacific*, the *Atlantic* and the *Northern Belle*. Together they competed with the CPR on the Georgian Bay/Lake Superior routes. But it was not long until there was more trouble.

On Friday, September 7, 1888, the *Baltic/Frances Smith* ran on the rocks at Elm Island in the North Channel just east of Clapperton Island.[4] All week long the weather had been fine,[5] but as the evenings cooled each autumn night, fog settled over the channel, greatly reducing visibility. As is normal, there was a light sea. Captain Robertson (who stayed

Top: The propeller steamer *Atlantic* was rebuilt from the hull of the old *Manitoulin* that burned in 1882. *Courtesy of the Owen Sound Marine and Rail Museum.*
Bottom: The *Pacific* at Sault Locks. The propeller steamer *Pacific* enters the locks at the Sault. The *Pacific* was owned and built for the Great Northern Transit Company and was originally a competitor of the *Frances Smith*. In 1887, the *Smith* joined the Great Northern and became part of their fleet as the *Baltic*. *Courtesy of the Sault Ste. Marie Public Library.*

with the ship when it was sold) was on watch, peering into the fog at
11:30 p.m., when the *Baltic* slammed into the Elm Island, a dozen kilometres (about seven-and-a-half miles) from the village of Kagawong
on Manitoulin. The steamer came to an abrupt stop. Canting on her
port beam, the ship was exposed to the possibility of being smashed to
bits by the waves although initial reports stated that there was no danger of serious damage where she rested, even if a storm blew up. The
forty passengers aboard were terrified.[6]

Tickets for the Great Northern Transit Company. After the *Frances Smith* joined the GNT as the *Baltic*, it was possible for passengers to purchase layover and open tickets for any ship on the line. *Courtesy of the Gore Bay Museum.*

Smith and Keighley's downbound steamer *Cambria* reported to Owen Sound on Monday, September 10, that the forward section of the ship was in about three feet of water and the stern in about five. In order to keep the ship from pounding onto the shore, Robertson opened the seacocks and flooded the hold. By early Saturday morning, the tug *Reid* was able to remove the frightened passengers, yet all the while, the stubborn and proud Robertson refused to signal passing ships for help. He was determined to wait for ships from his own line (Great Northern Line) to execute the rescue. The passengers, however, were not so reluctant; most wanted to reach safety as soon as possible. Along with the rescued passengers aboard the *Reid*, was the corpse of a Mrs. Bennet being taken to Collingwood for burial. As there was not room for everyone and the dead body on the tug, some of the passengers and the crew waited for one of the company ships to get them off the treacherous rocks.[7]

A few days later, two company ships, the *Atlantic* and the *Pacific*, of the Great Northern Line arrived on the scene. The remaining passengers were transferred, and the steamers set to work attempting to pull the *Baltic* from the rocks. They worked in tandem, using heavy chains to dislodge the steamer from her rocky perch. It was to no avail. The captains (Pete Campbell of the *Pacific*, R.D. Foote of the *Atlantic* and Tate Robertson of the *Baltic*) consulted and decided to bring the ageing *Northern Belle* under Captain W.J. Bassett, up from the Collingwood/Parry

Sound route for further assistance.[8] The water that had been pumped into the hold to prevent the *Baltic* from being smashed to bits was pumped out. Since no water flooded back into the hold, it was assumed she did not require major repairs below the waterline. The hold was once again filled with water while they waited. Once the *Belle* arrived, water was again pumped out from the hold and the load lightened. Eventually, all three vessels were able to drag the *Baltic* into deep water, only slightly the worse for wear.

The late 1880s were also a turning point in Captain Robertson's personal life. At the end of November 1888, he married an Owen Sound schoolteacher, Victoria Adelaide Creasor. The modest ceremony was held in the home of Victoria's father, the highly respected local lawyer, John Creasor. With the season completed, the newly wed captain was able to spend the winter months with his new wife before shipping out again next spring.

By June 1889 the new *Baltic* was well-integrated into the company and moving everything from bricks to furniture to Sault Ste. Marie.[9] She was also retracing her former excursion route to Mackinac Island on routine trips to the Sault. In mid-July, the *Baltic* made the fastest time on record for a trip from Sault Ste. Marie back to Collingwood, making all the scheduled stops. Captain Robertson, who was still in command, left Mackinac and St. Ignace early Thursday evening and arrived at Clapperton Channel before dark on Friday. He reached Collingwood just before 9 o'clock on Saturday evening, having waited at the Owen Sound dock for one hour and forty minutes. In order to accomplish this astounding feat, Robertson made unprecedented time from Killarney to Wiarton in seven hours and forty minutes.[10] It was a Great Lakes record.

Full of confidence after this fine demonstration of speed and skillful navigation Robertson pressed his luck with his now ageing vessel. On July 29, 1889, both the *Baltic* and the *Carmona* (the former 173-foot double-decked sidewheeler *Manitoba*) were taking passengers on board at Owen Sound. The *Baltic* loaded passengers and freight for Killarney and points north on her regular run. The *Carmona* took on excursionists for an evening cruise to Presqu'ile just a few kilometres from Owen Sound. The excitement on the dock was high because both ships seemed ready to depart at the same time. Despite cool weather, Captain La France and his crew managed to attract about one hundred excursionists.

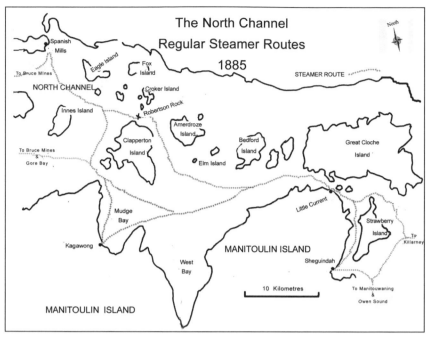

Map of the North Channel Regular Steamer Route, 1885. Steamers traced several routes through the dangerous waters of the North Channel to service the growing number of communities on Manitoulin Island and along the north shore.

Aboard both ships, passengers crowded against the railings to look down on the dock as the respective crews prepared to head out. On the *Baltic*, First Mate C. Hill hurried to have the gangway pulled up and the ropes let go. Robertson signalled with a couple of blasts on the whistle and they moved quickly away from the dock and pointed the bow north. The purser, A.G. Campbell, completed his cabin assignments and finished his accounting tasks. In the galley the cook, Arron Tripp, put the final touches on the evening meal, but everyone seemed to be out on deck.

Five minutes after the departure of the *Baltic*, the *Carmona* shoved off with Captain La France in the pilothouse. In the wake of the *Baltic*, he ordered full steam ahead in order to catch the record-breaking steamer. A few kilometres out, he began to overtake her. As La France was about to pass, Robertson started to zigzag back and forth, dangerously crossing the bow of the advancing *Carmona*.[11] The passengers crowded on the decks cheered as the two headstrong captains duelled it out as they headed for Georgian Bay. Smoke poured from the funnels.

The paddles churned water and foam from the rotating wheels was forced out of the air holes on the paddle boxes, kicking spray high into the air.

As his bow gained gradually on the *Baltic*, La France signalled to the Robertson to keep to one side. When his forward decks were just ahead of the *Baltic's* gangway, the two vessels inched nearer and nearer until passengers on the decks could almost shake hands. At this point the *Baltic* began to move even closer to the overtaking vessel in an attempt to cut her off. Seconds later the *Baltic* struck the paddle box of the *Carmona*. The ships bounced apart and hit again, causing some minor damage. The mood of the passengers turned from excitement and enthusiasm to fear, and for some, terror.

The excursionists blamed Robertson for his reckless behaviour.[12] The final results of the incident seem to end with the papers calling for an investigation, but no inquiry appears to have been initiated. The aggressive conduct of Robertson was in sharp contrast to the rookie captain of 1872 who seemed to have difficulty getting his crew to load wood at Leith.

14

Brutal Outrage on the *Baltic*

On Monday, August 26, 1889, Charles Hambly loaded freight into the *Baltic* at Meaford. There he met Joseph Ward, a fireman he had worked with on the barge *Kincardine* earlier that year. It was the last time Ward would see the young man. Hambly would be dead before midnight.

The shy and quiet sixteen-year-old farmer's son from the Bruce Peninsula left his father's farm in Albermarle Township outside Wiarton in early spring. His mother had died a year before and he was living with eight brothers and a sister. At the time he was about five feet six inches tall and a bit stout, his father, Thomas Hambly, said. He had curly brown hair, grey/blue eyes and was strong for his age. As a farm boy he had done strenuous work and was used to long hours. Like many lads his age he was injured working on the farm. One of his fingers had caught in an auger and when it healed, remained crooked.[1] He was too young to sport a moustache or a beard, as was the custom for young men of the time. His father said he was a good boy. He was mild mannered and he never swore. Charles belonged to the Sons of Temperance and had taken an oath never to drink alcohol.

The back twenty acres of Mr. Hambly's farm overlooked Colpoy's Bay, some two hundred metres below. The ground is rocky there, with only a thin layer of soil covering the dolomite cap of the Niagara Escarpment. Today the famous Bruce Trail winds along the edge of the cliff where Charles certainly watched heavy steamer and sail traffic move in and out of the bay as he worked the back fields.

In June, after working on the *Kincardine*, Charles shipped on board the *Favourite*, a newly launched package and passenger steamer out of Meaford. He worked on the ship for the early part of the summer and, when he became ill, left his job. Betty Gallagher, a passing acquaintance, said that she talked with Hambly at Mrs. Kelso's boarding house in Owen Sound on Sunday, August 18, and stated that he was then unemployed.[2] During the next week he got a job on the *Baltic* as a deckhand and ended up in Collingwood the following Sunday, August 25. That afternoon he was bathing with fourteen-year-old William Smalley, the mess room boy from the *Baltic*. Smalley observed later that Hambly did not swim. He compared his attempt at swimming to that of a young pig splashing about in the water.[3] On Monday morning the *Baltic* sailed for Owen Sound, where she was loaded for her trip to Wiarton, the Sault and Mackinac Island. First Mate Charles Odum Hill supervised the loading and noted that the deck crew were sober and doing their work as directed. When all freight was secure, he signalled Captain Robertson in the pilothouse and the ship cast off.

They steamed away from Owen Sound's wharf and passed the outer buoy at 8:20 p.m. as dusk settled. Although it was evening a low-lying fog sat over the water, obscuring the quiet lake below the hull. From the height of the wheelhouse, Captain Robertson and Second Mate John Montgomery could see over the fog and make out the darkened western shore. Robertson directed John Currie, the watchman, to steer on a prescribed time and course: sixty minutes to Pyette Point, twenty minutes to Cape Commodore, thirty minutes to White Cloud Island and a fourth leg to Wiarton. Currie turned the wheel over to Montgomery shortly after the first leg and did his rounds. First Mate Hill, his loading duties completed, was off watch. As they approached the end of the first course, he stood on the promenade deck for a few minutes before turning into bed.

Down in the engine room, Chief Engineer John Doran, a man with over thirty years' experience on the lakes, recorded the *Baltic's* steam pressure and vacuum pressure in his log book, noting that the paddle wheel was turning at nineteen rotations per minute, a moderate speed that would push them along at about twelve miles per hour. The captain, believing that everything was running smoothly up top, told Second Mate Montgomery that he was going to the office where Purser, A.G. Campbell was completing his accounts.

The deck crew, their work finished, returned to their quarters in the forecastle of the ship.[4] What happened next is not clear. Conflicting details of the "Brutal Outrage on the Baltic" emerged at the trials over the next few months. The results of the trials and the subsequent hearings about Captain Robertson's conduct were widely covered in the press. They were the meat of debate in the House of Commons and ultimately the deliberation of the Privy Council of Canada. The local community got into the affair and wrote letters to their member of parliament, Simon Dawson, the engineer who built the Dawson Road.

Early coverage of Hambly's death in *The Globe* attracted the attention of Inspector John Wilson Murray, the provincial detective and Canada's answer to Sherlock Holmes. Although the account in his memoirs published in 1904 is embellished to make a good story, his recollections about Hambly's (Inspector Murray refers to him as Tambly) death confuse rather than illuminate.[5]

John Wilson Murray, known as the "Great Detective," was Ontario's Chief Inspector and was reputed to be Canada's answer to Britain's Sherlock Holmes. The high profile Charles Hambly suicide brought him to Owen Sound. He later included an account of his investigation in one of his books. *Courtesy of the Ontario Provincial Police.*

Murray claimed that the crew had stolen some whisky, started to drink the stolen booty, and then tried to coerce the young "Son of Temperance" to participate. When Hambly refused, the drunken gang attempted to force the liquor down his throat.[6] The only corroboration of Murray's observation is revealed in the court testimony of Walter Jennings, a deckhand. Under examination by the Crown attorney, Alfred Frost, on September 19, 1889, Jennings stated, "The fireman [Andrew Tyman]...was the worse for liquor. I think Russell [the second engineer] was the worse for liquor." Jennings continued against the objection of the defense council, John Creasor, "...and Hambly told me he had had a drink and I told him...and as soon as the boat left the dock he had better go to bed." There are no other references to alcohol in the court documents.

Murray claimed Hambly was teased for his refusal to drink, then pushed to the ground and finally humiliated by being tarred and feathered. He further claimed that Hambly was chased around the decks until he eventually jumped overboard. That is not quite what happened.

What follows is a careful reconstruction of events based upon the statements of the officers, the crew and the passengers who were on board the *Baltic* the night of the outrage. It summarizes the conclusions of the court, the testimonies of investigating officers and the documents filed by Captain W.J. Meneilly, supervising inspector of steamboats for the government of Canada. Finally, it recapitulates the findings of Lieutenant Andrew Gordon R.N., who was appointed as commissioner by the Privy Council[7] to investigate the competency of the ship's officers.[8]

When John Currie turned the wheel over to Second Mate James Montgomery, he attended his rounds about the ship. In one of the saloons he heard some of the passengers talking about an incident that apparently had happened down on the main deck. He went to investigate. Just forward of the forward gangway, he saw George Daggett, the second cook, Kenneth McFadzen, the porter, Thomas Russell, the second engineer, and deckhand Charles Backhaus teasing young Hambly and pushing him around. Currie overheard Russell joke that they were going to tar and feather young Hambly. Currie, without success, told him to leave the boy alone.

The seasoned crew continued pushing the rookie deckhand about while others of the crew and a few passengers egged them on. When they refused to stop, Currie climbed the stairs to First Mate Hill's cabin to tell him what was happening below. Hill's response was, "I am just turning in, and it is not my watch."[9]

Although Currie persisted in asking for help, Hill dismissed his concerns. As a veteran on the lakes, he had seen this kind of hazing before. Currie then went back to the pilothouse and told Second Mate Montgomery about the ruckus. Montgomery's response was, "They won't kill him."[10]

Meanwhile the torment was about to be continued.

Currie went back to work on the promenade deck, while below him in the forecastle, Hambly was once again being assaulted, slapped about the face and shoved about by his tormenters. Other members of the deck crew (Walter Jennings, James Petch, and Charles Backhaus) joined in. Hambly struggled as best he could and shouted, "Damn it! Leave me alone!" He was crying while the crew attempted to unbutton his shirt and

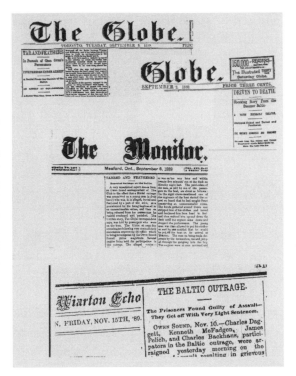

Headlines. Newspapers around Ontario ran front-page stories about the "Baltic Outrage" for several days after the event. The resulting trial was transcribed in detail for the reading public. *Courtesy of the Owen Sound Union Library.*

his trousers. By this time several passengers, including John Baxter of Collingwood, Joseph Cherry of Euphrasia, Jacob McInnes of Owen Sound, and Malcolm McEacheran of Stayner, had come to the main deck to see what was going on. Each would testify at the trial on September 16, 1889.

Russell was leading the abuse, and claimed to have witnessed Hambly performing "an unnatural act" with one of the horses. Although this thread runs through the documents as inference and subtext, there is absolutely no evidence to support the story. What seems more plausible is that Russell, a bully, was picking on a young and new member of the crew.

A mob mentality caused almost everyone on the now crowded deck to laugh and make jokes at Hambly's expense as he was held on the deck, kicking and fighting. The crew flipped Hambly onto his back and pinned him to the ground. By now he was completely naked and physically exhausted.

Several more male passengers came below and crowded around the crew to find out what all the commotion was about. After half an hour of abuse, Hambly seemed to give up the struggle and offered no resistance. He collapsed sobbing on the deck. Russell yanked Hambly to his feet and he stood there, unsteady, staring at the deck, his head bowed and his body bent forward.

One of the crew suggested that they bring up some tar for some more "fun," so Andrew Tyman went to fetch a tar bucket in the bow where the caulking was stored. He handed the pail to Russell who then started pouring tar over Hambly's head and shoulders. Soon he was entirely covered. The crew jeered and laughed as Hambly stood mute, dizzy and sobbing.

At this point, Hambly fell into a stack of boxes and then onto a pile of grain bags. As he stumbled around with tar being poured over his body from head to toe, the crew laughed even harder. Each time he bumped into grain bags, freight boxes and coils of rope, there was tar smeared over everything. Russell grabbed Hambly by the hair and straightened him up. The crew cursed Hambly as he staggered about from one side of the ship to the other, naked and weeping. Aaron Tripp, the chief cook, had by this time split open a pillow and dumped the contents into an empty fish box, which he then threw over the dazed Hambly. He was now covered entirely in feathers. Passenger Joseph Cherry said, "You have done enough already."

One of the passengers ran to the promenade deck's forward saloon and told the female passengers what was happening. "Many lady passengers gave expression to their feelings with hysterical cries."[11] There was a commotion in the ladies' saloon as the women screamed and demanded that someone do something. Two of the male passengers went

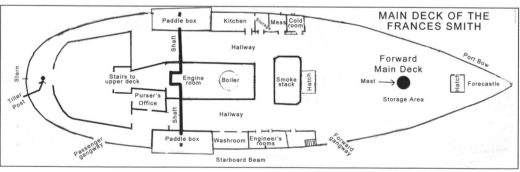

Sketch of the main deck of the *Frances Smith*. Deck passengers remained on the main deck, sleeping wherever they could. The shaft connecting the two paddlewheels through the engine room was an obstruction that required passengers step down below the rotating iron rod when moving from one part of the deck to another. Charles Hambly was assaulted on the forward main deck. He leapt to his death from an external stairway on the starboard side near the passenger entranceway. The sketch is based on a diagram by John Doran (engineer) for the trial of Arron Tripp *et al* in 1889.

searching for the captain and found him on his way to the main deck. It was not the first time Robertson had heard about the disturbance. Chief Engineer John Doran had told him about the trouble moments before while Robertson was still in the purser's office.

At this point Captain Robertson strode down the stairs, then marched to the forward part of the deck where the large crowd of twenty or thirty had gathered. He ordered his unruly crew to stop the hazing and directed Russell to assist Hambly to get his clothing back on.[12] Robertson later admitted that he was unable to distinguish crew members from passengers. There was a regular turnover of crew, he said, and it was the mate's responsibility to hire and recruit crew, not his.

He then instructed Hambly to go to the purser's office and collect his pay and turned on his heel and walked away. Hambly stood speechless picking feathers from his body as Russell and Tripp roughly pulled on his clothing. He appeared dazed; some said he seemed detached from events and his predicament. A few said he was insane.

By now, John Currie, the night watchman, had come down from the promenade deck carrying his lantern. He found Hambly dressed but still covered in feathers, standing with his valise in his hand. The chief engineer stuck his head out of the engine room and shouted at Hambly to go to the starboard side where the purser's office was located. Currie offered to take him there.

They walked to the starboard side near the after gangway, where a set of exterior iron stairs led to the promenade deck above. A number of crew and deck passengers followed.[13] Hambly then set his valise down, leaned against the bulwark just behind the paddle box, and stared into the darkness near the gangway door next to the office of Purser Campbell. When Currie rapped on the purser's window, Campbell opened it immediately and was told to get Hambly's money. At that moment, a fellow passenger asked Joseph Cherry for the time. "Seventeen minutes past ten" he replied, just as Charles Hambly climbed onto the rung of the iron ladder. From there he stepped onto the ship's rail, and leapt into Georgian Bay with a scream. Jack McMillan, a waiter who was standing at the rail, grabbed for Hambly as he went overboard, but was unable to hang on. There was a splash and then nothing was heard but the steady swash of the *Baltic's* paddles and the expelled air being pushed through the vents on the paddle box.

Starboard quarter of the *Frances Smith*. From the position just aft of the paddlewheel is the passenger gangway and exterior stairs to the promenade deck. Charles Hambly jumped to his death by standing on the rail near the stairs. *Courtesy of the Owen Sound Marine and Rail Museum.*

Those standing nearby said that the paddles turning at full speed swept him under. This seems unlikely given the location of Hambly when he jumped. It seems more likely he was pushed away in the wash of the revolving wheels.

Hector Lamont, a passenger standing beside Currie, shouted, "There's that man overboard! Stop the boat!"

Currie shouted for the engineer, John Doran, to stop the boat, then ran to the upper deck and threw a lifebuoy attached to a rope over the stern. Unfortunately, the lifebuoy was tied to a very short rope so it dragged uselessly ten metres behind the still moving steamer. In the engine room, Doran put the paddles into reverse for three revolutions. He feared that if he did more revolutions the wheelsman in the pilot-house would be hurt if the wheel spun out of control. Nobody else except the captain observed the paddle reversal. At court everyone agreed that the boat stopped some distance from the point where Hambly jumped. They did not all agree on how long the boat remained stopped.

As the vessel was brought to a halt, Hector Lamont ran aft. He climbed the stairs to the hurricane deck to get a better view but there was nothing to see except the pitch-black night. There was not a sound except small waves slapping against the hull and water dripping from the now motionless paddles. A haze hung over the water obscuring everything for about two metres above the bay.

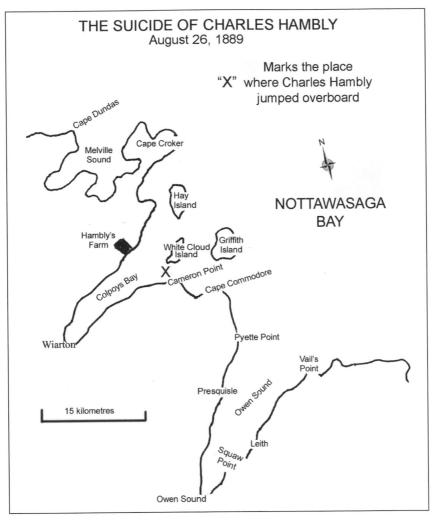

THE SUICIDE OF CHARLES HAMBLY
August 26, 1889

Marks the place
"X" where Charles Hambly
jumped overboard

Cape Dundas

Melville Sound

Cape Croker

N

Hay Island

NOTTAWASAGA BAY

Hambly's Farm

White Cloud Island

Griffith Island

X

Cameron Point

Cape Commodore

Colpoys Bay

Wiarton

Pyette Point

Vail's Point

Presquisle

Owen Sound

15 kilometres

Squaw Point

Leith

Owen Sound

Map showing where Charles Hambly died. Seventeen-year-old Charles Hambly jumped to his death from the stern of the *Baltic* within view of his father's farm on Colpoy's Bay. His tragic death spelled trouble for Captain Robertson and his crew.

Robertson, who by then was on the deck, ordered Montgomery to go below to find out why the engines had stopped. His immediate report was that someone was overboard. Captain Robertson then ordered Montgomery to remain there while he went to the purser's office. He claimed that after hearing the details, he ordered, "Stand by to lower a lifeboat." Nobody else heard the order. No lifeboats were lowered.

Robertson claimed that he thought the crew was waiting to lower the boat from the hurricane deck so he went above, but found nobody at the starboard lifeboat station. He swore in court that he did not go to the after part of the ship. After reporting to the lifeboat station, he said, he returned to the pilothouse.

Contrary to Robertson's oath, Lamont claimed Captain Robertson came aft and saw him (Lamont) staring over the stern into the water. According to Lamont, Robertson exclaimed, "Why has the ship stopped?" Lamont testified that he told him that a young man had jumped overboard. Lamont reported at the trial that Captain Robertson muttered, "What will I do? He needn't have taken a blackening of his hands and face so hard."[14]

Lamont said, "Captain, this man was stripped stark naked and tarred and feathered" Robertson responded angrily, "Nonsense!" to which Lamont retorted, "Not nonsense, I saw him so myself."

Captain Robertson replied, "Well he is gone: there's no use in stopping here."

At this point the *Baltic* was still sitting dead in the water, about eight hundred metres south of White Cloud Island. The dark outline of the island was visible above the haze.

Robertson later claimed that he conferred with his first mate, Charles Hill. Hill and Robertson agreed that because of the haze over the water, there was no chance of a rescue. The crew had still not reported to the lifeboat stations. Robertson speculated in a letter to the deputy minister of marine on April 25, 1890, that the crew was frightened and hiding in the forecastle because of the suicide. That was the reason for their failure to report, he believed.

After four to six minutes, Captain Robertson rang for full ahead.[15] There were no lifeboats lowered. There were no attempts to initiate a search and there were no orders to bring the *Baltic* around to look for Hambly. Charles Hambly was gone and that was that. Later in the week there was speculation in Collingwood that Hambly swam to the island because no body was found.[16] However, everyone knew Charlie Hambly was dead.

The *Baltic* arrived in Wiarton, forty-five minutes later. Captain Robertson sat down and wrote a letter of regret to Hambly's family. Unfortunately, he had Hambly's name wrong and wrote to the parents of Charles Owen.[17] Some remaining passengers stayed with the *Baltic*, depending on their destination. Those who wanted to go to other North Channel destinations like Providence Bay or Kagawong switched to another ship. Some disembarked at Wiarton. Joseph Cherry, in fact, switched to another line and Robertson claimed he suspected him of fabricating the story to give his competition a reason to run him and his company down. The crew, on Robertson's orders, said nothing.

On Tuesday, August 27, the *Baltic* continued her journey to Killarney, Manitowaning and Little Current as per her schedule. On her way back, she once again stopped in Wiarton where Robertson's father-in-law, lawyer John Creasor, boarded the *Baltic* en route to Owen Sound. His advice to Robertson was to leave the investigation to the authorities.

On September 1, Joseph Cherry arrived back at Owen Sound, downbound on the *Campana*. He gave his eyewitness information to Crown attorney Alfred Frost and Provincial Constable C. Pearse.[18] After taking his statement, a warrant was issued on September 2 for: Thomas Russell, second engineer; Aaron Tripp, first cook; George Dagget, second cook, and Kenneth McFadzen, second porter.

That same day, Chief Constable McAuley and C.C. Pearse left Owen Sound for Collingwood where the *Baltic* was by then at dockside. At Meaford, Chief Constable Daley met them and accompanied them. Mr. Cherry was with them as a witness. The four crew members were immediately identified, arrested and brought back to Owen Sound to stand before George Price J.P. He remanded them for a week for a preliminary hearing.

At dockside before leaving, Pearce interviewed Captain Robertson who was indifferent about the whole affair and uncooperative,[19] and

John Creasor Q.C., was politically active in Owen Sound. His daughter Victoria married William Tate Robertson a year before he was called to defend the crew of the *Baltic* after Hambly's death. *Photo courtesy of Maurice Rhodes.*

refused to answer questions. He again directed his crew not make any statements to the police or to the newspapers. Shortly afterwards, however, he mellowed and offered to give Constable Pearce and the other constables a "free ride" back to Owen Sound and an opportunity to search the ship. Later in the week the police made a public appeal to have passengers and eyewitnesses come forward with information about Hambly's death. Not much was forthcoming in their interrogation of the crew.

Joseph Cherry claimed that on the day of the arrests, Robertson called him aside on the main deck and said quietly to him, "Is this a put-up job?" What he apparently meant by this was, were the owners of the *Carmona*, the competition, encouraging Cherry to make his ship and his company look bad? Robertson then asked Cherry if the officers on the *Carmona* gave him any money or if he had told them about the Hambly affair on his downbound trip. Cherry replied, "No." Robertson reasoned with Cherry to talk about the accusations made about Hambly. Cherry then stated that Robertson told him to go and see Mr. Creasor and swear an affidavit about Hambly for which he "would see that I would be well paid."

Cherry replied, "I am not for sale." Robertson continued to reason with Cherry and when he realized that he was getting nowhere, he threatened to ruin him. "Even if it cost thousands of dollars and took ten years."[20]

Meanwhile, to add to the confusion and tight-lipped uncooperativeness of the crew involved in the events, Hambly was still being referred to mistakenly as Charles Owen in the press. *The Globe* ran a full column front-page story about the "Outrage on the Baltic" on September 2 and September 3 reporting on the death of "Charles Owen."

Captain Tate Robertson quickly mounted his defense, knowing that there would be trouble for him, the crew, and the company. He sent a terse rebuttal to *The Globe's* story in a letter to the editor. He also sent telegraphs to all the municipal telegraph offices around southern Georgian Bay on September 2.

EDITOR – The Globe – The sensational article in the Globe today is simply paragraph by paragraph untrue with the exception of an unknown man jumping overboard

W. Tate Robertson
Capt. Baltic[21]

His brusque and uncommitted statement to the papers was typical of Robertson's tight-lipped responses to the police during the early stages of the investigation.

Meanwhile, Provincial Detective John Wilson Murray was busy on the case. Murray had a reputation as a tireless and highly successful investigator whose skills and international fame added drama to the case. Murray interviewed the crew, the passengers, and then went to visit Hambly's home near Wiarton. His reports and interviews were important in the prosecution's argument, especially when crewmembers "forgot" details or made contradictory statements during the trial.

J.M. Fyfe, a commercial traveller who often sailed on the *Baltic*, wrote a spirited defense about her officers and crew in *The Globe*. He accused their reporter of errors in details about the *Baltic* (he was correct) and attributed the misrepresentation to the rivalry that existed between Collingwood and Owen Sound as well as an attempt to injure the character of the good Captain.[22] He disputed *The Globe* report that the crew was "maddened with liquor." He maintained that there was no bar on the *Baltic* and that the sale of liquor was prohibited on the Line.

On September 9 the four prisoners (Daggett, Tripp, Russell and McFadzen) who were now in jail were formally charged with the death of Charles Hambly. They were remanded for another week. An argument then ensued between the defence and the prosecution about who would be a witness at the trial. Constable Pearse reported that some of the crew were foreigners and were under the control of the captain. The captain, he stated, intimidated them to keep quiet and they should therefore be held in custody until the trial.

Pearce stated to the judge that the master of the *Baltic* was present on September 2 when the initial arrests were made and that Captain Robertson had said, "I am not in the habit of swearing Pearse, but by – , if any passenger or hand on this boat gives any evidence in this case, or a man lays an information or has anything to do with this prosecution, I will follow him, if it takes me ten years and costs me thousands of dollars, and I will ruin him in business and every other way."[23] He further reported that some of the witnesses had told him that Captain Robertson told them to say that they knew nothing of the affair.

Andrew Tyman, the fireman, was arrested on September 10 in Little Current when Constable Pearse went up to Manitoulin Island on the *Carmona* to catch up to the *Baltic,* which by now was continuing her regular schedule.[24]

By September 12, nine more members of the crew were arrested as witnesses in the death of Hambly. They included: John Currie, Charles Backhaus, James Petch, Jack McMillan and Walter Jennings. The preliminary hearing began on September 16 before George Price, Justice of the Peace; George Spencer, Police Magistrate, and John Rutherford, Justice of the Peace. The crew members originally arrested (Daggett, Tripp, Russell and McFadzen) were refused bail and held in the Owen Sound jail while arguments about the nature of the charges were debated.

Once the hearing began before the Grand Jury, the defence council, John Creasor, objected to the "bulldozing " of his client John Currie, the night watchman, whose testimony on the stand was vague and did not match the statements he initially made to Detective John Murray. Currie was unable to remember details or the sequence of events.

In response to Creasor's objection, the judges observed, "It appears that all these boatmen have been either intimidated or bribed. They are most unwilling to give evidence. It seems to us that the bulldozing has been the other way. We think the Crown Counsel should have a good deal of license with adverse witnesses."[25] The tone for the trial was set.

Over the next week, confusing evidence, contradictory testimony and forgetful witnesses appeared in the court, but the essential details were tabled. The preliminary court found enough evidence to have them sent for trial. As a result Charles Daggett, Kenneth McFadzen, James Petch, Thomas Russell, Aaron Tripp and Charles Backhaus were charged with manslaughter.

They appeared before the provincial court of Judge Wilson C.J. Armour. Each pleaded not guilty. The defence argued that, although Charles Hambly had been tarred and feathered, there was no case that his drowning was a direct result of the outrage. Defence lawyers argued that the defendants be found not guilty of manslaughter.

Alfred Frost argued for the Crown, that if the outrage had caused the boy to become insane, then the outrage was the cause of the drowning.[26] He argued that the accused be found guilty. The judge agreed there was no evidence that Tripp and Russell had followed Hambly to the location on the ship where he jumped overboard. On a point of law, he found that they did not directly cause Hambly's suicide and he advised the jury to find them not guilty. For the same reason, the other four were also found not guilty.

The six were then arraigned on an indictment of aggravated assault. Daggett, McFadzen, Petch and Backhaus again pleaded not guilty. Russell and Tripp entered a plea of guilty. In the end, all were found guilty of the lesser charge.[27] Tripp and Russell were sent to hard labour in Central Prison in Toronto for one year each. The other four, Daggett, McFadzen, Petch and Backhaus were sentenced to six months hard labour in the same prison. The court dismissed charges against others of the crew, although it noted that Jennings had taken part in stripping Hambly.

When the trials closed, the local newspapers were inflamed at the lenient sentences, claiming that the behaviour of the crew "speaks badly on men." *The Meaford Monitor* complained, "It is painful to think that our race is so degraded as not to have the manliness and courage to stand up against such outrage."[28]

As an addendum, Judge Armour, on the advice of the jury, made several observations about the role of Captain Robertson. He stated, "There is no evidence to show that any person had informed the captain of what was going on, but as soon as it came to his knowledge, it was his duty to make enquiry, and if he found anything unlawful had taken place, then it was his duty to hand the offending parties over to the authorities." His Lordship continued, "In regard to the charge of intimidating witnesses, I can only say that I shall look into the matter and instruct the crown attorney to see what course ought to be pursued...As to stopping the boat," he stated, "I suppose that would have little effect as far as the poor boy was concerned, but it would have struck one as being humane at all events to made some effort to save the unfortunate lad." He concluded, "Throughout the whole of the investigation it struck me painfully that no person interfered to save the boy."[29]

The court notified the Minister of Marine and Fisheries, Sir Charles Tupper, about the conduct of Captain Robertson and his lack of cooperation with the court. As a result Deputy Minister of Marine William Smith sent a memo to the Supervising Inspector of Steamboats, Captain W.J. Meneilly, requesting that he gather information about the behaviour of Robertson and his officers. He filed his initial report in early January 1890. In his second report on February 4, he concluded

Sir Charles Tupper, dressed in full regalia as the Minister of Marine in the cabinet of Sir John A. Macdonald. Despite the fact that he was personally acquainted with Captain Robertson and received heavy political pressure from Grey County Conservatives, he refused to interfere with the suspension of Robertson's ticket as a master on the Great Lakes. *Courtesy of William James Topley, Library and Archives Canada, C-011351.*

that Captain Robertson was "remiss in his duties" and that he "endeavored to hinder or obstruct the proper inquiries ...by those seeking justice." Of particular concern was the fact that the lifeboats were not lowered and that Roberson had not performed the routine lifeboat training as required under the statues covering steamer operation.

The next day, February 5, 1890, Sir Charles Tupper appointed Lieutenant A.R. Gordon R.N. to lead an investigation into the conduct of the captain and his mate. Gordon had a solid reputation as a sea captain in the Arctic and as an administrator. He had participated in international conferences concerning shipping along the east coast of Canada and the United States and received special government commendations for his work. He brought with him integrity and a sound reputation for knowledge about shipboard command. His investigation was a no-nonsense inquiry.

As soon as Gordon's recommendation (see Appendix D) to suspend Robertson's master's license for a year was made public, Robertson's political friends in Owen Sound and Collingwood rushed to his defence. John Creasor, Q.C., the defence lawyer for the crew of the *Baltic*, wrote a letter on his behalf directly to the prime minister on April 17.

Creasor was a powerful figure in Owen Sound political circles and an ardent Tory. He would receive his appointment to the bench from Sir John A. Macdonald within the year. His connections in Ottawa were solid and it was believed that he could influence the government. Charles Cameron, general manager of the Great Northern Transit Company, major shareholder of the company, life member of the Free Masons, deputy reeve of Simcoe County (1872) and staunch Conservative also wrote to Macdonald. An even more forceful letter of support for Captain Robertson was sent to Sir John A. from the pen of the Anglican Archdeacon at St. George's Church in Owen Sound. Early in his career Archdeacon A.R. Mulholland had met Archbishop Strachan and Lord Elgin, and he likely assumed he could pressure the government of Canada with his ancient, if long dead, connections:

Owen Sound
2nd April, 1890
PRIVATE
The Right Honourable
Sir John Macdonald G.C.B.
Ottawa

My dear Sir John Macdonald,
About a month ago Doctor Landerkin M.P. made a motion in the House of Commons to inquire into Captain Robertson's conduct on the "Stm. Baltic" on what has been designated by the "Globe" newspaper as the "Baltic outrage." The Minister of Marine appointed a commission to investigate the matter – I attach an excerpt from the "Empire" in reference to this investigation which shows positively that Captain Robertson knew nothing whatever about the outrage until all was over. It was shown through evidence that Captain Robertson & all other Captains had violated the "Wreck & Salvage" Act by not drilling the crews regularly as required by that act. – Now it may be possible that action injurious to Capt. Robertson may be

taken and I would respectfully draw your attention to the fact that
Capt. Robertson is well connected and closely related to John Creasor Esq. & other town prominent citizens & it would be unwise for
the Minister of Marine to cause irritation as I feel convinced that
very many Conservatives could resent any such action upon this part
of the Minister of Marine as they feel convinced that Capt. Robertson should not be made a scapegoat by political enemies – I assure
you nothing would be gained & a great deal lost . The matter is prac-
tically a matter of the past & the guilty parties are now in Central
prison. – pardon me my dear Sir John Macdonald, for taking the
liberty of writing to you on this matter.

I am an old Tory & I have been forty years Rector of Owen Sound
& I know well the views of the people & it would grieve me to the
heart if the action of the Minister of Marine would cause any to leave
the Conservative ranks.

> I have the honour to be yours most faithfully.
> A.R. Mulholland
> Archdeacon of Grey
> Diocese of Huron[30]

Sir John A. responded to the entreaties with a standard thank you letter to each, assuring them the matter would be considered once again.
He referred the matter directly back to Charles Tupper who clearly was
asked to review the government's position in order to satisfy the Tory
heavyweights of Grey and Simcoe counties.

Robertson mounted an aggressive letter campaign including a long
personal apologetica of a dozen pages claiming that Lieutenant Gordon did not understand inland navigation, that other captains did not
follow the rules about lifeboats, that he was the "victim of circumstance,"
that because First Mate Hill was not censured neither should he be censured, and that he was being deprived of earning a living.

John Long, an owner of the company, and the customs officer in
Collingwood each wrote character references for Robertson. Meanwhile
behind the scenes, the member of parliament was attempting to have
Robertson retain at least his mate's papers so that he could continue to
sail. Memos flew back and forth from the clerk of the Privy Council to
the deputy minister and back to M.P. Simon Dawson.

It was all to no avail. The minister's decision was final and unequivocal in his response to the prime minister:

Minister Of Fisheries
Ottawa, Canada
22nd May, 1890

My dear Sir John Macdonald,
Upon my return from Washington I received the letter in reference to Captain Robertson's Certificate which you transferred to me from Mr. John Creasor, Q.C., of Owen Sound.

In reply I beg to say that circumstances under which Captain Robertson was suspended are embodied in the following finding of Lieut. A.R. Gordon R.N., who was appointed Commissioner to investigate the conduct of the late Master of the "Baltic":

(1) Captain Robertson failed to comply with the requirements of the Steamboat Inspection Act.

(2) That no proper efforts were made for the rescue of the unfortunate man when he had fallen overboard.

(3) That while Captain Robertson had no knowledge of the actions of his crew which would have enabled him to prevent the outrage, I cannot help coming to the conclusion that he did threaten the witness Cherry, and that he failed in his duty when he did not report the occurrence to the local authorities at Owen Sound.

After going very carefully over all the papers, evidence, &c, connected with this matter, I felt obliged to confirm the finding, which I did under Sec 13, Chap. 73, Revised Statues of Canada. I am therefore, as you will see, "funtus officio," and under the circumstances it would cause grave scandal were I to reverse this action.

Believe me,
Yours faithfully,
Charles H. Tupper[31]

Despite Mulholland's warnings about political fallout in the riding of Grey North, the Conservatives in Owen Sound re-elected incumbent James Masson in 1891 with a wider margin than in 1887. The Great Northern Transit Company (formerly Collingwood Lake Superior Line)

Reverend Robert Mulholland (1823–1902)
represented the establishment's views from
his position in the Church of England at
the diocese in Owen Sound for forty years.
*Courtesy of St. George's Anglican Church,
Owen Sound, Ontario.*

continued to advertise Captain Robertson as the captain of the *Baltic* in *The Collingwood Enterprise* of May 15 and, until May 23, 1890, in *The Meaford Monitor*, despite the fact that his license had been suspended for a year on May 1 of that year.

It is interesting to note that the *Baltic* crashed into the wharf in Meaford, smashing a hole in her bow on Monday, May 5, 1890, four days after Robertson's suspension.[32] If there was someone else at the helm, they obviously did not have the skill of the former captain. Robertson remained on board the ship during the year without the official capacity of master. *The Manitoulin Expositor* reported that Robertson was at the helm during the summer. Tate Robertson, it seems, simply disregarded the suspension.

However, by 1891 he was returned to his full command on the *Baltic*, a position it appears he never really relinquished, and the steamer continued a regular run to Duluth. Captain Robertson remained as master until his retirement in 1892 whereupon he became the customs agent for the port of Owen Sound. He was later appointed vice consul for the United States at Owen Sound in 1908, where he remained until his death in 1912.

15

Farewell to the *Baltic*

DESPITE THE DISASTERS faced as a result of ship losses in the 1880s, the Great Northern Transit Company managed to maintain almost full control over Georgian Bay shipping until the mid-1890s. The company's high freight rates were particularly annoying to lumber interests along the eastern coast of the bay, so it was no surprise that a new company was formed to challenge them. Once again the Dodge lumber interests were involved, along with support from Captain W.J. Bassett of Collingwood and several shareholders from Barrie, Collingwood and Toronto.[1] The newly formed company, called the North Shore Navigation Company, acquired the *City of Midland* as their first vessel. By painting her black, the company came to be known as the Black Line in contrast to the Great Northern Transit's white ships. In 1892, they entered into an agreement with the Meaford Transportation Company to lease their ship, the *Favourite*.[2] By 1894 they had purchased the vessel and renamed her the *City of Parry Sound* in 1895.[3] That same year they added the 150-foot steamer *City of Toronto* to the fleet, while to meet the upstart's challenge, the Great Northern Transit Company added the *Majestic* to its line. She, naturally, was painted white.

In the face of increased competition from more modern steamers, the *Baltic* remained active only until 1893. In that last year she took passengers to the World's Fair at Chicago over the summer. Once she was tied up in the fall, she never sailed again. The *Baltic* was mothballed at the

The *Baltic* steams out of Little Current in 1891 or 1892. This is one of the last known photos of the former *Frances Smith. The estate of W.D. Ritchie, courtesy of Sandy McGillvery.*

Collingwood dock and tied to the small wharf at the foot of Hurontario Street. Unattended and unmanned except for a watchman's periodic inspections, the ship sat idle and dark for two years. Her furnishings were removed and all operational materials for passenger service were taken ashore. On the morning of Saturday September 5, 1896, fire broke out on board the *Baltic.* The blaze was noticed about a quarter to three in the morning and, within hours, the ship was burned to the waterline.[4]

Fortunately for the town, there was only a moderate wind from the southeast, or the town itself could have been set ablaze. The old wooden steamer sent flames high into the night sky before anyone was aware of the dangerous situation. Sparks and embers blew toward Georgian Bay and away from the wooden warehouses huddled on the dock. Smoke billowed out of the hull as the vessel was entirely engulfed, spewing fire from the upper decks. As Collingwood's commercial areas along First Street and Hurontario Street were safe, crowds quickly filled the streets to see the conflagration. Roaring flames and burning particles missed landing on the grain elevator located on the railway wharf where, as the *Frances Smith,* the *Baltic* had loaded troops heading to fight Riel in 1870. Despite their prompt arrival, the firemen were hampered by the fact that the steam fire engine would not work.[5] With the help of spectators now spilling onto the wharf, they eventually attached a hose to a hydrant at the end of the slip and pumped water on the old

The *Baltic* at dockside, Owen Sound, circa 1890. Toward the end of her commercial life, the steamer showed clear signs of wear. After her last trip to Chicago in 1893, the vessel was stripped of all her internal fittings and mothballed at the Collingwood dock. *Courtesy of the Owen Sound Marine and Rail Museum.*

ship. It was no use. By late morning the *Baltic* was a burnt mass, floating in the shallow water. The docks were charred on both the east and west side of the smoldering hulk.[6] All ropes were gone and only the anchor chains held her in place. In the water, bits of charcoal, burned planks and small flecks of grey ash bobbed around the ruin.

At the end of her life the *Baltic* was nothing but a sad shell, her white body now a blackened hulk. The once gleaming "splendid and commodious" steamer of the upper lakes awaited disposal of her charred remains. With her inner machinery and metal parts visible, the scorched ruin was barely afloat.

Within days, *The Collingwood Bulletin* reported manager Charles Cameron's statement that his company, the Great Northern Transit Company, (White Line) had almost completed the sale of the *Baltic* to the Brown Line of Windsor, and that M.W.J. Brown had arrived in Collingwood on September 4 to close the deal. Later in the week, *The Owen Sound Times* speculated that arson was involved.[7] The ship carried $15,000 insurance split among several insurance companies. This may have been a generous valuation for a mothballed vessel that had not been on the open water since 1893. There had been no fires in the boiler for months and the only person to keep an eye on the vessel was a watchman. He had inspected the boat at half-past eight the night of the fire and reported nothing amiss. "The fire was no doubt the work of an incendiary," claimed *The Owen Sound Times*, in a rather smug report of the sad end.[8]

```
DURING MONTHS OF
JUNE, JULY and AUGUST
THE MAGNIFICENTLY EQUIPPED SIDE-WHEEL
STEAMER "BALTIC"
LIGHTED THROUGHOUT BY ELECTRICITY
Will be put into service between COLLINGWOOD,
          OWEN SOUND, WIARTON and

Columbian Exposition, Chicago
Making Special Trips every Two Weeks.
Lying at Special Dock at South Chicago
~~→ FOR SIX DAYS ←~~
Within one hundred feet of Electric Railway, which runs
every five minutes to Exposition.  Fare five cents,
        or by Illinois Central R.R. (see map).

DATES OF SAILINGS
June 14     July 12    August 9 ⎫
  "  28       "  26      "  23  ⎬ WEDNESDAYS

Round Trip Rates, including Berth and Meals,
while lying in Chicago.

$40.00,    -    $45.00,    -    $50.00
ACCORDING TO LOCATION OF STATEROOM.

And from Toronto, Hamilton and London,
BY G. T. R. OR C. P. R.
$44.00      -    $49.00          $54.00

Accommodation limited to 100 Passengers
Capacity of Steamer  -  -  - 150    "

Stateroom accommodation should be secured as
early as possible.

For full particulars apply to
THOS. LONG,              CHAS. CAMERON,
  Sec.-Treas.,               Manager,
  COLLINGWOOD.               COLLINGWOOD.
```

The last handbill to advertise the *Baltic*'s
excursion to Chicago in 1873. *Courtesy of
Phillip Smith.*

Given this climate of suspicion, the high valuation of the old boat and the condition of the *Baltic*, the insurance consortium refused to pay the claim for $15,000. Cameron and the Great Northern sued. The case was heard in the Assize Court before Judge Armour in Toronto in September 1897. It became a battle of conflicting testimony, acrimony and marine expert versus marine expert. The insurance companies claimed that the *Baltic* was supposed to have been running in 1896, yet she was tied up to the dock all season. Because she was not running, the claim for insurance was invalid, they contended. Besides, they claimed, she was "condemned by the government inspector" and was in a state of "rotten, decayed, and unseaworthy condition."9 At the hearing, the insurance company called several of the former crew, including Captain John Simpson and the ship carpenter, Henry Woods, to state that the conditions on board the *Baltic* were below standard for the times.

The White Line, in turn, called marine experts who testified that the ship was an admirable vessel and was regarded as one of the finest on Georgian Bay. It was indeed a magnificent floating palace and not the potential coffin described by the insurance companies. Former crew testified to the *Baltic's* good qualities as a ship they were once proud to serve upon. At the conclusion of testimony, Judge Armour directed the jury to consider only the value of the vessel at the time of the boat's destruction. The judge ruled out the insurance consortium's claim that "a ship is not covered by the policy while tied to the dock or at anchor." Such a contention if sustained, he said, would annul the insurance policies of all ships when not under sail.

The jury's deliberations were difficult, given the conflicting testimony of the former crew and the "experts." The jury eventually decided to award Cameron and company $12,000, the sum based on the full value of the policy minus the value of the boilers. The boilers were salvaged for $3,000.

In 1898, the insurance companies appealed the verdict to the Ontario Court of Appeal. Although the justices were equally divided, the initial judgment was upheld. One of the insurance companies in the consortium, the Alliance Insurance Company, paid their portion of the claim. The remaining five companies appealed again, this time to the Supreme Court of Canada. The appeal was granted in a complex decision that only lawyers are able to appreciate (see Appendix E). The upshot was that the White Line lost the case over the *Baltic* fire, meaning that the remaining insurance companies did not have to pay up. It was a serious blow to the Great Northern.

Within a year, the North Shore Navigation Company bought out the Great Northern Transit Company, renaming themselves the Northern Navigation Company. The new company became one of the most prestigious shipping lines on the Great Lakes for another four decades. However, by the early 1940s steamers like the *Noronic*, and *Hamonic* were having a difficult time financially. The *Noronic* burned in Toronto in September 1949. The *Hamonic* was scrapped in 1946. The *Huronic* was scrapped in 1950. The CPR ships *Assiniboia* and *Keewatin* (built in 1907) were nearing the end of their lives too. The little steamers like the *Caribou* owned by the Owen Sound Transportation Company worked away serving Owen Sound and Manitoulin and some of the

Directors of the Great Northern Transit Company, 1896. *Back row, left to right:* James Beatty, Thomas Long, "Black Pete" Campbell, Henry Eberts Smith; *Front row, left to right:* Charles Cameron, W. Krough, John Long. *Courtesy of Stuart Robertson.*

north shore ports, but even they were aged and within a few years not sustainable after the road developments in the 1950s and 1960s.

For almost fifty years, after the *Baltic* burned, the old Collingwood fishermen remembered the bass and perch that swam amid the wreck of the her charred ribs near One Tree Island.[10] Now, more than a hundred years away from the glory days of this grand steamer, the ribs are gone and the memory fades. She has gone to be with "the finny tribes" that William H. Smith talked about on the day she was launched. The waves of Georgian Bay continue to wash the rocky shore, but splendid steamers like the *Frances Smith* will never return. The era is gone.

Our modern world has not been kind to the old passenger steamers of the Great Lakes. The debris of their broken bodies is scattered around the lake bottoms. Occasionally adventuresome divers visit their underwater remains. Sometimes curious summer museum visitors take a moment to look at photographs and posters or other bits and pieces saved by steamboat aficionados. These tokens of our heritage only hint at the importance steamboats played in our past. Their stories are still waiting to be told.

Appendix A

Six Models of the *Frances Smith*

During my research into the story of the *Frances Smith*, I discovered six wonderful models of the vessel. Each has an interesting story.

In the Collingwood museum, displayed in prominent view, is a delightful model of the *Baltic*. It is classic folk art without slavish attention to absolute dimension. The model is a beauty. There is life and vitality in every part of the model from the stem to the fantail. An almost whimsical character to the design summons up the joy of hundreds of people on excursions to Mackinac Island and the anticipation of thousands more heading west to begin a new life in Manitoba.

The model is made from wood taken from the rudder of the burned out *Baltic* before she was towed to her grave more than a century ago. Hugh Myler, a long time marine engineer and crew member of the *Baltic*, presented his masterpiece to the Huron Institute, the precursor of the Collingwood Museum back in 1949. His gift is special to all who love our Great Lakes heritage. When the Huron Institute burned, this gem was somehow saved.

Staring at Myler's model from every angle is a time transporting experience. One can hear the splashing paddles and the steady thumping of the rocking beam on the hurricane deck. It is easy to imagine Captain Robertson peering from his pilothouse into fog-bound Neebish Channel or a cabin passenger strolling along the promenade deck so carefully recreated by Mr. Myler. The struts holding the deck above the hull are carefully reproduced. Everything is in its place, making this my personal favourite.

Top: The model of the *Baltic* crafted by Hugh Myler survived a fire at the Huron Institute and is now on permanent display at the Collingwood Museum. *Centre:* The model of the *Frances Smith* originally donated by T.W. Douglas of Owen Sound is one of the most accurate representations of the *Frances Smith*. It is on permanent display at the Owen Sound Marine and Rail Museum. *Bottom:* Joan Hyslop, curator of the Grey Roots Museum, displays the model of the *Frances Smith* donated to the museum by Phillip Smith on behalf of family of William H. Smith. *All photos by Scott Cameron.*

Top left: The half model on the wall, known as the Cook model, is said to have hung in a bar in Clarksburg, Ontario, at one time. Pictured (l-r): Elmer Cook, Clara Cook and Helen Dobson. *Courtesy of H. Elmer Cook's daughters, Helen (Dobson) and Sharon DeBoard. Top right:* Mr. Norman Smith of Little Current proudly holds his model of the *Frances Smith* while standing at his front door. *Photo by Scott Cameron.* *Bottom:* The Thunder Bay model is believed to have been carved by Erle Smith. It is located at the Thunder Bay Historical Museum. *Courtesy of Dr. Tory Tronrud, Thunder Bay Historical Museum.*

At the Owen Sound Marine and Rail Museum, mounted in a glass case on the wall, is the Douglas model, so named for the donor of the ship. It sat in the office of the T.W. Douglas clothing store for many years before it was donated by T.W.'s son, Stewart, sometime in the 1950s. T.W.'s son Ken Douglas told me that he suspects that his great-uncle Fred, who was a boat builder, may have made it. Stewart repainted the model before donating it to the museum. Like the model of the *Baltic*, it is well-preserved, and well-cared for. It is finer, less robust in appearance and more accurate in its colours and design than Collingwood's Myler model. However, because it is a half model it is not as approachable as the Collingwood model.

Grey Roots is the new centre that houses both the Grey County Archives Collection and Museum Collection, located just outside Owen Sound, Ontario. Deep in their vaults is possibly the oldest model of the *Frances Smith*. The family of William H. Smith donated it several decades ago and it has not been on display for more than a dozen years, much to the dismay of the family. They feel that this wonderful artifact, which has not been shown to the public for so many years, deserves to be front and centre in the museum gallery. The positive part of the story is that it is well-preserved. The curator will, on request, take a researcher to the vaults to see the masterpiece. I consider myself fortunate to have gazed for over an hour at the model. I want to go back.

This Smith model is also a half model, mounted on black velvet. What a delicate thing it is! Its lines are graceful and as close as any model can be to the accurate reflection of the ship. Contrary to what the owners thought, this is not the architect's model. Because the two stacks are not shown and the texas cabin behind the pilothouse are part of the model, it had to have been made sometime after 1869. Its paint scheme is possibly the most authentic of all models, although the red on the hull is a bit garish. Looking at this model from all angles, top, side and bottom was most helpful in understanding the interior design as well as the deck patterns.

The Cook model is in the private hands of an Ontario collector. I saw it once while it was at the Meaford Museum. Apparently the model was purchased in a bar in Clarksburg, Ontario, by a man who then passed it on to Elmer Cook, now deceased. The model was donated to the Meaford Museum in the early 1990s. Unfortunately, it was not "restored" to the satisfaction of the collector's family and a lawsuit ensued. The half model was returned to the family.

Mr. Norman Smith of Little Current, Ontario, is an "old" sailor. His little house is on a hill above the main part of town almost in view of the docks. He said he liked the name of the *Frances Smith* so he decided to make a model. It sits in his living room and acts as a light stand. The model is a true primitive work and is an interesting addition to the models of the steamer.

The Erle Smith model is located at the Thunder Bay Historical Museum. Erle Smith was a civil engineer who worked for the city of Port Arthur beginning in 1907 and later for the C.D. Howe Company. By 1934 he was district engineer for the Department of Northern Development (later the Department of Highways). He was a founding member of the Association of Professional Engineers of Ontario in 1922. Curator Dr. Tory Tronrud's efforts to find out more about the vessel were to no avail. He graciously took photos of the boat for this book. I have yet to see the real thing.

Appendix B

List of Ships Identified in the Text

Name of Vessel	Built	Length x Width in feet	Deregulation Date	Comment
Admiral	?	?	?	Schooner.
Africa	1873	136x25	1895	Propeller, sank in gale near Cove Island, 13 dead.
Alabama	1862	220x32	1863	Commerce raider captured/sank over 50 northern U.S. vessels, sunk by enemy fire in France.
Alberta	1883	263x38	1947	Propeller, CPR steamer built in Scotland, scrapped.
Algoma	1841	127x43	1877	Paddlewheel, aka *City of Toronto* and also *Racine*, abandoned & sunk at Collingwood, Ontario.
Algoma	1883	263x38	1885	Propeller, CPR steamer built in Scotland, wrecked at Isle Royale, 37 died.
Annie L. Craig	1870	184x32	1881	Propeller aka *City of Winnipeg*, burned at Duluth, Minnesota, 4 deaths.
Asia	1873	173x28	1882	Propeller, sunk in Georgian Bay with 100 persons.
Assiniboia	1907	336x44	1969	Propeller (CPR), built in Scotland, burned, scrapped in New Jersey.
Athabasca	1883	263x38	1947	Propeller, CPR steamer built in Scotland, scrapped at Hamilton, Ontario.

Name of Vessel	Built	Length x Width in feet	Deregulation Date	Comment
Atlantic		See *Manitoulin* below		
Baltic		See *Frances Smith* below		
Bonnie Maggie	1859	111x19	1869	Paddlewheel, aka *Bonnie Boat*, wrecked near Kincardine, Ontario.
Brooklyn	1866	133x26	1874	Propeller, boilers exploded, approx. 22 did near Wyandotte, Michigan. (unconfirmed data)
Cambria	1888	131x23	1903	Paddlewheel, aka *Champion* and *Champion II*. Rebuilt to 175 feet, broken up.
Campana	1873	241x35	1909	Propeller, aka *North*. British registry, wrecked near Quebec.
Canadian	1853	162x47	1868	Paddlewheel, launched as *Canadian Lily* became a tow barge, broken up.
Cascaden	?	?	1871	Schooner, wrecked near Tobermory, Ontario.
Champion	1877	See *Cambria* above		
Chi-Cheemaun	1974	365x72	still sailing	Ferry between Manitoulin Island and Bruce Peninsula, Ontario.
Chicora	1864	221x26	1938	Paddlewheel, aka *Let Her B*, rebuilt. foundered as a barge.
City of Owen Sound	1875	172x31	1909	Propeller, sank in North Channel 1887, raised 1891 and renamed *Saturn*, foundered again near Southampton, Ontario.
City of Winnipeg		See *Annie L. Craig* above		
Clifton	1853	187x26	1867	Paddlewheel, became a barge engine placed in *Frances Smith*.
Collingwood		See *Kaloolah* below.		
Conrad Reid	1862	?	1875	Schooner, all hands lost near Port Stanley, Ontario.
Cumberland	1871	205x26	1877	Paddlewheel, wrecked at Isle Royale, Lake Superior.
Edmund Fitzgerald	1956	711x75	1976	Propeller, lost with all hands on Lake Superior, Nov. 1975.

Name of Vessel	Built	Length x Width in feet	Deregulation Date	Comment
Favourite	1889	130x25	1900	Propeller, aka *City of Parry Sound*, burned at Collingwood, Ontario.
Frances Smith	1867	181x28	1896	Paddlewheel aka *Baltic*, burned at Collingwood, Ontario.
Gore	1839	125x16	1852	Paddlewheel, aka *Goderich*, retired.
Hubbard	1856	131x36	1875	Schooner, sunk near Muskegon, Michigan.
Hunter	1867	192x30	?	Propeller, burned in 1861 & rebuilt.
Illinois	1853	269x29	?	Paddlewheel, 1855, foundered near Lakeport, Michigan.
Jessie Drummond	1865	134x23	1902	Schooner wrecked on Lake Ontario, crew saved.
Kaloolah	1853	188x25	1862	Paddlewheel, aka *Collingwood*, wrecked near Southampton, Ontario.
Keewatin	1907	336x44	1965	Propeller, retired to a museum at Sauguatuck, Michigan.
Kincardine	1871	107x20	1892	Propeller, stranded near Cabot Head, Georgian Bay.
Lady Elgin	1851	252x32	1860	Paddlewheel, collision in Lake Michigan, 267 lives lost.
Magnet	1847	173x26	1928	Paddlewheel, rebuilt and reregistered several times, ended up as a barge.
Majestic	1895	235x35	1915	Propeller, burned at Point Edward, Ontario.
Manitoba	1871	173x25	1903	Paddlewheel, aka *Carmona*, burned while tied up at Windsor, Ontario.
Manitoba	1889	303x38	1951	Propeller, CPR, replacement engine from CPR *Algoma*, broken up.
Manitoulin	1880	152x30	1903	Propeller, burned near Manitouwaning, Ontario, in 1882, rebuilt and renamed *Atlantic*, burned near Parry Sound, Ontario.

Name of Vessel	Built	Length x Width in feet	Deregulation Date	Comment
Mary Ann Lydon	1874	121x26	1912	Schooner, driven ashore on Lake Ontario.
Minnie Williams	1862	135x26	1875	Schooner, sunk near Ludington, Michigan, 8 hands lost.
Montgomery	1856	204x33	1901	Propeller changed to barge, wrecked on Lake Superior.
Mazeppa	1851	?	1856	Paddlewheel, wrecked near Southampton, Ontario.
Mystic Star	c.1873	141x29	1892	Schooner, sunk.
Nellie Sherwood	1867	77x22	1882	Schooner, lost near Tobermory, Ontario, 5 deaths.
Niagara	1845	230x34	1856	Paddlewheel, burned while bound from Chicago to Collingwood, about 70 deaths.
Noronic	1913	363x52	1949	Propeller, burned in Toronto, Ontario, 119 died.
Northern Belle	1875	129x23	1898	Propeller, aka *Gladys*, burned at Byng Inlet, Georgian Bay.
Northern Queen	1872	149x28	1915	Propeller, returned to U.S. registry in 1882, burned at Sturgeon Bay, Wisconsin.
Okonra	1868	60x13	1879	Tug, burned near Wiarton, Ontario.
Ontario	1874	181x35	1899	Propeller, wrecked on Lake Superior.
Ontonagon	?	?	?	no data
Oxford	1853	90x?	1855	Propeller, wrecked on the Bruce Peninsula.
Pacific	1883	179x31	1898	Propeller. burned at Collingwood, Ontario.
Penetanguishene	1833	?	1838	Paddlewheel, retired.
Planet	1855	265x33	1863	Paddlewheel, sunk in Lake Superior with 35 persons.
Ploughboy	1851	170x28	1870	Paddlewheel, aka *T.F. Park*, burned at Detroit, Michigan.
Quebec	1874	186x35	1885	Propeller, sunk near St. Joseph Island, Ontario, raised and reregistered in U.S. until 1922. Sunk at Alpena, Michigan.
Rescue	1855	122x23	1876	Propeller, armour plated gunboat, scrapped.

Name of Vessel	Built	Length x Width in feet	Deregulation Date	Comment
Robert Holland	See *Northern Queen* above			
Silver Spray	1864	134x17	1874	Paddlewheel, burned at Owen Sound, Ontario.
South American	1914	290x47	1967	Propeller, scrapped in 1974 at Baltimore, New Jersey.
Sovereign	1873	140x24	1891	Propeller, foundered in Lake Superior.
St. Louis	1864	203x31	1914	Propeller, stranded at Cape St. Vincent, New York.
Sulter Girl	1863	?	1875	Scow schooner, all hands lost near Port Stanley, Ontario.
T.J. Scott	1909	64x16	1958	Tug, aka *Eureka*, sold to the Harrisons of Owen Sound, scrapped in Toronto.
Waubuno	1865	135x19	1879	Paddlewheel, sunk near Parry Sound, Ontario, 24 lives lost.

Sources:

Information for this chart has been taken from the following sources in 2005:

1   The personal files of the author

2   The private database of William McNeil

3   David Swayze's Shipwreck File site: www.baillod.com/shipwreck/swayze/default.asp and also at http://great-lakeshistory.homestead.com/Alpha.html.

4   Walter Lewis' Maritime History of the Great Lakes site: www.hhpl.on.ca/GreatLakes/search/Search.asp.

5   Marine Museum of the Great Lakes site: http://db.library.queensu.ca/mar-mus/mills/index.html.

Note: Often several vessels had the same name. Attempts have been made to verify that the descriptions of vessels mentioned above are indeed the correct vessels. Where there is doubt or where information is lacking, a "no data" entry and a "?" are shown.

Appendix C

Presentation to W.H. Smith on April 30, 1867

To
William Henry Smith Esquire
Proprietor and Commander of the Steamer
Frances Smith

Dear Sir:
We your fellow townsmen beg to say that we participate in the pleasure which you must this day enjoy, in the successful completion of a project, which for some time has been the object of your ambition, i.e. the construction of this splendid vessel.

Your efforts heretofore in providing us with a speedy and commodious means of transit, conferred upon us as a boon possessed by few other towns, we beg to assure you that we are not unmindful of the favours received, and that we feel much satisfaction in witnessing in the launch today, the substantial results of the enterprising spirit possessed by you. During your residence among us, the exhibition of the spirit, by you, has elicited our warmest commendation. That same ambition has built our cities and towns, made fine farms of the wilderness, intersected our country with railroads and canals, and erected into a wealthy and prosperous Dominion – a land that was comparatively recent, one gloomy forest.

Your preserving and honourable efforts for the advancement of your personal interests have been such that we as a community have shared the benefits accruing therefrom, our labouring men and mechanics have been largely employed, the business of our town increased, and the farming community of the surrounding country have been enabled to obtain an increased reward for their labour.

We have met today to acknowledge our appreciation of those qualities, which we see in you, those qualities have secured you to our respect and admiration and in testimony of the esteem in which we hold you, we beg to present you with this SETT OF COLOURS, to be borne by this splendid steamer, the launch of which we are this day to witness, her beautiful model, great strength, the superior workmanship displayed upon her, attest to the skill and ability of her architect and under the command of yourself THE TRAVELLING PUBLIC may rest assured of safety, speed and comfort, together with kind and courteous attention.

To conclude – We heartily wish you success in this undertaking, We hope and trust that it may prove profitable to you and that your esteemed family may long enjoy the fruits of your preserving energy.

Done at Owen Sound
The thirtieth Day of April
AD 1867

Captain Smith replied:

Mr. Mayor and fellow townsmen:
For the appropriate and highly esteemed present as well as your kind address, either of which would in itself be sufficient to inspire with feelings of grateful remembrance of the many kind favours I have already received at your hands – accept my heartfelt thanks and I trust that the future will not find me unmindful of what can, and must of necessity be done, in order to develop even some of the great natural resources of our town and surrounding country. In fact, this is the only place in which there can be a dockyard conveniently established for the construction and needy repairs of the merchant marine, which is likely at no distant day to spring up in this north-westerly portion of the great Dominion of Canada.

I feel, gentlemen, that my first effort at building may and will be followed by many others; and should this noble vessel astonish the finny tribes of Georgian Bay by her speed, as I am sure she will, the entire credit will be due to her designer and builder, Mr. Simpson.

Gentlemen, I again most cheerfully thank you for your magnificent present, and kind wishes for myself and my family, and I trust that the new ship may long be spared to float those beautiful colours to the gentle breeze.

Source: *The Owen Sound Comet*, May 3, 1867.

Appendix D

Shipping Rates for the *Frances Smith,* 1870

MONTREAL TO OWEN SOUND

Item	Per 100 Pounds
Freight and General merchandise	40 cents
Bar Iron and Nails	30 cents
Pig Iron	25 cents

TORONTO TO OWEN SOUND

Item	Per 100 Pounds
Classified Freight	
1st Class	40 cents
2nd Class	32 cents
3rd Class	25 cents
Wheat, Peas and Beans in lots of 360 bu. (60 pound bu.)	7 cents
Barley and Buckwheat in lots of 450 bu.	6 cents
Flour in lots of 100 bu. per barrel	4 1/2 cents
Flour in bag in lots of 200	15 cents
Adult through ticket to Toronto on Northern Railway	4.00 dollars
Adult return Ticket good for 6 days	6.00 dollars

Source: *The Meaford Monitor*, April 28, 1870.

Appendix E

Dates of Post Office Openings on Georgian Bay and Lake Superior

Community Name	Date of First P.O.
Algoma Mills	May 1, 1882
Batchawana	November 1, 1865
Blind River	July 1, 1877
Bruce Mines	1853
Cape Rich	June 1, 1853
Cockburn Island	July 1, 1880
Collingwood	July 1, 1853
Garden River	June 1, 1866
Kagawong	July 1, 1876
Killarney	June 1, 1854
Little Current	July 1, 1864
Manitowaning	1854
Meaford	July 6, 1841
Michipicoten	August 1, 1865
Nipegon (Nipigon)	October 1, 1872
Owen Sound	July 6, 1846
Pointe aux Pins	August 1, 1870
Port Arthur	November 1, 1869
Sault Ste. Marie	1853

Community Name	Date of First P.O.
Silver Islet	January 1, 1871
Spanish Mills	September 1, 1868
Thessalon	August 1, 1874
Tobermory	September 1, 1881
Wiarton	August 1, 1868

Source: Library and Archives Canada postal database searchable Web site at www.collectionscanada.ca/archivianet/02010902_e.html, accessed Dec. 3, 2004.

Appendix F

Report of A.R. Gordon

Sessional Papers
Volume 15
Fourth Session of the Sixth Parliament
Of the
Dominion Of Canada
Session 1890
Volume XXIII
53 Victoria.   Sessional Papers (No. 87B.)   A. 1890

REPORT

Of Lieut. Gordon, R.N., [Royal Navy] into the conduct of the master
and mate of the steamship "Baltic," in connection with the outrage perpetrated on one Charles Hambley (sic), a deck-hand of the said vessel,
on the 26th August, 1889.

Meteorological Service, Toronto, 24th April, 1890.
Sir, – I have the honour to report that I have now completed the investigation into the conduct of the master and mate of the S.S. "Baltic," in
connection with the outrage perpetrated on one Charles Hambley (sic),
a deck-hand on said vessel, on the 26th of August, 1889.

I held court one day in Owen Sound, and two days in Collingwood,
examining in all eight witnesses; a copy of the evidence taken is for-
warded herewith.

The court has been formally adjourned till Saturday next the 5th April, when it will be opened at the office of the Inspector of Steamboats, in the Custom House, Toronto, when the decision will be given in open court. In regard to Charles Odlum Hill, holding a master's certificate of competency, who was mate on board the "Baltic," I find that no blame whatsoever attaches to him in connection with this unfortunate affair. He had been on duty all the day, and retired to rest when the ship left Owen Sound. He was only awakened some time after the unfortunate had gone overboard, and on having been told what had happened, concluded that at that time it would be of no use to lower a boat. The crew seem to have all been sober and in good working trim, and there was nothing in their conduct to cause Mr. Hill to anticipate any disturbance. Mr. Hill, is therefore completely exonerated from all blame in connection with this outrage, and I have returned his certificate, which during the investigation was in the custody of the court.

In reference to Captain Tait (sic) Robertson. The questions to consider are:

First: Were all due precautions taken On board the "Baltic" for the saving of life in the event of any one falling overboard?

Second: Did Captain Robertson use every effort to rescue the unfortunate victim?

Third: Did Captain Robertson in any way obstruct or impede the officers of justice in the discharge of their duties?

In regard to the first question the evidence of Captain Robertson and Mr. Hill is distinct, that the boats on the "Baltic" were never lowered by the crew for the purposes of familiarizing them with the work, boats being only lowered on three occasions during the season, once when the inspector visited the ship. Again, the chief officer says he lowered one boat in Collingwood to do some painting, and the third time was when the vessel broke her shaft, and was anchored in the north channel at the latter end of the season. The object of the enactment of sub-section 4 of clause 29 of Chap. 78 of the Revised Statutes, is that the crew may be familiarized with the method of getting boats in the water, and this is doubly necessary on the inland waters where the deck-hands are so frequently changed.

If the crew of the "Baltic" had been drilled as prescribed by the Act, there would probably have been little, if any, difficulty in getting a boat lowered.

I, therefore, find that Captain Robertson is in fault in that he did not carry out the instruction to masters of vessels contained in the section of statute above quoted.

It also appears from the evidence that this enactment is almost completely disregarded by our lake shipping.

Second : As to using every effort to rescue the unfortunate man after he was overboard, both Captain Robertson and Mate Montgomery seem to have lost their presence of mind, and to have gone rushing about the ship. Captain Robertson admits that he stood by the boat on the hurricane deck with a lot of people on the quarter just below him, and yet he never hailed them to come up and assist to get a boat away.

Second Mate Montgomery says he cleared away one fall of the boat the captain was at, but the captain says he never saw him there. Mr. Lamont, a passenger, whose evidence seems entitled to credence, says the captain stood near him for a minute at the after end of the hurricane deck, and altogether the mental strain and annoyance seems to have confused Captain Robertson, so that he did not act with the promptness which should characterize a seaman in an emergency of the kind. He took no steps to ascertain if his vessel had been brought to a dead stand, and the evidence shows that the life-buoy was towing after the vessel only a few yards astern, and was therefore useless. It is also shown that the vessel had continued to range ahead notwithstanding that the engineer had given her three or four strokes astern.

I am of opinion that with a crew properly drilled in handling the boats, especially if the captain had come astern on his vessel, which he might safely have done in the calm night described, that it might have been possible to save the man. But in the case as it stood absolutely nothing was done for the rescue of the unfortunate, and, for this, Captain Robertson cannot escape responsibility.

In regard to Captain Robertson's knowledge of what had occurred on his ship, I find that neither he nor Mr. Hill had any knowledge of the actual treatment the boy had received, until after the unfortunate was drowned. It seems extraordinary that a number of passengers and crew who must be aware that there is always an officer on deck, should have witnessed such brutal conduct, and yet have failed to report it to some one in authority. On hearing what had happened, the chief engineer went and reported to the captain, who went forward and found the boy dressed, but with tar on his hands.

Captain Robertson swears that he did not on this occasion tell the boy to go and get his money, and also says that he was first told of the action of his men by someone when he was on the promenade deck.

Whilst, as against this, Mate Montgomery says the captain had informed him that he had told the boy to go and get his money, a fact borne out by the actions of the boy and of watchman Currie. And as the chief engineer also contradicts the captain as to informing him, I cannot come to any other conclusion than that Captain Robertson's recollections of the night are somewhat confused. I find that Captain Robertson had no knowledge of the outrage in time to have prevented its occurrence, but I have to find that Captain Robertson did not exercise sound judgment and did not make all possible efforts to save the life of the unfortunate man who was overboard.

Third: in regard to the question of obstructing or failing to aid the peace officers in the discharge of their duties.

Captain Robertson admits in his evidence that when they returned to Owen Sound on the Saturday evening after the event, he had heard from passengers and others, details of the treatment to which the boy had been subjected, and under the circumstances, I consider that he failed in his duty when he did not voluntarily communicate with the Crown authorities. He says he consulted a Mr. Creasor, at Owen Sound, a barrister, and was guided by his advice, but I cannot think that this relieves him from the responsibility which accrues to him from the do-nothing policy which he pursued at first.

Constable Pierce [Pearce] and Mr. J.G. Cherry, one examined in Owen Sound, and the other in Collingwood, both agree with great accuracy in the evidence they give, as to the threats made use of by Captain Robertson at the time of the arrest of Russell and Tripp in Collingwood. I cannot help giving full weight to this testimony, though Captain Robertson's recollection of the matter seems to be at fault. I regret to have to conclude that Captain Robertson did thus, in general terms, threaten the witness, Cherry; though he subsequently seems to have realized what was his duty, and to have aided the authorities by all the means in his power, granting passage to the detectives and constables, and keeping his crew together while required as witnesses.

To summarize, then, I find that (1) Captain Robertson failed to comply with the requirements of the Steamboat Inspection Act. (2.) That no proper efforts were made for the rescue for the unfortunate man when he had fallen overboard. (3.) That while Captain Robertson had no knowledge of the actions of his crew which would have enabled him to prevent the outrage, I cannot help coming to the conclusion that he did threaten the witness, Cherry, and that he failed in his duty when he did not report the occurrence to the local authorities at Owen Sound.

I, therefore, adjudge that the certificate of service, as master on the inland waters, of the said William Tait (sic) Robertson, be suspended for the period of twelve calendar months, to date from 4th March, 1890. I have the honour, &c
ANDREW R. GORDON.

NOTE – I have been enabled to take a somewhat lenient view of the threat made by Captain Robertson from two considerations, viz.: – 1st, that he at first supposed Cherry to have been instigated in the proceedings by the people on a rival line of steamers; and 2nd, that on realizing the position of affairs he afterwards endeavoured in every way to aid the peace authorities in the prosecution of their duties.
A.R.G.

W.M. Smith, Esq., Deputy Minister of Marine, Ottawa.
I confirm the Commissioner's finding, and approve his sentence.
Charles H. Tupper.

Source: *Sessional Papers*. Volume 15, Fourth Session of the Sixth Parliament, The Dominion of Canada, Session 1890. Volume XXIII, Fourth Session of the Sixth parliament, The Dominion of Canada, Session 1890 (No. 87B.) located at King's College Library, Windsor, Nova Scotia.

Appendix G

Supreme Court Decision

THE LONDON ASSURANCE CORPORATION
(DEFENDANT)   APPELLANT;
THE GREAT NORTHERN TRANSIT
COMPANY (PLAINTIFF)   RESPONDENT
ON APPEAL FROM THE COURT OF APPEAL FOR ONTARIO

A policy issued in 1895 insured against fire the hull of S.S. *Baltic* including engines &c., "whilst running on the inland lakes, rivers and canals during the season of navigation. To be laid up in a place of safety during winter months from any extra hazardous building." The *Baltic* was laid up in 1893 and was never afterwards sent to sea. In 1896 she was destroyed by fire.

Held, reversing the judgment of the Court of Appeal (25 Ont.App.R.393) that the policy never attached; that the steamship was only insured while employed on inland waters during the navigation season or laid up in safety during the winter months.

Held also, that the above stipulation was not a condition but rather a description of the subject matter of the insurance and did not come within sec.115 of the Ontario Insurance Act relating to variations from statutory conditions.

Appeal from the decision of the Court of Appeal for Ontario (1) affirming by an equal division of the court the judgment at the trail in favour of the plaintiff.

The plaintiff brought actions against seven insurance companies on policies insuring his S.S. *Baltic* against loss by fire. The action against the Alliance Assurance Co. was tried and resulted in a verdict for the plaintiff, and on the company appealing it was agreed that the evidence on that trial should be treated as the evidence in all cases. The appeal resulted in the verdict at the trial being sustained by an equal division in the Court of Appeal. The Alliance Assurance Co. then settled with the plaintiff, the other six companies joining in an appeal to this court.

Wallace Nesbitt and McKay for the appellant referred to Slinkard v. Manchester Fire Assur. Co. (1): Benicia Agricultural Works v. Germania Ins. Co. (2); Pearson v. Commercial Union Assur. Co. (3).

Osler Q.C. and Douglas for the respondent cited Wanless v. Lancashire Ins. Co (4); Goring v. London Mutual Fire Ins Co. (5); Parsons v. Queens In. Co, (6)

The judgment of the court was delivered by:

SEDGEWICK, J. – On the 5th September 1896, the steamer *Baltic* owned by the Great Northern Transit Company, Limited, the present respondents, was burned while in dock at Collingwood, Georgian Bay. At the time of the fire she was insured against fire to the amount of $11,000 in seven companies, all of them except the Alliance Assurance Company being the present appellants. The companies having disputed their liability actions were brought and one of these cases was tried before Armour C.J., with a jury at Toronto in September 1897. Judgment was there given in favour of the plaintiffs, which judgment was sustained upon appeal by an equally divided court, Maclennan and Moss, JJ being of opinion that the judgment should stand, the Chief Justice and Osler, dissenting. The appeal is from the judgment to this court.

(1) 55 Pac.Rep.417.

(2) 97 Cal. 468.

(3) 1 App.Cas. 498.

(4) 23 Ont. App. R.224.

(5) 10 O.R. 236.

(6) 2 O.R. 45.

It is an admitted fact that the last trip of the *Baltic* was made in the season of 1893. In September of 1893 she was laid up at Collingwood and from that date she never again went to sea. It also appeared that during 1894, 1895 and 1896 she never obtained a certificate of inspection provided by the Dominion Act without which she could not have been run; that her planking, her frames and her engine bed were in such condition that it would have been impossible for her to have been moved from her position by her own motive power; that her electric light plant and certain portions of her furniture had been removed, and that she was in such condition that she could not in any sense be described as a running boat. Only two questions are raised; first, as to whether at the time of the fire the vessel insured came within the risk described in the policy; and secondly, as to whether the provisions of the Ontario Fire Insurance Act in regard to the conditions had been or should have been complied with. The wording of the description of the risk in each of the policies is identical and is as follows:

On the hull of the S.S. *Baltic*, including engines, boilers and appurtenances thereto, anchors, chains, masts, spars, rigging, sails, cabin and office furniture, beds, bedding, linen, silverware and platedware, cutlery, china, glassware and earthenware, looking glasses, mirrors, wheelbarrows, trucks, clocks and apparel on board said steamer whilst running on the inland lakes, rivers and canals during the season of navigation.
To be laid up in a place of safety during winter months from any extra hazardous building.

Ordinary outfit to be allowed in winter and spring.

It is understood and agreed that the steamer insured under this policy has permission to carry merchandise, hazardous and non hazardous, as freight from port to port with one barrel of coal oil for steamer's use. And the controversy mainly turns upon interpretation to be given to the words "whilst running on the inland lakes, rivers and canals during the season of navigation."

Three contentions have been put forward:

The first (and it is that upon which the judgment of the trial judge is based and is followed by Mr. Justice Maclennan in the Court of Appeal) is that the clause was intended to confine risk to fire whilst the vessel was inland, whether on the lakes, rivers or canals during the season of navigation, but not on the ocean or ocean port." Another interpretation is that the phrase "whilst running" &c., applies to and qualifies not the S.S. *Baltic* itself but only some of the property and articles intended to be included in the risk. The third interpretation is that by the words in question the companies undertook to insure not a vessel laid up during the season of navigation but a vessel actively engaged or employed during that period upon the inland lakes, rivers or canals – that during the season of navigation she must be a vessel in use or as they say 'in commission," (a term applicable to national ships of war) – with the necessary ship's papers and properly provided with master, crew and everything requisite for the ordinary prosecution of the business of a merchant vessel.

I am not able to agree with the view of the learned Chief Justice of the Queen's Bench Division. IT is true that the word "inland" is an emphatic word confining the risk so far as locality is concerned to inland lakes, rivers and canals. So that if the loss should occur while the vessel happened to be say, at Halifax or any other Atlantic port or on the high seas, she would not be covered. But there are, it seems to me, other equally emphatic words and one of these words is "running." The Learned Chief Justice's interpretation gives no effect to it. But not only that; it necessarily introduces into the clause an idea which is opposed to the idea conveyed by the word "running." Namely, the idea that whether the ship was "running," that is, in active employment or use, or whether she was laid up either at anchor or in the dock or upon dry land, she was still within the words of the policy. This I think is not interpreting the contract but enlarging it, making a contract not contemplated by the parties. I have not been able to appreciate the second interpretation given to this clause to which I have referred. It is a clause qualifying either the word "Baltic," or the word "steamer." It contemplates not engines, anchors, office furniture, etc. running, but a steamer running, nothing more, nothing less.

The third interpretation is. I think the correct one. It is an element of importance that this is a fire policy not a marine policy. Two elements much more important in a fire policy than in a marine policy are those of locality and mode of use. The risk of a thing being burned depends not so much upon the thing itself as upon its location and the uses to which it is put. A wooden building used for the manufacture of Dynamite in a crowded city surrounded by factories continually emitting sparks from their chimneys or smokestacks may be absolutely uninsurable. The same structure removed for farming purposes to the open prairie might be insured at an almost nominal sum. Now this is not a "time" policy. A time policy is a phrase used only in marine insurance to distinguish it from a voyage policy. IT in no material respect differs from a policy upon a building or upon anything else capable of insurance against fire. Neither is it a policy insuring the subject matter from one definite period to another. It is rather a policy insuring it during such periods within two defined points of time as she may happen to come within the description and terms of the risk. In the present case she is insured, first, whilst running upon the inland lakes, rivers and canals during the season of navigation, and secondly, whilst she is laid up in a place of safety during winter months (removed) from any extra-hazardous building. There may be within the year many periods, longer or shorter, in which she is not covered at all. She may during the season of navigation be running on the high seas. Whilst so occupied she is not insured. So likewise during the winter months she may be running either on the high seas or upon the unfrozen waters of inland lakes, or at the City of Quebec engaged as a ferry from one side of the St. Lawrence to the other. Still she is not insured. I do not know and it is not material to determine to what extent the element of locality influenced the insurance companies in making these policies. I do not know whether navigation upon salt water is carried on at a greater risk than on fresh water or why the operations of this steamer were confined to the latter but admitting that the parties in limiting the operations of the vessel to inland waters had in view the prohibition of navigation in ocean waters, it is perfectly clear that they had also in contemplation two distinct classes of risk, namely, the risk of fire whilst she was in actual use during the season of navigation and likewise the risk of fire whilst she was not in use but laid up in a place of safety during the winter months. The mode of use in both cases was material to the risk. In the summer months no special provision was made for her safety. Then she would be running. She would have her master and crew; she would have her life saving and fire saving apparatus; she would be under constant supervision and the danger of fire would be reduced to a minimum. In the winter months, however, she must be laid up. She may be laid up anywhere, whether in an inland port or an ocean port, but wherever laid up it must be in a place of safety and removed from and extra hazardous building. Looking at the whole clause it seems to me that the words 'running during the season of navigation' are mainly used in contrast to the words "laid up during the winter months." She is only covered by the clause whilst during the season of navigation she is running and whilst during the winter months she is laid up in a place of safety. This, it seems to me, is the true construction of the clause. It gives a natural and reasonable meaning to each of its words and it does not necessitate as the first interpretation does the insertion of the additional stipulation to which I have referred in order to give effect to it. If the view I take is incorrect and the first interpretation is the correct one; if it is not necessary that during the season of navigation the vessel should be in actual use; if all that was contemplated by the parties was that during the season the vessel should exist in situ whether running or laid up then she might be laid up anywhere, whiter in a place of safety or no; she might be anchored or even let run adrift upon the open lakes; she might be moored or hauled up high and dry in immediate proximity to any factory or building no matter how dangerous such proximity might be. Surely, as I view it, this consideration alone shows the untenable character of he ground upon which the judgment below is based.

One other point remains. It is contended that the stipulation contained in the words "whilst running, "&c., is a condition within the meaning of the Ontario Insurance Act. and inasmuch as it varies from or is in addition to the conditions by that Act made statutory, the policy should comply with section 115 of the Act which provides that such variations or additions should be printed in conspicuous type and in ink of different colour. So far as this point is concerned I entirely agree with the view taken by the learned Chief Justice of the Court of Appeal and Mr. Justice Osler. The stipulation in question is in no sense a condition but rather a description of he subject matter insured. It is descriptive of and has reference solely to the risk covered by the policy and not to the happening of an event which by the stature, therefore, does not apply.

On the whole I am of the opinion that the appeal should be allowed and the action dismissed; all costs to follow in the usual course.

Appeal allowed with costs*

Solicitors for the appellant: Beatty, Blackstock, Nesbitt, Chadwick & Riddell.

Solicitors for the respondent: McCarthy, Osler, Hoskin & Creelman.

* Leave to appeal from the judgment to the Judicial Committee of the Privy Council has been refused.

Source: "Reports of Cases decided in the Court of Appeal, During the Year 1898," Reported under the Authority of the Law Society of Upper Canada, Volume XXV (Toronto: Boswell & Hutchison, 1899) 577-84.

Notes

1 STEAMBOATS ON THE UPPER LAKES

1 *The Collingwood Enterprise Bulletin* (Collingwood), March 17, 1949.

2 Walter White, a commercial fisherman from Collingwood, remembers the island from the days he sailed and fished with his father before 1949.

3 When first built, the upper cabins of the *Frances Smith* were much narrower and there was no transom above. That modification along with the addition of a "texas" cabin behind the pilothouse was part of a general reconstruction of the upper decks two years after the initial launch. Author's note: A "texas" was an extension of the pilothouse and was sometimes used as quarters for the captain. It is unclear where the term came from, but some scholars claim it was so named because it was a "large cabin," but I have not been able to verify this.

4 The twin arched windows were also part of the reconstruction in 1869. Prior to that cabin windows and the windows in the pilothouse were rectangular in shape.

5 The Crimean War was between Russia and an alliance of Great Britain, France, Sardinia and Turkey (1853–56). Much of the fighting took place in the Crimean, a peninsula of the Ukraine, lying between the Sea of Azou and the Black Sea. Florence Nightingale (1820–1910) English nurse and medical reformer, became famous during the Crimean War for her work in improving medical procedures and standards of care in army hospitals.

Lord Raglan was commander-in-chief at the Battle of Balaklava in the Crimea in October 1854. Lord Lucan was in command of the cavalry and his brother-in-law, Lord Cardigan (detested by Lucan) was responsible for a light cavalry brigade. Lucan, responding to what he mistakenly took to be Raglan's orders, commanded Cardigan to charge into a valley controlled on three sides by the Russians. Cardigan protested but followed orders. It was suicidal. The British troops were mowed down. Alfred, Lord Tennyson's "Charge of the Light Brigade" was the British epitaph for what they later claimed was a victory.

6   The *Penetanguishene* was the first paddlewheeler built on Georgian Bay at Pene-
    tanguishene in 1833. It had eight berths for gentlemen, and six berths for ladies.
    The captain was Captain Borland. The owner was a Mr. Thompson, who pos-
    sibly was one of the builders. The vessel ran from Penetanguishene to St. Joseph
    Island near Sault Ste. Marie, but sank in 1839 in a collision on the Detroit River.
    See *Toronto Courier British American Journal*, Tuesday, September 23, 1834, and
    Canada Company Records Series A 4, A-4-5 Vol. 1, Ontario Archives, and the
    Mills List at the Marine Museum of the Great Lakes.

7   Robert Cunningham, *Algoma Central Corporation: The Centennial Anniversary His-
    tory 1899–1999* (Sault Ste. Marie, ON: Algoma Central Corporation, 1999) 8.

8   *The Meaford Monitor*, Jan. 13, 1882.

9   James Barry, *Georgian Bay: An Illustrated History* (Toronto: Stoddart, 1992) 33.

10 From an excerpt of "Diary of Mrs. Anna Jameson" in James Barry, *Georgian
    Bay: The Sixth Great Lake* (Toronto: Stoddart, 1995) 114.

11 Sydenham was renamed Owen Sound by an act of Parliament in 1856.

12 Captain J.W. Hall, *Marine Disasters of the Western Lakes During the Navigation
    of 1871 with the Loss of Property, Vessels Bought and Sold, the Old and New Ton-
    nage, with the Names of Vessels Laid Up at Various Lake Ports also important Marine
    History* (Detroit Free Press Book and Job Printing Establishment, 1872). Taken
    from Walter Lewis' Web site, "Disasters on the Western Lakes During 1871,"
    at www.hhpl.on.ca./GreatLakes/Documents/shiplists/Halls1871/default.asp,
    accessed May 5, 2005. Captain Hall compiled ship disasters over several years
    and published annual records.

13 Personal communication with Walter White of Collingwood in the spring of
    2004 and again in the spring of 2005. He is still fishing but will soon retire after
    over 40 years on the bay. He is the son of an old-time fisherman who knew the
    waters of southern Georgian Bay like the back of his hand.

14 Kerosene replaced whale oil in illuminating lighthouse lamps in the 1880s, accord-
    ing to Florence Kern. See "Lighthousing in the 1890s," in *The Bulletin*, U.S.
    Coast Guard Academy Alumni Association, Vol. 40, No. 6, 1978.

15 Taken from www.sos.state.mi.us/history/museum/musewil/chlight.html, accessed
    November 25, 2004.

16 Taken from www.tc.gc.ca/aboutus/pubs/ourstory/1936-menu.htm, accessed Sept.
    20, 2003.

17 Lieutenant Henry Wolsey Bayfield, born in 1795, served with the British Navy
    from 1816 to 1856. He was recruited by Captain William Owen, Royal Naval
    Surveyor, to assist in mapping the Great Lakes. They began in the St. Lawrence
    River in 1816 and, by 1822, Bayfield was making maps of Lake Huron, Geor-
    gian Bay and Lake Superior. The surveys were taken back to London, England,
    in 1824 and the first maps were produced by 1826. He returned to Canada and
    mapped the Bay of Fundy and the Gulf of St. Lawrence. Bayfield is recognized
    as a pioneer in Canadian hydrology. See *Dictionary of Canadian Biography*, Vol.
    XL (Toronto: University of Toronto Press, 1976) 54–56.

18 Lieutenant Bayfield's original map is located in the manuscript room at the British Library, London, U.K.

19 Cousins James and Henry Beatty formed the North West Transportation Company in 1871, sailing ships from Sarnia to the Lakehead. Over the next decade, they owned the *Waubuno,* the *Asia*, the *Quebec*, the *Manitoba* and the *Ontario*. Their connections with the Grand Trunk Railway at Sarnia made them a major competitor to the *Frances Smith* and her alliance with the *Cumberland* and *Chicora* on the route to Lake Superior sailing out of Collingwood. These cousins were descendants of the Beatty family who immigrated to Canada from Ireland in 1836, settled in Thorold, Ontario, and ultimately acquired timber rights in the Parry Sound area. William Beatty Sr. and his sons William and James Hughes prospered in the lumber business. William Beatty Jr. is considered the founder of Parry Sound, Ontario. For more on the Beatty family, see Adrian Hayes, *Parry Sound: Gateway to Northern Ontario* (Toronto: Natural Heritage Books, 2005).

20 *The Owen Sound Times*, Nov. 8, 1878.

21 One fathom is equal to six feet.

22 *The Port Arthur Weekly Sentinel*, July 31, 1885.

23 *The Tobermory Shipwrecks* (Tobermory, ON: The Blue Heron Co., 1996) 45.

24 Letter from William Tate Robertson to Alexander Rocke Robertson, August 27, 1877. The letter is in the private collection of Stuart Robertson.

25 *The Thunder Bay Sentinel* (Prince Arthur's Landing), Sept. 2, 1881.

26 Ibid, June 29, 1882.

27 The three blasts signal of 1890 has now been changed to meet international standard signals. Today, the signal for fog is a single blast every three minutes.

28 Thos. S. Thompson, *Thompson's Coast Pilot for the Upper Lakes*, 5th edition (Detroit, MI: Detroit Free Press, 1869) 12.

29 W.A. McEwen and A.H. Lewis, *Encyclopedia of Nautical Knowledge* (Cambridge, MA: Cornell Maritime Press, 1953) 101. Elmer Ambrose Sperry was born in Courtland, New York, on Oct. 12, 1860, and died June 16, 1930. He is credited with inventing the Gyroscopic Compass, Patent Number 1,242,065.

30 "History of the Development of the Life Preserver," (unpublished), U.S. Coast Guard, 1943, a page of photocopied material mailed to the author by the U.S. Coast Guard.

31 James C. Mills, *Our Inland Seas: Their Shipping & Commerce for Three Centuries* (Cleveland, OH: Freshwater Press Inc., 1976) 109. Originally published by A.C. McClurg & Co. of Chicago, Illinois, in 1910.

32 Paul Hancock, *Shipwrecks of the Great Lakes* (London: PRC Publishing Ltd., 2001) 20.

33 Mills List, *Frances Smith*, Mills Number: [018870], Maritime Museum, Kingston. Taken from www.marmus.ca/dbtw-wpd/exec/dbtwpub.dll, accessed January 28, 2005.

34 There is a local legend that in 1863, Captain W.H. Smith, by cunning and persistence, convinced the government of Canada West (Ontario) to dredge the harbour of Owen Sound. The Sydenham River flowed into the harbour and often

created a bar (or sandbar), blocking navigation to the town site. This obstacle was of considerable inconvenience to the community, as large vessels with deep draft had to dock outside the town. If the government of Canada West could be convinced that the river was at least sometimes navigable, they would have to assume responsibility for dredging the harbour for the port of Owen Sound.

Apparently Captain Smith maneouvred his boat (sometimes it was claimed to be the *Clifton* while at other times it was the *Canadian*) to the far side of the bar, whereupon he had his crew carry the anchor toward the town. He then started a donkey engine to winch his boat over the bar towards a pool of water in the river behind the bar. After repeatedly performing the action, his vessel was dragged into the river to float freely in the pool.

He reportedly took a photo of the ship in the pool. The vessel was turned around and winched back into the outer harbour, using barrels and logs to roll the boat back over the bar. He then personally took the photo to government officials in Ottawa to prove that they had a responsibility to improve Owen Sound's inadequate harbour. As the legend has it, the government was forced to assume the responsibility for funding subsequent dredging in 1860. He, therefore, gained access to his dock at the edge of town.

In 1860, the harbour was dredged to a depth of twelve feet and one hundred feet wide in 1860 at a cost of $25,000. The government contributed $12,000. It now was possible for vessels to move into a basin near the swing bridge at the centre of town. See W. Wye Smith, *Gazetteer of the County of Grey for the Year 1865–6* (Toronto: Globe Stream Press, 1865) 237.

Despite an exhaustive search of newspapers of the day, no evidence has been found to corroborate the legend. Most local "historians" know the legend and are able to spin a great story around the event. The story has been retold without documentation in several well-known books about the Georgian Bay.

35   *The Thunder Bay Sentinel* (Prince Arthur's Landing), May 18, 1876.

36   *The Duluth Minnesotan*, Nov. 22, 1873.

37   *The Thunder Bay Sentinel* (Prince Arthur's Landing), Nov. 19, 1880.

38   Ibid.

39   Ibid.

40   John Weichel, *Forgotten Times*, Volume 2 (Southampton, ON: Bruce County Museum & Archives, n.d.) 421.

2 CAPTAIN W.H. SMITH ARRIVES ON GEORGIAN BAY

1   Captain W.H. Smith was born on May 7, 1826. He and his wife Frances Eberts had seven children: Henry Eberts, Charlotte Cornelia, Annie (died in infancy), Frances Jane Brodie, Elisa Louisa Isabella (died at age three), Horace Bruce and William Henry. Information is from personal communication with Phillip Smith, great-grandson of William Henry Smith.

2   Taken from the obituary of W.H. Smith in *The Owen Sound Times,* Nov. 10, 1871. The Eberts family owned the *Ploughboy* in 1851 and sold it to Thomas F.

Park in 1854 according to the official records. There were three Park brothers, John R., Theodore J., and Thomas. They were very well-to-do businessmen in the Windsor area and owned several ships. There is a Park House Museum in Amherstburg. Ontario, with a collection of Park family memorabilia.

3   At the time the Bruce Peninsula was called the Indian Peninsula, the Saugeen Peninsula and sometimes the Ojibway Peninsula. Newspapers of the time called it the Indian Peninsula. According to *Place Names of Ontario,* the "Ojibway called it Saugink or Sauking, hence the name Saugeen Peninsula, which was often used in the early part of the 20th Century. It had earlier been known as the Indian Peninsula." See Alan Rayburn, *Place Names of Ontario* (Toronto: University of Toronto Press, 1997) 46.

4   *The Chatham Planet,* Dec. 20, 1855, quoted in Hancock, *Forgotten Times,* 418. The original newsletters were called *Bruce Coast Fo'cs'le* and were published from November 1992 to May 1996.

5   Hancock, *Forgotten Times*, 421.

6   *The Northern Advance* (Barrie), Jan. 31, 1856.

7   Ibid.

8.   William Gibbard was of the area, having lived in both Barrie and Collingwood for awhile. A surveyor, he laid out the town of Thornbury. He also had an exceptional town plan for Collingwood, modelled on that of Bath, England. He was appointed inspector of fisheries in Georgian Bay by the government of Upper Canada and looked after delivering treaty money to the Indians of Manitoulin Island. He was murdered by persons unknown. W.H. Smith conducted the inquest.

9   F. Charles Thompson was a businessman who was reported in the Barrie newspapers as being involved with the syndicate.

10   *The Northern Advance* (Barrie), Feb. 21, 1856.

11   Ibid, April 23, 1857.

12   *The Barrie Herald*, April 22, 1857.

13   From the *Bruce Coast Fo'c'sle*, Number 57, May 1996, published in Southampton. Butterworth eventually went to work for Captain Smith, and was the master of the *Clifton* during the summer of 1866 while Smith was preparing for the construction of the *Frances Smith*. (Butterworth died of a heart attack on board the *Clifton* in September 1866. From *The Owen Sound Comet*, September 14, 1866.)

   A week later the *Clifton* was in an accident with the schooner *Restless.* The vessel had run aground in Owen Sound harbour and a rope was placed across the river to secure it for the night. As the *Clifton* steamed past the *Restless*, she caught the rope and swung the schooner about. The bowsprit of the schooner was destroyed and damage was inflicted to her hull. The *Clifton* had her cookhouse smashed.

14   *The Barrie Herald*, May 21, 1857.

15   R.C. Plumb, "The 1857 Depression on the Lakes," in *Inland Seas*, Vol. 10.4 (1954) 290–91. *Inland Seas* is the periodical of The Great Lakes Historical Society, published in Vermilion, Ohio.

16   R.C. Plumb, in "The 1857 Depression on the Lakes," was referring to William
      Smith's steamer line that was chartered by the Northern Railway (officially
      known as the Ontario, Simcoe and Huron Union Railway). Frederic William
      Cumberland was born in London, England, in 1820. He lived in Toronto after
      coming to Canada in 1848. He was the driving force behind the construction of
      the railway. In 1855, he chartered five ships from the United States Lake Supe-
      rior Line to run three times per week from Collingwood to Chicago and weekly
      to Green Bay, Wisconsin. He had calculated that he could deliver freight from
      New York to Chicago for less than any U.S. railroad and less than existing Cana-
      dian railways. The ships were the *Lady Elgin*, *Montgomery*, *Ontanogon*, *Hunter*
      and *Niagara*. He lost money on the both railway and the steamer service that
      year and again in 1856. The company ended up in receivership in 1859.
           Meanwhile, W.H. Smith was providing his ferry service from Owen Sound
      to Collingwood with his steamer, the *Canadian* (later replaced by the *Clifton*), sail-
      ing under the under the flag of the Collingwood Line. Cumberland reorganized
      the Northern Railway and, by 1862, was again ready to charter ships. However,
      the whole plan was scuttled because of the Civil War and the shortage of vessels
      available for charter. Instead, he negotiated with an American firm to haul freight
      from Collingwood to Chicago. See Dana Ashdown, *Railway Steamships of Ontario*
      (Erin, ON: Boston Mills Press, 1988) 39–40. At the same time, Smith's ship was
      chartered by the Collingwood Line to haul freight along the southern shore of
      Georgian Bay from the Northern Railway's terminal at Collingwood.

17   Plumb, "The 1857 Depression on the Lakes," 290–91.

18   Grey County Registry Office, Owen Sound, Ontario, "Report of the Standing
      Committee on Finance," Grey County Council, Spring 1858.

19   Ibid, November Session, 1858, 73.

20   *The Barrie Herald*, May 21, 1857.

21   Grey Roots, Grey County Archival Collection, "Owen Sound Council Records
      of 1859–60."

      22   *The Kingston Daily News*, Oct. 10, 1859, taken from www.hhpl.on.ca/scripts/-
      as_web.exe?KingNews+D+1467725, accessed on July 12, 2003.

23   Peter Fuller's Diary, entry for September 29, 1859, unpublished. Peter Fuller's Diary
      is in the private collection of Stanley Knight Limited, Meaford, Ontario. Fuller
      arrived in Meaford in 1852 and became a sawmill owner and community leader.

24   *The Leader* (Toronto), July 5, 1859.

25   A "walking beam" was a metal structure mounted on the top deck and was driven
      by a piston from the engine in the hold. Metal rods, were attached to this beam
      which rocked ("walked") back and forth. The rods were attached to a crank
      which in turn was attached to the paddlewheels that drove the ship.

26   *The Weekly Chronicle & News* (Kingston), July 8 1859, taken from
      www.hhpl.on.ca/Great Lakes/Scripts/News/Article.asp?ID=15084, accessed on
      June 15, 2005.

27   *The Owen Sound Comet*, Aug. 23, 1860.

28   Author's note: Information accessed on July 15, 2003, at http://129.1.59.220/cgi-win/lak952.exe differs from the 92-foot length source mentioned in Kingston Maritime Museum. I believe the length to be 187 feet.

29   The logbook of the *Clifton* is located in the Grey Roots Archival Collection, Owen Sound, Ontario.

3 ECONOMIC PROSPECTS AROUND GEORGIAN BAY, 1865

1   From a speech by William Henry Seward, October 25, 1858. Seward was speaking about the problem of slavery in the United States when he stated, "It is an irrepressible conflict between opposing and enduring forces, and it means that the United States must and will, sooner or later, become either entirely a slave-holding nation, or entirely a free-labor nation." He was in fact predicting the Civil War three years before it began. He was a member of the U.S. Senate and was the unsuccessful candidate for the Presidency in 1860 against Abraham Lincoln. He later served in Lincoln's cabinet.

2   William Wye Smith, *Gazetteer and Directory of the County of Grey for the Year 1865–6* (Toronto: Globe Steam Press, 1865) 215.

3   *The Owen Sound Comet*, Oct. 11, 1861.

4   For a discussion on the rivalry between Owen Sound and Collingwood and the evils plaguing a new community, see Paul White, *Owen Sound: The Port City* (Toronto: Natural Heritage Books, 2000) chapters 18 and 19.

5   The Harrison brothers (John, William and Robert) arrived in Owen Sound in the 1840s and by the 1850s had set up their businesses along the Sydenham River where the Mill Dam is located today. One of the legacies of the family is the expansive Harrison Park in Owen Sound, Ontario.

6   Pearl ash or potash was derived from the ashes of burned wood and was used in the making of soap.

7   Mr. W.C. Boyd was a pioneer entrepreneur and merchant in Owen Sound when he built his wharf in 1844 near the present-day Bayshore Arena. The wharf, constructed so he could receive supplies for his local businesses, remained the major deepwater wharf for Owen Sound for two decades, even after the harbour was initially dredged in 1860. For more on W.C. Boyd see, Paul White, *Owen Sound: The Port City*, chapters 4 and 7.

8   The unpublished Frank Harding papers in the Meaford Library were the source for much of the information about Meaford. See also, *St. Vincent: A Beautiful Land*, published in 2004 by the St. Vincent Heritage Association of Thornbury, Ontario.

9   Cyrus R. Sing was born in Ireland, then emigrated to Canada where he initially lived in Prince Edward County. In the 1860s, he and his brother James moved to St. Vincent Township. His bother left, but Cyrus remained and became a major land developer and politician in the area. The village of Singhampton near Collingwood was named for him.

10   Information for this section was obtained from reading Collingwood and Simcoe County newspapers for 1865 (*The Northern Advance, The Collingwood Enterprise, The Collingwood Daily Review, The Examiner, South Simcoe News*).

11   The Indian name *Shebahonaning* was still in common use in 1865 and would remain so for another decade before the hamlet was renamed Killarney.

12   Ontario Heritage Foundation, Government of Ontario Plaque, Little Current. Viewed on site 2004.

13   Cornishmen were miners with extensive experience gleaned from working the tin mines in Cornwall, England. They were the obvious choice for a new mining operation. Although conditions at Bruce Mines were not particularly good they were better than those back in the depressed mining communities in Cornwall.

4 THE CONSTRUCTION OF THE *FRANCES SMITH*

1   *The Kingston Daily News*, Mar 13, 1865. Taken from www.hhpl.on.ca/Great-Lakes/Scripts/News/Article.asp?ID=15377, accessed on December 24, 2004.

2   Gerry Ouderkirk, "The Shipbuilding Simpsons," unpublished, 1987. Gerry Ouderkirk is an amateur historian, tugboat enthusiast and captain on the Toronto Island Ferry. Author's Note: It was Gerry who got me started on this quest of the *Frances Smith*. We have exchanged much communication over the years.

3   Fred Landon, *Lake Huron: The American Lakes Series* (Indianapolis, IN: Bobs-Merrill Company, 1944) 308.

4   Author's Note: According to Patrick Labadie, this was the name given to this structure. The modern term is pilothouse. Throughout the text "pilothouse" and "wheelhouse" are used interchangeably.

5   *The Owen Sound Comet*, May 3, 1867.

6   A "sett of colours" was given to every ship upon launching to be flown as a ship identifier. In essence it was the ship's flag.

7   *The Daily Leader* (Toronto), May 1, 1867.

8   *The Owen Sound Comet*, May 3, 1867.

9   Ibid.

10   *Ibid,* May 17, 1867.

11   If you are a relative of one of the deceased members of the village or of St. Vincent Township and have a gravesite to visit, you may be able to gain access by contacting the military base at Land Force Central Training Area, Camp Meaford.

12   *The Owen Sound Comet*, May 31, 1867.

5 AGROUND IN GEORGIAN BAY

1   *The Trilogy* (Owen Sound), Jan. 21, 1976.

2   Andrea Gutsche *et al.*, *Alone in the Night* (Toronto: Lynx Images, 1996) 113.

3   The original map by Captain Bayfield and the updated 1863 map are located in the British Museum, London, U.K.

4   *The Kingston Daily News*, Dec. 1, 1868, taken from www.hhpl.on.ca/scripts/-as_web.exe?KingNews+D+3380633, accessed on July 10, 2003.

5   Ibid, Dec. 18, 1868, taken from www.hhpl.on.ca/scripts/as_web.exe?-KingNews+D+3391539, accessed on July 10, 2003.

6   Ibid, Nov. 30, 1868, taken from www.hhpl.on.ca/GreatLakes/Scripts/News/Article.asp?ID=15568, accessed on Dec. 24, 2004.

7   *The Barrie Examiner*, May 6, 1869.

8   *The Trilogy* (Owen Sound), Jan. 21, 1976.

9   *The Chicago Tribune*, May 7, 1869. The Campbell & Owen shipyard soon after became the Detroit Drydock Company, one of America's most innovative Great Lakes shipbuilding yards.

10   *The Meaford Monitor*, May 7, 1869.

11   Ibid, June 4, 1869.

12   Ibid, June 18, 1869.

13   Ibid.

14   Ibid, Sept. 10, 1869.

6 THE RED RIVER AFFAIR

1   Not to be confused with Thomas Scott, mayor of Owen Sound and later Member of Parliament, this Thomas Scott was born in Ireland and came to Canada West in 1863. He was an active Orangeman and member of the 49th Hastings Battalion of Rifles. He eventually ended up working as one of the Simon Dawson's men, building a road to the Red River, but was fired for leading a strike. While unemployed, he came under the influence of John Schultz, the leader of a small Anglophone party that advocated annexation of the Red River to Canada. Because of his resistance to Riel's Métis movement, Riel imprisoned him along with a number of other men. He escaped prison only to be captured again by the Métis. In prison he insulted his captors who took him outside Fort Garry and beat him. He was subsequently tried for insubordination and shot by firing squad. Orangemen across Ontario demanded that the government of Canada avenge his "murder" and stop the Red River from falling into the popish influence of the Métis and their Catholic leaders. See *Dictionary of Canadian Biography*, Vol. IX, (Toronto: University of Toronto Press, 1976) 707.

2   George F.G. Stanley, *Toil & Trouble: Military Expedition to Red River* (Toronto: Dundurn Press, 1989) 85–86.

3   *The Owen Sound Advertiser,* as reported in *The Meaford Monitor*, April 14, 1870.

4   *The Meaford Monitor*, April 21, 1870.

5   An observation given on Smith's character on occasion of his death, *The Owen Sound Times*, Nov. 10, 1871.

6   *The Meaford Monitor*, April 21, 1870.

7   For rates see Appendix 1.

8   Garnet Joseph Wolseley was born in 1833 in Ireland. He had served in the Crimea, as well as India and China, before being posted to Canada in 1861. He was promoted to the rank of colonel in 1865 and was recognized as a superb organizer. After commanding the 1870 expedition to the Red River, he returned to England and subsequently served in Africa. See *Dictionary of Canadian Biography*, Vol. XIV (Toronto: University of Toronto Press, 1998) 1077.

9   Stanley, *Toil & Trouble*, 91.

10 Ibid, 95.

11 James Barry, "The Wolseley Expedition Crosses the Great Lakes," in *Inland Seas*, 1968, Vol. 24.2, 95.

12 Taken from www.mhs.mb.ca/docs/transactions/3/unitedstatesredriver.shtml., accessed on May 23, 2004.

13 Ibid.

14 Stanley, *Toil & Trouble*, 98.

15 Taken from www.shingwauk.auc.ca/Wilson_MissWork/MissWork_Chapter_9.html, accessed on Oct. 17, 2004.

16 Captain G.L. Huyshe, *The Red River Expedition* (Toronto: Macmillan, 1871) 32.

17 Taken from Barlow Cumberland, *A Century of Sail and Steam on the Niagara River* (Toronto: The Musson Book Company Limited, 1913) online at www.hhpl.on.ca/GreatLakes/Documents/Cumberland/default.asp?ID=co11#p1 89, accessed on Oct. 20, 2004.

18 Report of the Committee of the Privy Council, January 28, 1870.

19 Rev. Edward F. Wilson, *Missionary Work among the Ojibway*, 1886. Project Gutenberg online book at www.gutenberg.org/etext/6983, accessed March 25, 2005.

20 *The Meaford Monitor,* May 19, 1870.

21 *The Owen Sound Advertiser*, May 26, 1870.

22 *The Globe* of May 23, 1871, claimed that Collingwood was transformed from a "dreamy quiet town" into a "miniature Chicago."

23 *The Owen Sound Advertiser*, May 26, 1870.

24 The 60th Rifles were well-equipped, especially trained regular soldiers under the command of the British. They had rifles rather than smooth-bore muskets and wore snappy, dark green uniforms. Attached to them were members of the Royal Artillery, Royal Engineers and an Army Service Corps. From Stanley, *Toil & Trouble*, 84.

25 *The Owen Sound Advertiser*, May 26, 1870.

26 James Barry, "The Wolseley Expedition crosses the Great Lakes," in *Inland Seas,* 1968, Vol. 24.2, 101.

27 *The Meaford Monitor*, June 2, 1870.

28 James Barry, "The Wolseley Expedition," 101.

29 *The Meaford Monitor*, June 2, 1870.

30 Letter from Captain Smith to Lieutenant Colonel Boulton, May 24, 1870. Captain Smith's concerns regarding his ship may have been coloured by the fact that there was a genuine fear of Fenians and their potential "terrorist" actions against Canadian targets. Both the Owen Sound and Collingwood newspapers, as well as *The Globe* in Toronto, carried long articles about Fenian dangers between 1867 and 1870. In Owen Sound the militia trained for the invasion and at Collingwood a battery of three guns was set up to protect the harbour, *The Owen Sound Comet,* June 7, 1867. Referenced in "Correspondence Relative to the Recent Expedition to the Red River Settlement with Journal of Operations," Presented to

the Houses of Parliament by Command of Her Majesty, 1871, London, Harrison and Sons, 1871. Located at Library and Archives Canada (LAC), Edward Harrison fonds, R7772-0-6-E, 31.

31   Provincial Archives of Manitoba, MG6 A-1, Walsh Papers, "Journal of Advance party of Mounted Police under J.M. Walsh."

32   *The Owen Sound Times*, Oct. 24, 1873.

33   Ibid.

7   ABOARD A PALACE STEAMER IN THE 1870s–80s

1   *The Collingwood Enterprise*, quoted in *The Owen Sound Advertiser*, Aug. 11, 1881.

2   *The Owen Sound Advertiser,* Aug. 11, 1881.

3   Ibid, July 10, 1884.

4   Taken from www.gutenberg.org./etext/7099, accessed on June 20, 2005. Title: A Trip to Manitoba; Author: Mary FitzGibbon (1851–1915). Release Date: December 2004, [EBook #7099].

5   In the 1860s aboard the *Clifton*, Captain Smith did record the names of his passengers, possibly because there were so few.

6   *The Globe* (Toronto), Aug. 1, 1878.

7   The *Clifton* made a total of 161 trips between Owen Sound and Collingwood in 1862, 136 trips in 1863 and 141 trips in 1864. Information is from the logbook of the *Clifton*, housed at Grey Roots, Owen Sound, Ontario.

8   *The Meaford Monitor*, July 25, 1872.

9   Sir Sandford Fleming (1827–1915) was born in Kirkaldy, Scotland. He immigrated to Canada and settled in the Peterborough area of Ontario. Later, as an engineer and surveyor, he worked with Frederic Cumberland to develop the Ontario, Simcoe and Huron Union Railway (Northern Railroad). The two fell out of friendship and parted ways. Fleming went on to become the engineer-in-chief of Canada's Intercolonial Railway until 1876. His extensive travels on Canadian railways made him realize the importance of standardizing time to resolve the confusion of local time systems in North America and Europe. To that end he devoted much of his efforts in the 1880s until the concept of standard time was universally accepted.

10   Rev. George M. Grant, *Ocean to Ocean: Sir Sandford Fleming's Expedition Through Canada in 1872* (Toronto: James Campbell and Son, 1873) 13–27.

11   Ibid.

12   "An Early Manitoba Diary: Extracts from J.W. Harris's Private Account of Events and Personalities," taken from www.mhs.mb.ca/docs/transactions/3/manitoba-diary.shtml, accessed on May 5, 2004.

13   *The Renfrew Mercury*, Aug. 14, 1874.

14   Ibid, Aug. 21, 1874.

15   *The Owen Sound Advertiser*, May 1, 1873.

16   The Smiths and Robertsons purchased the *Silver Spray* in 1874.

17   *The Owen Sound Advertiser*, December 5, 1872.

18   Ibid, May 1, 1873.

19   Members of the British press included: Mr. Sydney Hall, *London Graphic*; Mr. Austin, *London Times*; Mr. Charles Roche, *London News*; Mr. McFarlane, *Edinburgh Scotsman*.

20   *The Morning Herald* (Halifax), July 11, 1881.

21   *The Quebec Chronicle*, July 19, 1881.

22   *The Globe* (Toronto), July 23, 1881.

23   W.H. Williams, *Manitoba and the North West: Journal of a Trip* (Toronto: Hunter Rose & Company, 1882) 11.

24   Ibid.

25   Ibid, 14.

26   *The Globe* (Toronto), July 30, 1881.

27   Williams, *Manitoba and the North West*, 15.

28   Chief Shingwauk (1773–1854) fought alongside the British in the War of 1812. As a respected Ojibwe chief, he developed a strategy to protect Aboriginal rights and governance. This strategy included the development of "Teaching Wigwams" in which European and First Nation traditional knowledge would be synthesized. On his death he was succeeded by Chief Augustin Shingwauk (1800–1890) who, along with missionary Edward Wilson, started the Shingwauk Home for Native children at Garden River, Ontario. In 1774, the Shingwauk residential school, named in honour of the earlier chief and operated by the Anglican Church, was set up just east of Sault Ste. Marie, Ontario. The school closed in 1970 and the land is now the home of Algoma University. Taken from www.shingwauk.auc.ca/shingwauktrust/shingwauktrust2.html, accessed on May 31, 2005.

29   Williams, *Manitoba and the North West*, 16.

30   *The Thunder Bay Sentinel* (Port Arthur's Landing), July 29, 1881.

31   Ibid.

32   Williams, *Manitoba and the North West*, 17.

33   Silver Islet, on the northwest corner of Lake Superior, was the world's richest silver mine in the 1870s. By the mid-1880s the mine was closed because it was no longer profitable. During its brief but productive history, the mine was subject to constant flooding during Superior's violent storms. At one time there were over 170 men, many of them Cornish, employed on the tiny island mine.

34   Williams, *Manitoba and the North West*, 17.

35   *The Duluth Tribune*, July 29, 1881.

36   Ibid.

37   Ibid.

38   *The Meaford Monitor*, July 2, 1869.

39   Ibid.

40   *The Collingwood Bulletin*, Aug. 30, 1871.

41   *The Owen Sound Advertiser*, Sept. 14, 1871.

42   Ibid.

43   *The Detroit Daily Post*, Sept. 2, 1871, as reported in *The Owen Sound Advertiser*, Sept. 14, 1871

44   *The Meaford Monitor*, Sept. 14, 1871.

45 Ibid.

46 Government of Ontario Death Register, MS 935 Reel 2, Record 1449471. See also *Burial Records*, St. George's Anglican Church, Owen Sound, November 1871.

47 It is interesting to note that there is no record of the burial at Greenwood Cemetery in Owen Sound, but W.H. Smith's gravestone clearly notes his burial there, as do the local papers.

48 *The Owen Sound Times*, June 28, 1878.

49 *The Meaford Monitor*, July 5, 1878.

50 Ibid.

51 With apologies to Stephen Leacock. Stephen Leacock (1869–1944) was first of all an academic. A professor of economics at McGill University in Montreal, he began writing parodies and satire in the early 20th century and was acclaimed for his delightfully witty and humorous sketches of a small town in Ontario. Leacock's fictional Mariposa is generally accepted as being based on the town of Orillia. An award for the best humorous book by a Canadian is made annually in his name.

52 *The Meaford Monitor*, June 21, 1878.

53 Ibid.

54 Ibid, July 5, 1878.

55 See Stephen Leacock, "The Marine Excursions of the Knights of Pythias," in *Sunshine Sketches of a Little Town* (Toronto: McClelland & Stewart, 1948) 65–94.

56 *The Owen Sound Times*, June 29, 1893.

8 THE GREAT STORM OF '75

1 *The Meaford Monitor*, Oct. 26, 1875.

2 Roderick Cunningham, *Algoma Central Corporation: The Centennial History 1899–1999* (Sault Ste. Marie, ON: Algoma Central Corporation, 1999) 72.

3 The McGuffins, in their beautiful book, *Superior: Journeys on an Inland Sea* (Erin, ON: Boston Mills Press, 1995), relate the story of how Nanabijou buried the silver deposits away from the white man's lust for precious metal and how Nanabijou was finally turned to stone to become the Sleeping Giant.

4 Val Eichenlaub, *Weather and Climate of the Great Lakes Region* (Notre Dame, IN: Notre Dame Press, 1979) 287.

5 Standard time in time zones began in Canada and the United States in November 1883, and became official in Canada in January 1885. Before then, time was a local matter regulated by the town clock or some jeweller's clock in a shop window.

6 David G. Brown, *White Hurricane: A Great Lakes November Gale and America's Deadliest Maritime Disaster* (Camden, ME: Ragged Mountain Press/McGraw-Hill, 2002) 12.

7 Ibid, 6, 7.

8 The barometer from the *Frances Smith* is preserved at Grey Roots Museum Collection, Owen Sound, Ontario.

9 "Record of Shipments" made from Owen Sound Harbour 1874–76, Grey Roots, Archival Collection, Owen Sound, Ontario.

10   Bob Whittier, *Paddle Wheel Steamers and Their Engines* (Duxbury, MA: Seamaster Boats Inc., 1983) 23.

11   Captain William Fitzwilliam Owen (1774–1857) of the Royal Navy sailed his schooner, the *Huron*, within 14 kilometres (about nine miles) of Owen Sound during his survey of the region in 1815. His family's names are sprinkled around the southern shore of Georgian Bay. Included in the list are Cape Rich, Fitzwilliam Island and Owen Sound.

12   "Public Instrument of Protest," sworn before Charles Gaumon of Collingwood, Nov. 11, 1875, by James Christopher Orr, master of the *Cumberland*, hereinafter referred to as Public Instrument of Protest.

13   Ibid.

14   *The Meaford Monitor*, Nov. 12, 1875.

15   Public Instrument of Protest.

16   *The Owen Sound Advertiser*, April 24, 1873.

17   *The Meaford Monitor*, Nov. 19, 1875.

18   Ibid.

19   Brown, *White Hurricane*, 140.

20   Andrea Gutsche and Cindy Bisaillon, *Mysterious Islands: Forgotten Tales of the Great Lakes* (Toronto: Lynx Images, 1999) 245.

21   Taken from www.terrypepper.com/lights/superior/menagerie, accessed on Feb. 16, 2003.

22   *The Meaford Monitor*, Nov. 19, 1875.

23   Ibid.

24   Ibid.

25   *The Thunder Bay Sentinel* (Port Arthur's Landing), Nov. 4, 1875. Reported in *The Owen Sound Advertiser*, Nov. 11, 1875.

26   *The Owen Sound Advertiser,* Nov. 11, 1875. The complete poem by Alex Speers is presented here:

CHRISTMAS ADDRESS   (To His Friends and Patrons)
On Lake Superior's stormy wave,
The Frances Smith was toss'd,
Her timbers creaked, her decks gave way,
And all gave up for lost.

The cattle overboard were thrown,
Our sheep and all were drowned,
While crates of fowl with ducks and geese
Were swimming all around.

Our Loss, 'tis true, was very great
To sink beneath the wave,
But all was done our ship to right,

The human lives to save.
A year of storms and wreck of ships,
When many lives were lost,
But Christmas comes with its good cheer,
And finds us at our post.

Year after year we still are here,
You all know where to go
To get the best that can be got
For every Christmas show.

In Beef we always do excel,
Our Princess is the best,
Just come and see her pedigree
She beats out all the rest.

Some twenty head of Cattle
As fat as fat can be
With flocks of Sheep and Lambs
Just come along and see.

Prize Pork and Sausage, all you want,
Turkeys and Geese this way,
Ducks and Chickens, first Stall to right,
Please do not go astray.

Just come around and see our Bear,
T'will neither scratch nor bite,
We paid the money brought him here
That you might have a sight.

Our hearty thanks to all our friends,
For kindness in the past,
Your orders now we want to fill
And long may favorites last.

And when around your board,
At Christmas and New Years,
Please don't forget your thanks to give,
And still remember Speers.

27 *The Owen Sound Advertiser*, May 4, 1876.
28 Ibid.

9 SERIOUS CHALLENGES

1   Frederic William Cumberland (1820–1881) was a British architect and engineer who, after moving to Canada, designed many of Toronto's well-known buildings of the 1850s. His interests also included the development of railways and he became the manager of the Ontario, Simcoe and Huron Union Railway.

2   Dana Ashdown, *Railway Steamships of Ontario, 1850–1950* (Erin, ON: Boston Mills Press, 1988) 41.

3   *The Owen Sound Advertiser*, July 31, 1873.

4   The National Policy was developed as early as 1876 by the Conservative Party. The policy was implemented in 1878 with the re-election of John A. Macdonald. It continued to evolve for several years as a high tariff policy and as a policy supporting infrastructure in Canada such as railways.

5   Horace Greeley (1811–1872) launched the *New York Tribune* in 1841. Through his paper he advocated free government land to settlers who would "Go West."

6   LAC, RG17, Vol. 162, Docket 16884, Montreal Telegraph Company, Fred Cumberland to John Lowe.

7   *The Globe* (Toronto), July 11, 1878.

8   *The Meaford Monitor,* May 4, 1871.

9   *The Northern Advance* (Barrie), June 3, 1875.

10 Ibid, Aug. 23, 1877.

11 Richard Palmer, "The Age of Sail Ended On Ontario," in *Inland Seas*, Vol. 46, (Winter 1990) 6–10.

12 W.R. Wightman, "The Canadian steam packet service of the upper lakes," in *Inland Seas*, Vol. 46:4 (1990), 254.

13 *The Meaford Monitor*, Aug. 9, 1878.

14 Robert Passfield (Sheila Ascroft ed.), *Technology in Transition: The 'Soo' Ship Canal 1889–1995* (Ottawa: published under the Authority of the Minister of the Environment, 1989) 14.

15 In Tate Robertson's letters to his older brother Alex, he often wrote about his walks on the deck and chats with charming "ladies." He played court whist with them in the saloons, sang with them around the piano and invited some to dine quietly in the dining room before bedtime. In one letter dated August 27, 1877, he claimed, "I am in love with about fifty...splendid ladies." Letters cited are in the Stuart Robertson Collection.

16 Letter, Tate Robertson to Alex Robertson, dated Jan. 27, 1874.

17 *The Owen Sound Advertiser*, April 24, 1873.

18 Ibid, Dec. 8, 1874.

19 Ibid, August 27, 1877.

20 *The Owen Sound Times*, April 5, 1877.

21 Letter from Tate Robertson to Alex Robertson, dated Dec. 2, 1878.

22 Ibid, Dec. 13, 1879.

23 Ibid, Sept. 22, 1881.

24 Ibid, Sept. 25, 1881.

25 Craig Heron, *Booze: A Distilled History* (Toronto: Between the Lines, 2003) 136.

26 *The Manitoulin Expositor* (Little Current), May 14, 1881.

27 "Montana" Charlie Wallace, originally the chief of police in Michipicoten, became the leader of an outlaw gang that included prison fugitives from the United States and Canada. See Harold Horwood and Edward Butts, *Pirates and Outlaws of Canada* (Toronto: Doubleday, 1984) 198. See also Pierre Berton, *The Last Spike: The Great Railway 1881–1885* (Toronto: McClelland & Stewart, 1971) 278–79.

28 *The Globe* (Toronto), Nov. 4, 1884.

29 Ibid.

30 *The Duluth Tribune*, July 22, 1881.

31 Ibid.

32 *The Meaford Monitor*, July 29, 1881.

33 *The Bulletin* (Collingwood), Sept. 28, 1881.

34 Ron Beaupre, "Ship of the Month," *The Scanner*, The Monthly News Bulletin of the Toronto Marine Historical Society, Vol. XIX, No. 6, 6.

35 *The Northern Advance* (Barrie), Nov. 3, 1881.

36 *The Owen Sound Advertiser*, Dec. 1, 1881.

37 Ibid, Dec. 13, 1881.

38 *The Meaford Monitor,* Nov. 7, 1881.

39 Ibid.

40 *The Herald and Lake Superior Journal* (Port Arthur), May 16, 1882.

41 *The Enterprise* (Collingwood), April 27, 1882.

10 DELIVERING THE ROYAL MAIL

1 Robert Parsons, *Steamboat Mail in Eastern Canada* (Waterdown, ON: Bill Longley Auctions, 1995) Chapter 5.

2 *The Meaford Monitor*, Jan. 15, 1872.

3 See Appendix E for a chart showing the dates of post office openings along the shores of Georgian Bay and Lake Superior.

4 LAC, RG2, Privy Council Office, Series A-1-d, Volume 6270, Reel 3300.

5 James and Henry Beatty had lumbering and steamer interests in Georgian Bay. They decided to establish a steam-passenger line at Sarnia in 1871.

6 The Collingwood Line had to promise business people of Hamilton and London that they would have the same through rates as businesses in Toronto in order to protect their right to handle the traffic through Lake Huron to Lake Superior.

7 LAC, RG3, B4, Volume 104, Reel 2267, 161, Matthew Sweetham to Postmaster General (PMG), July 6, 1875.

8 The *Cumberland* was built in 1872 to replace the aging *Algoma*, which had been built in 1839.

9 The Privy Council extended the route to include Duluth in 1873.

10 LAC, RG3, B4, Volume 104, Reel 2267, 161, Sweetham to PMG, July 6, 1875.

11 The office of the Postmaster General was in a bit of confusion in 1875. When the Hon. Donald Alexander Macdonald stepped down from the position on May 17, 1875, the post of PMG was left vacant for two days until the Hon. Telephone Fournier was appointed on May 19, 1875. He was only temporary and lasted until Oct. 7, 1875, whereupon Hon. Lucius Seth Huntington replaced him two days later.

12 LAC, RG3, B4, Volume 104, Reel 2267, 161, Sweetham to PMG dated July 6 1875.

13 LAC, RG3, B4, Volume 104, Reel 2267, 208, Sweetham to PMG, dated July 29, 1875.

14 Ibid.

15 LAC, RG3, B4, Volume 104, Reel 2267, 223. Sweetham to PMG, dated Aug. 17, 1875. In this correspondence, Sweetham tells the PMG what is contained in letters he sent and received to/from Robertson.

16 Postal Inspector Matthew Sweetham calculated that on some runs it cost $1.75 to deliver a letter with a three-cent postage stamp.

17 By this time James Beatty of Sarnia was on the Board of the Great Northern Transit Company.

18 Cockburn Island is located to the east of False Detour Channel and west of Manitoulin Island. Today the island is deserted except for a few summer cottages and a small Ojibwe First Nation Reserve. In the 1880s, there were almost one thousand permanent residents. As the lumber that sustained the community gave out and the steamers stopped running in 1963, people moved away because of the isolation.

19 LAC, RG3, B4, Volume 110, Reel 2270, 87, Sweetham to PMG, dated May 25, 1885.

20 LAC, RG3, Series D, Volume 112, Reel 2271, 709, Sweetham to PMG, dated Sept. 16, 1885.

21 LAC, RG3, B4, Series D, Volume 112, Reel 2271, 934, Robertson to PMG, dated April 22, 1886.

22 Ibid, W. Tate Robertson to PMG, April 22, 1886.

23 Ibid, W. Sweetham to PMG, May 7, 1886.

24 *The Owen Sound Advertiser*, Nov. 17, 1887.

11 TROUBLES ON THE LAKES

1 *The Enterprise* (Collingwood), July 20, 1882.

2 *The Meaford Monitor*, Oct. 13, 1883.

3 *The Herald* (Port Arthur), Sept. 23, 1882.

4 According to *The British Whig Standard* of Kingston (Sept. 19), McGregor got to Owen Sound from Collingwood on the 16th. Upon hearing about the *Asia* tragedy, he boarded a tug and reached Parry Sound on September 17. He passed the Limestone Islands en route and found a trunk from the *Asia*. Apparently Captain McGregor lost his son on the *Asia*. He must have returned to Owen Sound by the 20th in order to arrive in Duluth on board the *Frances Smith* by September 22.

5   *The Herald* (Port Arthur), Sept. 23, 1882.

6   Ibid.

7   The navigation season for 1883 was a disaster, according to J.B. Mansfield (ed.), "Great Lakes, 1896," in *History of the Great Lakes*, Vol. 1 (Chicago: J.H. Beers & Co., 1899): "53 vessels were a complete loss, 123 lives were lost and damages for the year were over two million dollars." To date, this is still considered a high rate of sinking for a year, taken from www.hhpl.on.ca/GreatLakes/Documents/HGL/default.asp?ID=s092, accessed on June 1, 2005. *The Weekly Herald and Lake Superior Mining Journal* of October 17, 1882, reported that in the previous three years over 470 lives were lost on the Canadian Great Lakes.

8   Dana Ashdown, *Railway Steamships of Ontario,* 34.

9   *The Herald* (Port Arthur), Oct. 25, 1882.

10 *The Owen Sound Advertiser*, July 19, 1883.

11 Ibid, April 24, 1884.

12 In 1870, in England, a patent for a communication device was applied for by William Chadburn and his father. By 1875 the father and son were in production in Liverpool, England, making the brass signal device used to communicate from the pilothouse to the engine room on ships. By 1884 over 3,000 vessels were equipped with the Chadburn Telegraph, however there were few of these on the Great Lakes ships. The CPR steamers were among the first, and conceivably the first, to have this "modern" device on the Great Lakes.

13 A.F. Hunter, *The History of Simcoe County*, Vol. 1, (Barrie, ON: Simcoe County Council, 1909) 192.

14 *The Thunder Bay Weekly Sentinel* (Port Arthur), May 31, 1884.

15 *The Herald* (Port Arthur), July 1, 1882.

16 *The Thunder Bay Weekly Sentinel* (Port Arthur), June 25, 1885.

12 CONFRONTATION WITH UNITED STATES CUSTOMS

1   *The Owen Sound Advertiser*, July 23, 1885.

2   *The Wiarton Echo*, Aug. 13, 1886.

3   Affidavit of Robert C. Parrott sworn before John Creasor, Notary Public for the Province of Ontario, November 23, 1886.

4   U.S. National Archives and Records Administration (Chicago), U.S. District Court, West District of Michigan, Northern Division, "The United States vs. Frances Smith," Report of John McQuewan, U.S. Commissioner, Jan. 12, 1887.

5   Ibid.

6   U.S. National Archives and Records Administration (Chicago). D.O. Watson, " To C.S. Fairchild, Acting Secretary of State," Aug. 6, 1886.

7   Ibid, Hugh L.S. Thompson. "To Collector of Customs, Grand Haven Michigan," Aug. 7, 1886.

8   *The Globe* (Toronto), Aug. 18, 1886.

9   *The Wiarton Echo*, Aug. 20, 1886.

10   U.S. National Archives and Records Administration (Chicago). The President of the United States of America, "To the Marshal of the Western District of Michigan," dated Sept. 10, 1886.

11   It is interesting to note that William Tate Robertson was appointed U.S. Vice consul at Owen Sound in 1908 after he retired from his role as a captain on the lakes. His first-hand experiences at Mackinac were no doubt valuable for this final phase of his career.

13   CHANGING FORTUNES

1   *The Globe* (Toronto), Sept. 2, 1887.

2   Ron Beaupre, *The Scanner*, Monthly News Bulletin of the Toronto Marine Historical Society, Vol. XIX, No 6, March 1987, 8.

3   The *City of Owen Sound* sat on the bottom for three years. She was eventually salvaged by the Collins Bay Rafting Company and towed to Little Current. There the ship was rebuilt as a steam barge and renamed the *Saturn* in 1896 – ready to sail again. She sank for a final time near Southampton in September 1901.

4   *The Owen Sound Advertiser*, Oct 4, 1888.

5   "Diary of Charles Ellis," 1888, unpublished, in the private collection of David Ellis of Meaford, Ontario,

6   *The Wiarton Echo*, Sept. 14, 1888.

7   *Through the Years*, Mid-North Printers and Publishers, Gore Bay, March 1988, Vol. V, Number V. The magazine is no longer in production. Author's names were not recorded.

8   *The British Whig* (Kingston), Sept. 19, 1888.

9   *The Meaford Monitor*, June 21, 1889.

10   Ibid, July 21, 1889.

11   *The Owen Sound Times*, Aug. 1, 1889.

12   Ibid.

14   BRUTAL OUTRAGE ON THE *BALTIC*

1   LAC, RG12, Vol. 15, File 8702-37, Vol. 1, Department of Transport, Government of Canada, Testimony of Thomas Hambly, Queen vs. Thomas Tripp, *et al.*, Sept. 16, 1889. Hereinafter referred to as LAC, Department of Transport, Testimony.

2   *The Wiarton Echo*, Sept. 20, 1889.

3   LAC, Department of Transport, Testimony, Testimony of William Smalley, Queen vs. Thomas Tripp, *et al.*, Sept. 18, 1889.

4   To access the crew's quarters in the forecastle, a hatch door was opened forward in the main deck and a set of stairs led to the bunks and lockers below.

5   John Wilson Murray, *Memoirs of a Great Detective* (Toronto: Collins, 1977) 136–139. Originally published as *Memoirs of a Great Detective: Incidents in the Life of John Wilson Murray* by William Heineman Ltd. of London, U.K., 1904.

6 *The Globe* of September 2, 1889 reported, "…and those engaged in their work, maddened with liquor, determined to complete their work."

7 Andrew Gordon's appointment was formalized in the Report of the Privy Council, March 4, 1890.

8 References and quotations are based on LAC, Department of Transport, Testimony.

9 *The Wiarton Echo*, Sept. 27, 1889.

10 *The Owen Sound Times*, Sept. 26, 1889.

11 *The Globe* (Toronto), Sept. 2, 1889.

12 Robertson's testimony conflicted with others at this point. Robertson said at court in March 1890 that there were few people on the forward deck. He asked what the matter was several times and got no answer. He claimed to have said, "I'll have no rows on my ship." Then he noticed a blackened Hambly and told him, "If any one ever attempts to hurt or molest you, no matter how low your rank, or humble you may be never hesitate to come to me, at all hours of the night, and I want my crew to understand that remember…that kind words and kind acts cost nothing." LAC, Department of Transport, Testimony. This particular quote is from the evidence given at the court on March 24, 1890.

13 Estimates of the size of the following crowd vary between 20 and 40. Many were deck passengers whose ticket only allowed them on the main deck.

14 *The Wiarton Echo*, Sept. 20, 1889.

15 Captain Robertson and Engineer Doran said twenty to twenty-five minutes.

16 *The Owen Sound Advertiser*, Sept. 5, 1889.

17 This wrong name would persist in the court records

18 *The Owen Sound Times*, Sept. 5, 1889.

19 *The Meaford Monitor*, Sept. 2, 1889.

20 LAC, Department of Transport, Testimony.

21 *The Globe* (Toronto), Sept. 2, 1889.

22 Ibid, Sept. 3, 1889.

23 Author's note: To me this curious echo of his conversation with Cherry lends credence to the quotation.

24 *The Owen Sound Times*, Sept. 19, 1889.

25 *The Wiarton Echo*, Sept. 27, 1889.

26 *The Owen Sound Times*, Nov. 14, 1889.

27 Ibid.

28 *The Meaford Monitor*, Nov. 15, 1889.

29 *The Owen Sound Times*, Nov. 14, 1889.

30 LAC, Reel C1800, Vol. 484, 241319–241323, Letter from A.R. Mulholland to J.A. Macdonald, dated April 2, 1890.

31 LAC, Reel 1689, Vol. 287, 131410–131412, Letter from Charles H. Tupper to J.A. Macdonald, dated May 22, 1890.

32 *The Meaford Monitor*, May 9, 1890.

15 FAREWELL TO THE *BALTIC*

1   Huron Institute, *Papers and Records*, Collingwood, ON: Huron Institute, 1909, Vol. 1, 51. The Huron Institute was an historical society in Collingwood at the turn of the century, which produced a journal. Unfortunately, a fire burned the museum and everything therein…except one or 2 volumes of the journal. This journal is in the Simcoe County Archives.

2   Ibid, 52.

3   Taken from http://db.library.queensu.ca/marmus, accessed on November 12, 2004.

4   *The Owen Sound Times*, Sept. 10, 1896.

5   *The Collingwood Messenger*, Sept. 10, 1896.

6   *The Owen Sound Advertiser*, Sept. 8, 1896.

7   *The Owen Sound Times*, Sept. 17, 1896.

8   Ibid, Sept. 30, 1896.

9   Ibid, Sept. 30, 1897. The quotation is from the subsequent hearing a year after the fire.

10   *The Ontario Historical Society Papers and Records*, (Toronto, 1913, Vol. 11, 60) notes that the one tree on One Tree Island, located in Nottawasaga Bay, was an ash tree and that it blew down in 1894.

Resources

ARTICLES

Barry, James P., "The First Georgian Bay Steamers," in *Inland Seas*, Vol. 23, 1967.

_____, "Wolseley Expedition crosses the Great Lakes," in *Inland Seas*, Vol. 24.2, 1968.

Palmer, Richard F., "The Age Of Sail Ended On Ontario," in *Inland Seas,* Vol. 46.1, 1990: 6–10.

_____, "Cost of Steamboating 1830s–1840s" in *Inland Seas*, Vol. 48.1, 1992: 49–58.

Wightman, W.R., "The Canadian steam packet service of the Upper Lakes," in *Inland Seas*, Vol. 46.4, 1990.

Waterbury, George A., "Woodburners," in *Inland Seas*, Vol. 3.4, 1947.

BOOKS

Amyot, Chantal, Bianca Gendreau and John Willis, *Special Delivery: Canada's Postal Heritage*. Fredericton: Goose Lane Editions, 2000.

Ashdown, Dana William, *Railway Steamships of Ontario 1850–1950*. Erin, ON: Boston Mills Press, 1988.

Barry, James P., *Georgian Bay: The Sixth Great Lake*. Toronto: Clarke Irwin & Company, 1978.

_____, *Georgian Bay: An Illustrated History*. Erin, ON: Boston Mills Press, 1992.

Berton, Pierre, *The Last Spike: The Great Railway 1881–1885*. Toronto: McClelland & Stewart, 1971.

Brown, David G., *White Hurricane: A Great Lakes November Gale and America's Deadliest Maritime Disaster*. Camden, ME: Ragged Mountain Press/McGraw-Hill, 2002.

Campbell, William, *Northeastern Georgian Bay and Its People*. Britt, ON: self-published, 1982.

Charlebois, Dr. Peter, *Sternwheelers and Sidewheelers: The Romance of Steamdriven Paddleboats in Canada*. Toronto: N.C. Press Ltd., 1978.

Croft, Melba, *Fourth Entrance to Huronia: The History of Owen Sound*. Owen Sound: ON: self-published, 1980.

Degler, Carl N., *Out of Our Past: The Forces that Shaped Modern America*. New York: Harper & Row, 1959.

Eichenlaub, Val L., *Weather and Climate of the Great Lakes Region*. Notre Dame: University of Notre Dame Press, 1979.

Folkes, Patrick, "Cooks and Ladies Maids: Women in Sail and Steam on the Great Lakes in the Nineteenth Century," in Victoria Brehm (ed.), *A Fully Accredited Ocean: Essays on the Great Lakes*. Ann Arbor, MI: The University of Michigan Press, 1998.

Grant, Rev. George M., *Ocean to Ocean: Sir Sandford Fleming's Expedition Through Canada in 1872: being a diary kept during a journey from Atlantic to Pacific*. Toronto: James Campbell and Son, 1873.

Hestor, Bill, *Georgian Bay Navigation 1847–1882*. Barrie, ON: self-published, 2002.

Historical Atlas of Grey County, 1880. Toronto: H. Beldon & Co. 1880.

Historical Atlas of Simcoe County 1881, Toronto: H. Beldon & Co., 1881. Reprint, Cumming Atlas reprints, Port Elgin, 1975.

Heron, Craig, *Booze: A Distilled History*. Toronto: Between the Lines, 2003.

Horwood, Harold & Ed Butts, *Pirates and Outlaws of Canada 1610–1932*. Toronto: Doubleday, 1984.

Hunter, Andrew F., *The History of Simcoe County*, Vol. 1, Barrie County Council, 1909.

Huyshe, Captain G.L., *The Red River Expedition*. Toronto: Macmillan, 1871.

Karamanski, Theodore J., *Schooner Passage: Sailing Ships and the Lake Michigan Frontier*. Detroit, MI: Wayne State University Press, 2000.

Mackey, Frank, *Steamboat Connections: Montreal to Upper Canada, 1816–1843*. Montreal & Kingston: McGill-Queen's University Press, 2000.

Miller, James C., *Our Inland Seas: Their Shipping and Commerce for Three Centuries*. Cleveland, OH: Freshwater Press. Inc., 1910. Reprinted 1976.

Monmonier, Mark, *Air Apparent: How Meteorologists Learned to Map, Predict and Dramatize Weather*. Chicago, IL: University of Chicago Press, 1999.

Morton, Desmond, *A Military History of Canada*. Edmonton, AB: Hurtig Publishers, 1990.

Murray, John Wilson, *Memoirs of a Great Detective: Incidents in the Life of John Wilson Murray*. London: William Heineman Ltd., 1904. Reprinted Collins, Toronto, 1977.

Parsons, Robert, *Steamboat Mail in Eastern Canada*. Waterdown, ON: Bill Longley Auctions, 1995.

Passfield, Robert W., *Technology in Transition: The "Soo" Ship Canal 1889–1885*. Ottawa, ON: Canadian Parks Service, Environment Canada, 1989.

Siggins, Maggie, *Riel: A Life of Revolution*, Toronto: HarperCollins, 1994.

Thompson, Thos. S., *Thompson's Coast Pilot for the Upper Lakes, on both shores from Chicago to Buffalo, Green Bay, Georgian Bay, and Lake Superior; Including the Rivers Detroit, St. Clair and Ste. Marie, with the Courses and Distances on Lake Ontario, and other information relative thereto*. Detroit, MI: self-published, 5th ed., 1869.

Stanley, George F.G., *Toil & Trouble: Military Expeditions to Red River*. Toronto: Dundurn Press, 1989.

Unwin, Peter, *The Wolf's Head: Writing Lake Superior*. Toronto: Viking Canada, 2003.

Urquart, M.C. (ed.), *Historical Statistics of Canada*. Toronto: Macmillan, 1965.

Williams, W.H., *Manitoba and the North-West: Journal of a Trip from Toronto to the Rocky Mountains*. Toronto: Hunter, Rose & Company, 1882.

Watts, Peter and Tracy Marsh, *W. Watts & Sons, Boat Builders: Canadian Designs for Work and Pleasure 1842–1946*. Oshawa, ON: Mackinaw Productions, 1997.

Walker, Frank N., *Four Whistles to Wood-up: Stories of the Northern Railway of Canada*. Toronto: Upper Canada Railway Society, 1953.

Wallace, Jim, *A Double Duty: The Decisive First Decade of the North West Mounted Police*. Winnipeg, MB: Bunker to Bunker Books, 1997.

White, Paul, *Owen Sound: The Port City*. Toronto: Natural Heritage Books, 2000.

Whittier, Bob, *Paddle Wheel Steamers and their Engines*. Duxbury, MA: Seamaster Boats Inc., 1983.

Wolff, Julius F., Jr., *Lake Superior Shipwrecks*. Duluth, MN: Lake Superior Port Cities Inc., 1979.

Young, Anna G., *Great Lakes Saga*. Owen Sound, ON: self-published, 1965.

MUSEUMS AND ARCHIVES (PROVIDING RESOURCES)

Alpena County George F. Fletcher Public Library
Archives of Ontario (AO)
Assiginack Museum
Bruce Mines Museum
Blind River Museum
Bruce County Museum and Archives
City of Thunder Bay Records Centre and Archives
Centennial Museum of Sheguiandah
Collingwood Museum
Collingwood Public Library
Gore Bay Museum
Great Lakes Shipwreck Museum, Whitefish Bay
Grey Roots Archival Collection and Museum Collection
Library and Archives Canada (LAC)
Marine Museum of the Great Lakes, Kingston
Meaford Museum
Minnesota History Center
Nova Scotia Archives
Ontario Provincial Police Archives
Owen Sound Union Library
Owen Sound Marine and Rail Museum
St. Edmunds Museum (Tobermory)
Toronto Reference Library, Baldwin Room
Sault Ste. Marie Museum
Sault Ste. Marie Public Library and Archives
Simcoe County Archives
The British Museum (London, U.K.)

The British National Library
The British Marine Museum
The Victoria and Albert Museum
The British Newspaper Archives
The U.S. Army Corps of Engineers Museum, Duluth

NEWSPAPERS

Over the time period covered by the story of the *Frances Smith*, newspapers in small towns across Ontario were in a constant state of changing ownership and nomenclature. Every effort has been made to identify the appropriate newspaper name in the Notes. In this list of resources, an outline of some of the major name changes is noted. For full details on newspaper name changes see, Brian Gilchrist, *Inventory of Newspapers 1793–1986* (Toronto: Micromedia Limited, 1987).

The Bulletin (Collingwood), also *The Collingwood Bulletin*, name varies
The Barrie Examiner
The British Whig, also known as *The Daily British Whig* (Kingston)
The Collingwood Review Herald
The Collingwood Enterprise and Messenger, The Enterprise, name varies
The Chatham Planet
The Daily Leader (Toronto)
The Daily News, name varies, *The Kingston Daily News, The Kingston News, The Chronicle and News*, published in conjunction with *The Daily News*
The Detroit Post and Tribune, The Duluth Tribune
The Duluth Minnesotian
The Globe (Toronto)
The Goderich Signal, The Goderich Huron Signal, name varies
The Manitoulin Expositor (Little Current)
The Owen Sound Advertiser, The Advertiser
The Owen Sound Comet, The Comet, name varies
The North Shore Miner (Prince Arthur's Landing, now Thunder Bay) absorbed to form *The Port Arthur Sentinel*, also known as *The Thunder Bay Sentinel*
The Meaford Monitor
The Renfrew Mercury
The Times (Owen Sound), *The Owen Sound Times,* name varies
The Wiarton Echo

PRIVATE PAPERS, DIARIES

"Peter Fuller's Diary," private collocation of Stanley Knight Ltd., Meaford, Ontario.
"Charles Ellis Diary," private collection of David Ellis, Meaford, Ontario.
Harding, Frank, "History of Meaford and St. Vincent," the transcribed papers are in the Meaford Public Library.
"Minute Book of Pythagoras Lodge," Meaford, Ontario.

Index

About the Author

Scott Cameron grew up in Sault Ste. Marie, Ontario. He received an undergraduate degree from the University of Western Ontario in 1959 and an M.Ed. from the University of Toronto in 1967. After a career as head of history and secondary school principal in Grey County, he created a successful home rental business in Europe. He has served on several boards and in 2005 was elected chair of the Owen Sound Marine and Rail Museum. He lectures and writes about marine related stories as well as about environmentalist John Muir.